About Island Press

Island Press is the only nonprofit organization in the United States whose principal purpose is the publication of books on environmental issues and natural resource management. We provide solutions-oriented information to professionals, public officials, business and community leaders, and concerned citizens who are shaping responses to environmental problems.

In 1998, Island Press celebrates its fourteenth anniversary as the leading provider of timely and practical books that take a multidisciplinary approach to critical environmental concerns. Our growing list of titles reflects our commitment to bringing the best of an expanding body of literature to the environmental community throughout North America and the world.

Support for Island Press is provided by The Jenifer Altman Foundation, The Bullitt Foundation, The Mary Flagler Cary Charitable Trust, The Nathan Cummings Foundation, The Geraldine R. Dodge Foundation, The Ford Foundation, The Vira I. Heinz Endowment, The W. Alton Jones Foundation, The John D. and Catherine T. MacArthur Foundation, The Andrew W. Mellon Foundation, The Charles Stewart Mott Foundation, The Curtis and Edith Munson Foundation, The National Fish and Wildlife Foundation, The National Science Foundation, The New-Land Foundation, The David and Lucile Packard Foundation, The Surdna Foundation, The Winslow Foundation, The Pew Charitable Trusts, and individual donors.

Planning for Biodiversity

Planning for Biodiversity

ISSUES AND EXAMPLES

Sheila Peck

ISLAND PRESS
Washington, D.C. ◆ Covelo, California

ISLAND PRESS is a trademark of The Center for Resource Economics.

Library of Congress Cataloging-in-Publication Data
Peck, Sheila.
    Planning for biodiversity : issues and examples / Sheila Peck.
        p.   cm.
    Includes bibliographical references and index.
    ISBN 1-55963-401-4
    1. Regional planning—Environmental aspects—United States.
    2. Biological diversity conservation—United States. I. Title.
HT392.P43   1998   98-10504
333.7'0973—dc21   CIP

Printed on recycled, acid-free paper ✺

Manufactured in the United States of America
10 9 8 7 6 5 4 3 2 1

To Ralph, for his constancy, and the music he brings to our lives

Contents

Acknowledgments

I would like to thank the many people who have contributed to this book. Their thoughts, time, support, and materials have improved its quality and increased my own understanding of the subject.

I am grateful to numerous ecologists and planners who reviewed chapters, or with whom I discussed my ideas. Maria Cacho, Allen Cooperrider, Ed Grumbine, Richard Harris, Richard Hobbs, Todd Hemingson, John Radke, Brenda Taylor, and Dean Urban in particular provided valuable comments, including suggestions of key concepts, ways to approach the material, and where I was or was not on track. Many other people sent useful responses to my e-mail queries, offering ideas for case studies, references, and/or their perspectives on aspects of biodiversity planning.

The twelve case studies featured in this book are fundamental to providing readers with a greater understanding of the ecological concepts and how they can be implemented by planners. I was fortunate to speak with a variety of people who were responsible for, or contributed to, these projects. All were extremely helpful, and I thank them for their long telephone calls, for their thoughts, and for sending me papers, photographs, slides, maps, and diagrams that further describe their work.

Planning for Biodiversity is an outgrowth of a previous work, *Landscape Conservation Planning: Preserving Ecosystems in Open Space Networks*, so I would also like to thank those who contributed to that earlier manuscript. Joe McBride, Randy Hester, and Paul Edelman offered initial suggestions and advice that helped guide my thinking and shape the form of the writing. Jim Bartolome, Conny Becker, Tim Duane, Andrea Mackenzie, Francesca Maltese, Sheila G. Peck, Denis Saunders, Arnold Schultz, Dan Smith, Richard Spotts, and Danai Thaitakoo reviewed all or portions of the manuscript. The Integrated Hardwood Range Management Program at the University of California funded a part of the work. Natalie Peck donated numerous hours for the design and layout of the first draft.

I am particularly grateful to my husband, Ralph Maltese, and my friend Maria Cacho for their support throughout the process, and to Heather Boyer, my editor at Island Press, for her ideas, comments, and patience.

Introduction

In 1948 it was a plan to make any city proud. Portland, Oregon's Forest Park established 4,200 acres of municipal parkland, offered recreation and education, preserved food and cover for wildlife, and protected the land from erosion and natural hazards. If you were to walk along one of several stream systems to the crest of the ridge, you might have encountered animals ranging from frogs and salamanders to owls and occasional black bears. Following the ridgeline north, you could travel through a variety of forest types, then out of the park through 100 miles of near wilderness to the Pacific Ocean. So effective was the original plan that later management updates in 1976 and 1991 could still advocate the preservation of this "undisturbed natural forest and park environment" within the City of Portland.

For the present, Forest Park may be considered a success. In the midst of a large, metropolitan area, this 7-mile peninsula supports largely native ecosystems, provides habitat to numerous rare and common species, and is highly prized by Portland residents. Yet how long will these ecosystems and species last? If we could revisit the park many generations from today, would we encounter a similar mix of plant communities? Could we still find salmon spawning in the streams, hawks and woodpeckers in the trees, and Roosevelt elk browsing along the ridgetop? Which issues need to be addressed now to ensure that such a variety of life survives? How can we preserve the ecological integrity of any open space area?

There are good reasons to ask these questions. We live in a time of extraordinary environmental change. All around us, natural landscapes continue to be reduced and fragmented. Essential relationships within ecosystems are different than they were just a century or two ago. The types and intensity of human development and resource use further influence these systems. One result of the changes has been a steep decline in biological diversity. We are losing diversity on a number of scales: We can expect fewer genetic combinations within

1

populations, fewer populations within species, fewer species within natural communities, fewer communities within landscapes, and fewer distinct landscapes.

Ecologists from a range of disciplines have become alarmed by the trend. A decrease in diversity—and the alteration of associated ecological processes—could impair ecosystem functions in countless unpredictable ways. It would narrow our own use and experience of the environment, and, more ominously, affect conditions that support our existence.[1] Over the past two decades, scientists have responded with an extensive effort to determine principles or concepts fundamental to preserving biological diversity. Essentially, they have sought to identify ecological "bottom lines" that can be incorporated into planning and policymaking. While it is still in the beginning stages, enough of the work has been completed to suggest useful guidelines.

Now the task is to ensure that these concepts move beyond the scientific journals and into the planning realm. *Planning for Biodiversity* was written to help ease this transfer. It further synthesizes the ecological concepts, and presents them in a useful, readable form. It is geared toward those currently involved in biodiversity planning. Among others, the word "planner," as used in the book, may denote a private citizen, a land trust member, a community activist, a resource agency staff member, or a developer, as well as a professional planner. The ideas covered in the book are valuable for developing new plans, and for assessing existing open space systems. They will help preserve treasures, like Forest Park, within functioning landscapes for the years to come.

❖

To effectively link planning and ecology, how the concepts in *Planning for Biodiversity* connect to each field should be clarified. One reason for this is simply to provide context: It helps to understand where the ideas fit in relation to the work of other environmental planners and from which scientific disciplines they were drawn. A second reason is to indicate how different professions have contributed to biodiversity planning. This new concentration inherits, on the one hand, a tradition of ecology-based planning, and on the other, an evolving framework of scientific thought.

In planning, the practice of collecting and analyzing landscape data has been standard for almost three decades. At the beginning of this period, Ian McHarg was the most prominent proponent of a holistic "ecological view." One of McHarg's greatest contributions was his insistence that designs be based on ecological processes. In *Design with Nature*, he demonstrated the practical value of recognizing these interactions and incorporating them into plans.[2] He also institutionalized comprehensive physical and biological inventories to identify the processes. To determine land use suitability, McHarg mapped landscape attributes on separate overlays. This geographic approach to analysis became fundamental to many objectives in ecological planning, including sustaining biodiversity. It foreshadowed modern computer-based geographic information systems.

Biodiversity planning also benefits from subsequent practitioners who expanded and developed ecological planning methods. Julius Fabos introduced the quantitative landscape model METLAND (Metropolitan Landscape Planning Model) to assess urban impacts and generate improved land use alternatives.[3] William Marsh's extensive textbook on landscape planning covers a range of environmental issues and techniques germane to biodiversity.[4] In *The Living Landscape*, Frederick Steiner develops a clear, useful planning process, complete with a variety of ecological analyses and suggestions for incorporating sociocultural information.[5]

Another relevant branch of planning is that which focuses on urban design and its relationship to landscape sustainability. Anne Spirn demonstrated that urban pollution and energy and resource use affect the wider regional ecology as well as our quality of life.[6] Michael Hough has sought to develop a new approach to urban design based on natural processes.[7] John Lyle and Robert Thayer have focused on creating sustainable designs for the systems and technologies that support our daily lives.[8] Their view is the most comprehensive, encompassing the built and unbuilt landscape, human and natural processes, and the importance of behaviors and values.

How is biodiversity planning related to these other concentrations? It might be considered a subset of ecological planning, since it focuses on the single issue of biodiversity conservation. Alternatively, due to the scope of the concept, it could be viewed as intertwined with most of ecological planning and many other branches of planning as well. Biological diversity, or biodiversity for short, has been defined as "the full range of variety and variability within and among living organisms, and the ecological complexes in which they occur; it encompasses ecosystem or community diversity, species diversity, and genetic diversity,"[9] or more simply, "the variety of life and its processes."[10] While both perspectives on biodiversity planning are valid, the two together may be most useful. It is a single issue, yet because it is associated with so many others, the extent to which it is maintained can help indicate the sustainability of different planning approaches.

Given its breadth, it is not surprising that biodiversity planning gleans information and ideas from many scientific fields. Depending on its objectives, a plan could incorporate findings from some combination of population ecology, community ecology, ecosystem ecology, landscape ecology, wildlife ecology, and plant ecology. Other disciplines also suggest significant patterns or processes. Population genetics, for example, has revealed relationships between genetic diversity and the fitness of populations and species, while bio-geography has helped explain the geographic distribution of organisms. Resource management professions such as forestry, wildlife management, fish-eries, and range management have also produced useful studies.

Within such an array of fields, the new discipline of conservation biology has become particularly valuable due to its focus on biodiversity. In fact, Michael Soulé, the first president of the Society for Conservation Biology, sug-gested that its purpose be "to provide the principles and tools for preserving biological diversity."[11] To this end, conservation biology draws members and ideas from all relevant sciences, including the basic research and applied fields noted above. Conservation biologists share a common commitment to envi-ronmental protection. Although it dates just to the late 1970s,[12] conservation biology can already be credited with synthesizing and developing a range of concepts practical for planning.[13]

Landscape ecology is also proving very useful. It addresses the spatial pat-terns of large groups of ecosystems; how species, energy, and materials move within these patterns; and how the patterns change over time.[14] Landscape ecology is similar to conservation biology in that it is a recent, synthetic disci-pline; it developed in Europe in the 1970s from geography and ecology.[15] It has focused scientific attention on the influence of varying spatial and tempo-ral scales, and especially on ecological interactions occurring over broad regions and long time periods. It provides a framework to assess how large-scale patterns and processes are related to biodiversity.

Over the past decade, closer relationships have developed between plan-ning and the ecological sciences. Journals such as *Landscape and Urban Plan-ning* routinely feature articles on landscape ecology, wildlife habitat, and species and ecosystem protection. Ecological design books have specifically addressed biodiversity issues.[16] Applied ecological journals, for example *Envi-ronmental Management*, have included pieces on planning, development, and the socioeconomic aspects of conservation. Planners have been plenary speak-ers at the International Association of Landscape Ecology.[17] Numerous articles on sustainability have been written for both planning and ecological publica-tions. Still, more links, better appreciation of each area's contributions, and increased collaboration will improve our ability to preserve the integrity of our landscapes.

❖

Planning for Biodiversity is a practical guide to ecological concepts necessary for maintaining biodiversity. Each chapter contains one or more case studies to demonstrate how the ideas have been implemented, as well as information on how to contact those involved for further information. Planning guidelines, which summarize the main points of the chapters, and a glossary are included at the end of the book.

Of the seven chapters, the first five cover principles to consider when framing a plan, while the last two pertain to specific aspects of the process. Chapter 1 introduces a framework to characterize biological diversity. It will help planners understand the range of biodiversity and then to address specific issues in the areas in which they work. Chapter 2 suggests conservation priorities among the numerous attributes of biodiversity. Chapter 3 explains concepts related to temporal changes in ecosystems, while the effects of landscape area and connectivity on habitat quality and species movement are covered in chapter 4. Chapter 5 addresses the elements of reserve design. Chapter 6 describes useful types of information to include in baseline data, as well as key sources. The causes of uncertainty in biodiversity planning, and the need for monitoring or adaptive management, are covered in chapter 7.

The principles offered in the book should be approached as guidelines, rather than as obligatory rules. The situations that planners encounter develop largely from local issues and ecology; local data may indicate that some concepts are especially relevant and render others less important. Also, the concepts are generalized from certain studies, and so will apply more to particular types of ecosystems, species, or geographic locations. In addition, plans are inevitably balancing acts among competing interests. Planners cannot preserve every aspect of biological diversity, and so must use their judgment to sustain the most significant attributes of ecosystems.

It is also helpful to remember—and accept—that uncertainty is inherent in biodiversity planning. We rarely have the resources to fully understand the areas in which we work: We lack studies on specific species or ecosystems; we have difficulty predicting the consequences of certain impacts; we cannot know which social, political, or economic issues will arise. Such uncertainty has several implications. It suggests, for example, that planning must be an ongoing process. Since we cannot fully predict the results of our plans, they will require monitoring, management, and reevaluation. They may require adaptive management, or some degree of experimentation to discern how a system operates. Uncertainty also compels us to be cautious in the changes we bring to landscapes and to weigh the risks of different types of actions. Sometimes using educated common sense may be an acceptable approach.

Ultimately, biodiversity planning must be oriented to creating sustainable societies. The ideas in this book help us toward this goal by indicating ecological limits and providing direction in our use and development of the environment. They offer strategies to protect biological diversity that can be imple-

mented today. To be truly effective, though, we must also address the root causes threatening biodiversity. These causes are generally economic, social, or
political. They involve our values, behaviors, and institutions—aspects of society which are more difficult and require more time to change. Both the immediate and long-term strategies will require our attention and creativity.

Chapter 1

Exploring Biodiversity

Mount Diablo, located in a state park east of San Francisco Bay, is known for its unique and varied species. The forty-minute drive to the top winds through numerous associations of oak, chaparral, pine, and grassland. The texture of the landscape is striking: a tapestry of interdigitating vegetation types, ranging from sparse blue oak savanna to tightly woven mats of brush. Shoots sprout from a recent burn, streams flow from winter rains, and exotic plants line the roadway. Image follows image, each one registering another facet of life on the mountain. Each is a part of the biodiversity of Mount Diablo.

How would one characterize biodiversity in this landscape? A way to begin would be to record the number and types of species, noting the presence of any that were rare or endangered. This approach, however, would yield only part of the picture. Another aspect of biodiversity is the ecological relationships that help establish and sustain species. For example, the vegetation patterns just observed and processes such as fire, water flow, and dispersal would all contribute to the present range of animals and plants. It is also important to portray biodiversity at different levels of biological organization. For instance, in addition to species, the description should include variations in the biotic communities of the mountain and in certain populations of species. Lastly, it should indicate how the different aspects of biodiversity fluctuate over time.

A biodiversity framework can be developed from these ideas.[1] It consists of the components, patterns, and processes of ecosystems, each existing at multiple levels of organization and all varying over time (figure 1.1). By incorporating all three ecosystem attributes (components, patterns, and processes), not only can specific variations in the biota be considered, but so can many other factors on which this diversity depends. Similarly, addressing different levels of

7

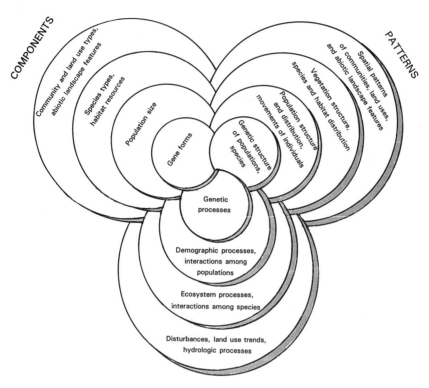

Figure 1.1. The biodiversity framework consists of the components, patterns, and processes of ecosystems, at multiple levels of organization. The diagram is shown in three dimensions to indicate that these ecological attributes also vary over time.

organization ensures that a range of these attributes is included. By estimating temporal variations, one can assess how representative today's conditions are of those that have occurred over a longer period of time.

This framework has several uses for planners. Most important, it promotes a comprehensive approach to biodiversity planning and management. It clarifies the extent of the concept and suggests a method to address biodiversity beyond legal requirements or immediate issues. In addition, it is helpful at specific stages of the planning process. It is useful for understanding which parts of an issue are significant and the relationships between these parts. It provides guidance in deciding which types of information to collect, which types of analysis might be important, and which aspects of the system should be monitored and over what period of time. It is basic to conserving biodiversity in the landscapes we value.

Components, Patterns, and Processes

For most people, the term *biodiversity* evokes images of species, especially charismatic mammals, on the road to extinction. Species are the components of ecological systems about which they care the most. The public is well aware that organisms are vanishing rapidly in many areas of the world. Locally, they may be involved in developing plans to conserve species diversity. These plans might prioritize biotic communities that support a high number of plants and animals. They might also target species that are ecologically valuable or vulnerable. On Mount Diablo, for example, riparian and oak woodlands include substantially more native species than those occuring in annual grasslands. Acorn woodpeckers are valuable because they excavate tree cavities and so create nesting habitat for other birds and small mammals. Other species might be included in a plan because they are endangered, occur only on the mountain, or exist here hundreds of miles from their nearest relatives.

Species, of course, are not the only levels at which an ecosystem exhibits diversity. Communities also vary. A biotic community is any group of plants, animals, bacteria, and fungi that occurs together at a particular place and time. Species themselves are comprised of populations, or subsets of individuals that regularly interbreed. The number of populations in a species and the number of individuals in a population can be great or small. Genetic diversity, or the differences contained in the genes of a species or population, can also range from high to low. Additionally, differences in abiotic, or nonliving, factors—such as land use, soils, geology, climate, slope, and aspect—influence biological diversity.

While the components of ecosystems are often the focus, biodiversity is more than these parts. Systems by definition are sets of interacting elements, and these elements cannot exist alone. Each living part of an ecosystem is related in numerous ways to other living and nonliving parts. Thus to conserve biodiversity, what is needed is a model that addresses not only the components of ecosystems, but the relationships that occurs among them. To do this, patterns and processes are added to components as the foundation of the framework (figure 1.2).

It is the pattern of the vegetation as much as its composition that one notices on Mount Diablo. Each hillside contains several distinct community types. Moreover, these vegetation patches clearly correspond to specific environmental conditions. Grasses predominate on the dry, sunny, south slopes, while the cooler north sides support chaparral. Coast live oak and bay laurel also grow on the north slopes and extend like fingers up the canyons where more moisture exists. Blue oak savanna covers the bottom of the mountain, while canyon

Figure 1.2. Ecosystem attributes on Mount Diablo include oak woodlands (a landscape component; top left), inter-mixed grasslands, shrublands, and wood-lands (a landscape pattern; top right), and fire (a landscape process; bottom left). (Photographs by Carl Nielson.)

live oaks occur only at the top. Intermittent and perennial streams support separate associations of vegetation. Along some patches edges are ecotones, or overlap zones between two communities, with their own hybrid suite of species.

Other ecological patterns can be found within biotic communities. Savannas, for example, have a two-storied structure consisting of overhead tree canopy and underlying grasses and forbs. Most other oak woodlands include a third layer of shrubs. Dense chaparral is a haven for small animals and can be virtually impenetrable to humans. Decomposing wood and leaf litter create structures at a microscale on the ground. Each of these patterns provides habitat for different groups of animals and plants.

Patterns also exist within and among species populations. The sex and age ratios of a population affect its reproductive success. It is influenced by its distance from other populations and by the type of habitat between them. For wildlife populations especially, maintaining opportunities to interbreed with other populations strengthens the group as a whole. In addition, varied genetic patterns occur in species, offering different opportunities for adaptation and evolution. Some species consist of populations that are similar across a broad geographic region. Others, with little ability to move and interbreed, exhibit significant genetic variation from one population to the next.

Ecological processes are the third major attribute of ecosystems and determinant of biodiversity. These are the interactions that take place among ecosystem components. Some processes are important because they create the initial conditions that allow species to colonize an area. Other processes maintain an environment conducive to the species' survival. The types of processes operating in a landscape govern which organisms it can support.

Most people are aware of many large-scale, dramatic processes because the processes affect their lives as well as their landscapes. Severe storms, for instance, produce flooding, landslides, and downed trees. Wildfires threaten homes in addition to burning large forest tracts. Swarms of insect pests leave hillsides of dead trees in their wake. Such landscape "disturbances" create more heterogeneous habitat, which supports a greater range of species.

Ecological processes also include routine, everyday occurrences. An animal seen in the distance might be foraging for plants, preying on other animals, or competing against a similar species. A young animal might be dispersing from its birth site to a new area or in the middle of migration. Seasonal flowers, cones, and shoots signal reproduction and regeneration. These are ongoing activities that maintain individuals, populations, and communities.

Still other processes are difficult to discern, but equally important for sustaining biodiversity. For example, it might take decades for a pond to fill in with reeds and grasses to become a meadow and ultimately a woodland. Similarly, we know that nutrients cycle among plants, animals, soils, water, and the atmosphere, although we cannot see them. A simple stream is shaped by incremental processes such as erosion and sediment deposition. A population long isolated may ultimately become a new species.

In addition to characterizing biodiversity, the three types of ecosystem attributes—components, patterns, and processes—are important for planning because they are interconnected. Each is linked to the others through a myriad of threads. To preserve a rare species, for example, a planner might consider attributes such as habitat area and structure, competing species, land uses, water and vegetation patterns in the landscape, distance between populations, reproductive characteristics, and genetic variations. To reduce nutrient infiltration into a river, the considerations might include width and length of the buffer zone, the types and productivity of buffer vegetation, slope, upland land uses, soils, and waterflow characteristics. Whatever the issue, its solution will involve a range of ecosystem components, patterns, and processes.

Biological Scaling

The next step in developing a framework is to distinguish within the three attribute types. This further organization helps planners identify more aspects of biodiversity and then focus on those particularly relevant to their situation. A useful approach is to think of an area in terms of biological scales. Different levels of biological organization are inherent in any landscape, and each has characteristic components, patterns, and processes.

The concept of a biological hierarchy is common in biology and ecology.[2] It involves a series of levels of structural complexity. Examples of these successive levels include atoms, molecules, cells, tissues, organs, organisms, populations, and communities. Each tier is a composite of those below and is itself nested within the tier above. Distinct properties exist at each scale, such that a given level is more than the sum of its parts.

For planning purposes, we can concentrate on the higher part of the hierarchy, populations and communities, and adapt it to reflect biodiversity concerns. Populations and communities are very useful scales, since they are basic biological units in parks and open spaces. To these we can add landscapes as the tier above communities. Among other components, landscapes are comprised of various communities and exhibit numerous patterns and processes essential to biodiversity. Underneath populations, the fourth tier is genetic. Although genetic diversity is relevant to maintaining populations, it is helpful to isolate it as a separate level as it includes a distinct set of ecosystem attributes (figure 1.3).

The landscape scale involves components and relationships that span large areas. For Mount Diablo, which covers about 30 square miles, either the mountain or the mountain and surrounding region might be considered the "landscape." Components at this scale include the biotic communities, as well as significant characteristics of them: for example, the proportions in which they occur, their rarity, productivity, and the diversity of species they support. Aspects of hydrology, such as streams, ponds, and springs, are other parts of the landscape. Abiotic components affecting biodiversity include climate, soils, geology, elevation, slope, and aspect. Land uses in and adjacent to the park and past and present management practices also influence the species mix.

Landscape patterns involve the spatial arrangement of components and processes. One type of pattern is the physical aspects of landscape patches. For instance, blue oak woodlands on Mount Diablo can be characterized in terms of their size, shape, or location. A second category includes relationships among different patch types. Communities can be adjacent to or separate from each other or correlated with specific abiotic factors. Recreational areas and campgrounds can be too close to sensitive habitats. The urban/wildland boundary has shifted significantly over the past few decades. A third type of pattern applies to the overall area. For example, the region can be classified in terms of the heterogeneity, or variety, of its vegetation or the degree to which its open space is connected.

Landscape processes produce changes in the components and patterns.

Figure 1.3. Ecosystem attributes from different scales on Mount Diablo: Mitchell Creek,
one of the few perennial streams (Landscape component; top left); regeneration follow-
ing a fire in chaparral (Community process; top right); fairy lantern, a plant endemic
to Mount Diablo (Population component; bottom left); deer with deformed antlers
(Genetic process; bottom right). (Mitchell Creek and regeneration photographs by Carl
Nielson; fairy lantern and deer photographs by John Pelonio.)

Some processes, such as a fire or intense storm, rapidly alter communities. Others result in slow, subtle changes. In the absence of fire, for example, chaparral plants may eventually overrun a grassland. Human land uses are also important processes at the landscape scale. One could examine the degree and rate at which land surrounding Mount Diablo is being developed or the effects of different grazing regimens throughout the park (table 1.1).

The community scale can also be associated with specific components, patterns, and processes. Here, the components include species and key habitat resources. Of particular interest are species that are endangered, rare, limited in distribution, ecologically valuable, or exotic. Tree snags, woody debris, rock outcrops, and perennial streams are examples of important habitat resources on Mount Diablo. Community patterns include characteristics of vegetation structure as well as the distribution of resources. Among the processes operating at this scale are those specifically associated with a vegetation type and those occurring between community organisms. For example, fire is inherent to California's chaparral, where even without human ignitions it recurs every ten

Table 1.1. The Attributes Compromising Biodiversity

	COMPONENTS	PATTERNS	PROCESSES
LANDSCAPES	Community types and significant character-istics (e.g., proportions, rarity, productivity, species diversity); hydrologic features; abiotic factors (e.g., climate, soils, geology, elevation, slope, aspect); land use types	Overall variety, connectivity, and fragmentation; patch sizes, shapes, and distributions; patch adjacencies and correlations	Disturbances (e.g., fires, floods, storms, landslides) and their characteristics (frequency, intensity, size, seasons); long-term changes in vege-tation and hydrologic features; nutrient flows; land use trends
COMMUNITY	Species types—that are ecologically valuable, endangered, rare, sensitive, exotic, or limited in distri-bution; key habitat resources (snags, woody debris, outcrops, perennial streams)	Vegetation struc-ture (e.g., density, layers, canopy closure, stand gaps); distribution of species and habitat resources	Smaller-scale disturb-ances and their char-acteristics; vegetation changes following disturbances (succes-sion); productivity, herbivory, predation, and parasitism; nutrient flows; human uses and impacts
POPULATION	Absolute or relative size of populations	Number and dis-tribution of popu-lations; distance between popu-lations; intent of individual ranges; migration patterns; population struc-tures	Reproduction, mor-tality, and regenera-tion; movement abilities and character-istics; immigration, emigration, and inter-breeding among populations
GENETIC	Variety of gene forms (alleles); rare or destructive forms of genes	Diversity within individual popu-lations; variations among populations	Rate of genetic change (due to chance, inbreeding, or interbreeding)

Adapted from R.F. Noss, "Indicators for Monitoring Biodiversity: A Hierarchal Approach," *Conservation Biology* 4, 4 (1990).

to forty years.[3] When a particular species is the target, a plan might also address community processes such as herbivory, predation, or parasitism.

The salamander ensatina (*Ensatina eschscholtzii*) is useful for illustrating population and genetic-scale attributes on Mount Diablo, since it is one of the few species on the mountain for which both types of data are available. Stebbins (1954) found approximately 100 ensatinas in an area near Mount Diablo, and estimated that 600 to 700 might occur in an acre of favorable habitat.[4] The size of a population, as well as its density, are population-scale components.[5] Noting overlapping color patterns in ensatina populations throughout California, Stebbins also deduced that individual animals traveled among the populations and interbred. Interbreeding, like reproduction, mortality and population growth, is an example of a population-scale process. Usually, however, the ensatinas moved within a limited oblong area averaging 70 to135 feet in length. In contrast to most amphibians, ensatinas do not migrate, nor do they depend on water sources to lay their eggs. Their movements appear to be limited to one site. They spend the dry months of the year underground or in leaf litter, emerge aboveground after the first autumn rain, breed in spring, and, as summer arrives, retreat again to moist areas. These types of individual movements constitute population-scale patterns.

Genetic variation in ensatinas was recently studied by Jackman and Wake (1994) and Moritz et al. (1992).[6] In this case, the researchers were not interested in specific genetic components, for example, rare or destructive forms of genes. Their primary focus was on the genetic patterns that characterized the populations and on the number of differences among these patterns. They discovered high levels of variation among populations and greater differences between populations separated by greater geographic distances. These patterns suggested information about genetic processes in ensatinas. For example, since the animals move very little, there is little gene flow among ensatina populations.

By subdividing ecosystem components, patterns, and processes according to biological scales, one can gain a better understanding of a range of aspects of biodiversity. This approach also helps identify attributes from different scales that might influence a specific concern. For example, to conserve a rare community type a planner might consider attributes at the landscape and population levels as well as the community scale. At the landscape level, abiotic factors constrain where vegetation grows, land-use pressures affect the rate at which it is developed, large-scale disturbances influence species diversity, and vegetation patterns govern the movements of community animals. At the population level, characteristics of regeneration, demographics, and movement affect the species and processes of the community. In general, diversity at any given level will be constrained by attributes associated with the level above and will exhibit properties that can be explained in part by the level below.[7] Because of these interactions, it is useful to consider and plan for biodiversity at multiple scales.

Biological Versus Spatial Scales

Intuitively, biological scales are associated with spatial scales. A landscape, being comprised of communities, is larger than its communities. Similarly, the size of a community is greater than its component populations. Genes, while not relevant in a spatial sense, are certainly smaller than populations or individuals. This relationship between biological and spatial scales makes the biological hierarchy attractive to planners. Planning depends on mapping physical entities, and involves obtaining and depicting data at specific spatial scales.

In reality, however, the levels of the biological hierarchy do not have any preordained size.[8] The space occupied by a population of bears, for example, is much larger than that occupied by a population of butterflies. The communities associated with these two species groups would also cover very different sized areas. In this case, the area of the butterfly community would actually be smaller than that of the bear population. Landscapes, watersheds, and ecosystems are also spatially vague. Each is determined differently according to specific situations. Defined as a community and its physical environment,[9] an ecosystem can be contained in a drop of water or be as large as a continent.

In addition, some ecosystem processes span multiple biological and spatial scales. Nutrient cycles and wildfires are examples of this type of phenomenon. Nitrogen in a tree's leaves, for example, falls to the ground, is freed through decomposition, and taken up again by the tree's roots. As the primary component of the atmosphere, however, nitrogen also cycles on scales up to the global level. A fire can affect species populations, a whole forest, and the broader landscape. The severity of its impact varies depending on the scale at which it is assessed. Such multiscale processes defy simple categorization.

It is helpful to think of ecosystem components, and selected ecosystem processes, as continuums. The spatial scale selected determines which types of attributes are considered. Different spatial scales will suggest different biological hierarchies. For Mount Diablo, a relatively large area, one would consider oak woodlands, chaparral, and grasslands as general communities. The species best assessed at this level would be large, wide-ranging animals or those broadly associated with a particular vegetation type. If a smaller area was considered, a more detailed set of communities and environmental variables could be defined. This greater data resolution would enable an assessment of other species, in particular small animals, that require specific habitat conditions.

Variation over Time

We have so far constructed a two-dimensional framework to characterize biodiversity in a given area. It is based on components, patterns, and processes, the primary attributes of ecosystems. These attributes were then subdivided according to levels in a biological hierarchy. The biological levels correspond in a general way to spatial scales. Populations, communities, landscapes, and certain processes, however, also span multiple spatial scales.

From the standpoint of biodiversity, the importance of these ecosystem attributes is that they are varied. At each level, there is a range of components. Several types of landscapes occur on and around Mount Diablo. On any portion of the mountain we can detect at least ten biotic communities. Within each community—and moving among communities—are untold numbers of populations. Each population and each species harbors unique genetic combinations.

Patterns and processes at each level also vary. Fires, floods, storms, and droughts recur on Mount Diablo at different frequencies and intensities. Following such ecosystem disturbances, different associations of vegetation appear, each with its characteristic plants and structure. The demographic patterns of populations vary, such that species that regenerate well one year may do poorly in the next. Depending on opportunities for interbreeding, genetic diversity can increase or decrease.

Each variation is caused by a process or group of processes. Some of these interactions are relatively continuous, but their characteristics and effects can change. From year to year, the rate at which a weedy species invades a community might be fast or slow. A bird can breed each spring but produce chicks with more or less success. Other processes are discrete events that recur at certain time intervals. Hurricanes on the south coast of Texas, for example, occur about every three years.[10] The bird population increases each spring, but decreases later in the year as the juveniles are caught by predators. As a result, biodiversity is not only the range of variation that can be seen today, but that which is expressed over a period of time. This variation over time gives a third dimension to the framework.

An awareness of temporal variations is fundamental to biodiversity planning. Planners should try to understand the full range of diversity for which they are responsible, not just as it appears at one point in time. Often the data used include a single satellite image, or one set of aerial photographs, and field data collected on just a few dates. Yet to fully describe biodiversity, information over a period of time is necessary. An obvious question is: Which additional dates should be selected, that is, how long does the interval need to be to detect a significant portion of an area's diversity?

In recent years, there has been great interest among ecologists in the significance of scale. Numerous researchers have examined patterns and processes at different spatial scales.[11] In addition, they have estimated the time over which these phenomena take place. Repeatedly, the studies have found correlations between spatial and temporal scales. Variations associated with large areas are manifested over relatively long time periods, while those associated with small areas can be observed in shorter intervals. This is so because the processes that influence these variations tend to be correlated in space and time (figure 1.4).

Following the 1988 fires in Yellowstone National Park, Romme and Despain (1989) studied burn patterns in that region over the past three hundred years.[12] They found that the last time such extensive, stand-replacing fires had occurred was in the early 1700s. Smaller fires, generally covering less than 100 hectares, have occurred approximately every few decades.[13] Romme and Despain suggest that the 250-year time interval of the stand-replacing fires is associated with the lifespan of lodgepole pines, the most common tree in the park. This was the amount of time required for the forest to reestablish from the fires of the 1700s and develop a late-successional structure. The old-growth forest contained lots of flammable woody debris; this in combination with the driest summer since 1886 was sufficient to produce the large fires. Based on this study, biodiversity at the landscape scale in Yellowstone National Park would vary over a period of several hundred years.

In contrast, Hobbs and Mooney (1994) studied a small serpentine grassland in California.[14] Here, the major processes affecting the composition and

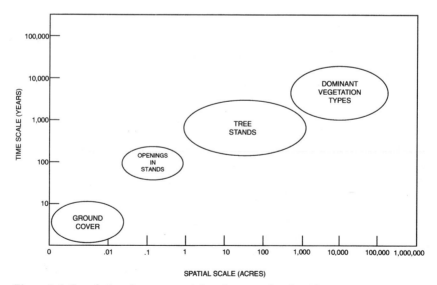

Figure 1.4. Correlations between spatial and temporal scales: The area over which ecological processes occur is related to the time period over which the processes vary. (Diagram adapted from Urban et al. (1987); scales were originally logarithmic.)

structure of the grassland were rainfall, gopher disturbance, and ants feeding on grass seed. The plants in the area were primarily annual grasses and forbs. Hobbs and Mooney estimate that diversity in this type of ecosystem would be expressed in just one to two decades.

These examples illustrate two important factors that affect the variation in biodiversity over time. The first involves the spatial scale of the processes: Lodgepole pine forests are influenced by large, landscape-scale fires. The grassland, on the other hand, is influenced by gophers and ants, factors operating on a scale of square feet. Variations in landscape-scale processes are often expressed in centuries, while variations in site-scale processes may require just a few years. The second factor is the lifespan of the dominant species in the community. The frequency at which plants or trees die affects the rate at which other species can establish and alter community composition. The annual grassland offers many opportunities each year for change, whereas significant change in the pine forest occurs at sporadic, multiyear intervals.

One way human-dominated landscapes differ from wilder ones is that they do not follow the space-time correlation.[15] Here, extensive areas can be altered in a short period of time. Many ecosystem attributes that existed before are modified, and new ones are introduced. These differences are due to the occurrence of different types of processes. Human-dominated landscapes are governed primarily by social, economic, and political concerns. In a natural grassland, for example, the composition of the community depends largely on the frequency and intensity of fire, on which species are able to colonize the area after a fire, and on competition between these species. If a housing complex was sited on the grassland, however, a new mixture of species would likely develop. For safety reasons, attempts would be made to control or eliminate fires. New exotic plants and pets would be introduced. These alterations would affect the viability of some of the original grassland species. The processes now influencing the grassland would be fire suppression, different forms of competition, and perhaps grazing or trampling from recreational activities. The time scale of these new processes has no relationship to the natural processes that previously dominated the grassland.

Temporal variation adds the final dimension to the framework, and with it we can characterize the full range of biodiversity. The variations associated with ecosystems are each expressed over some period of time. The amount of time depends on the processes that influence this diversity. In general, the components, patterns, and processes associated with larger spatial scales vary over longer time intervals than those at smaller spatial scales. Longer-lived species, and the communities they dominate, also vary over longer periods of time than do short-lived species and their communities. Human processes do not necessarily follow this generalization. They are not related to natural processes at the same scale. They also tend to occur faster and to disrupt the patterns of the natural processes. For these reasons, the time required for changes in human-dominated landscapes should be considered separately.

The Biodiversity Framework and Planning

The main purpose of developing this framework is to help planners develop a sense of biodiversity in the areas in which they work. They can create their own frameworks of landscapes, communities, and species populations, and of the types of patterns and processes that support these different components. This conceptual organization will help in considering biodiversity at different spatial scales, and how it might vary over different time intervals.

A second purpose of the framework is to help in the assessment of bio-diversity issues. Conserving a particular community or species, or overall biodiversity in an area, requires that a range of interrelated factors be addressed. A model that includes components, patterns, and processes at various scales will help identify the factors most significant to the situation.

One benefit of the framework is that it may uncover an issue that is important at certain spatial and temporal scales, but not at others. For example, a site might be developed in such a way as to protect a particular woodland. If the site was evaluated in terms of the broader landscape, however, one might see that the woodland was surrounded by residential development. This larger pattern would suggest that the woodland species were isolated from other populations and may decline over a longer period of time. Alternatively, a planner might be working in a region seemingly devastated by insect pests and wildfires. When viewed from the perspective of centuries, these processes might be revealed as inherent to the forest and not an ecological problem at all.

A potential problem with the framework is that it can be overwhelming. It demonstrates the complexity of biodiversity and how various aspects of it might be understood. Yet planners are always limited by resources and by the data and studies that are available. To be effective, they must focus on those portions of biodiversity that they have the capacity to address. Within these constraints, they can select priorities, as recommended in chapter 2.

Choosing appropriate spatial and temporal scales is a particular planning challenge. In most cases, one of these choices will be the landscape scale. Many planners, including land use or open space planners, are responsible for large regions, such as a county or regional park district. Biodiversity conservation groups—often comprised of planners, landowners, agency personnel, and academics—also address larger areas. In addition, many issues impacting biodiversity result from land uses that affect extended landscapes.

As noted earlier, the natural processes associated with landscapes tend to vary over intervals ranging from decades to centuries. This time span presents difficulties for data collection and analysis. Planners have addressed this issue by compiling historical data, such as old air photos, anecdotal information, and other data gathered in the past by resource agencies. Geographically based models can also be employed to assess long-term patterns and trends. While this information may be incomplete, it can still help indicate the ways in which a landscape might vary over time. Geographic information systems are being increasingly used for this purpose. (See chapters 3 and 6 for further discussion.)

The landscape-scale assessment and local biodiversity issues may suggest additional spatial scales for analysis. The broad assessment may highlight threatened areas or communities that are rare, have high species diversity, or are especially productive. Endangered, sensitive, or rare species or species and land uses particularly valued by the public may be a special concern. Community and population-scale attributes could be considered in these types of situations using more detailed data. Again, it is important to estimate the time intervals over which these attributes might vary.

This chapter has explored the broad concept of biodiversity. As was done for Mount Diablo, each of us can begin to develop a framework to characterize and conserve biodiversity in our own areas. Subsequent chapters of the book present more information to help with specific aspects of this process. They elaborate on key components, patterns, and processes and show how planners have incorporated ecosystem attributes into conservation strategies.

Multiscale Planning for a Threatened Landscape

The Cosumnes River Project, California

LOCATION MAP

CALIFORNIA

The Cosumnes River is the last undammed river flowing from the Sierra Nevada into California's great Central Valley. Its 1,250 square-mile watershed supports a variety of biotic communities, ranging from high altitude red fir forests to the riparian woodlands and wetlands at the river's confluence with the Sacramento–San Joaquin Delta. The floodplain includes the best remnants of valley oak riparian forest left in the state. The area also supports tens of thousands of migratory waterfowl, neotropical songbirds, and many rare fish species. In the future, however, these ecological values will be increasingly jeopardized by urbanization and water diversions. Most of the watershed lies in Sacramento and El Dorado counties, two of the fastest growing counties in the state. In anticipation of the threat, The Nature Conservancy (TNC) and eight partner organizations have developed a comprehensive conservation plan. Their goal is to preserve the natural communities along the river corridor as one large sustainable ecosystem.

The project started with a more limited vision and scope. Its initial focus was the Cosumnes River floodplain, identified by California's Natural Diversity Data Base as an outstanding example of Central Valley wetlands and riparian forest (figure 1.5). Extremely valuable biologically, these two communities have been reduced to 6 percent and 2 percent of their original distributions. TNC and partner Ducks Unlimited responded in 1986 by establishing a 1,400-acre floodplain preserve, including freshwater wetlands, riparian forest, and adjacent agricultural lands. At that point, conservation efforts were concentrated solely on specific valley bottom communities and species.

The project expanded dramatically in 1990. By this time it was apparent that the floodplain communities were dependent on watershed-scale patterns and processes. The shift coincided with an overall change at The Nature Conservancy to a broader, ecosystem approach to conservation. Since riparian forests and wetlands are sustained by seasonal flows and flooding, TNC ecologists argued that the entire river should be included in the plan. In considering the larger watershed, project designers discovered additional biotic communities and landscape patterns that merited protection. The foothills, for example, support rare Ione chaparral, vernal pools, and blue oak woodlands, a poorly regenerating habitat used by numerous vertebrate species. The configuration of communities in the landscape also appeared important in maintaining top

Figure 1.5. Conserving wetlands and riparian forests along the Cosumnes River requires preserving watershed-scale patterns and processes. (Photographs courtesy of The Nature Conservancy.)

predators and terrestrial migratory species. These realizations prompted a reassessment of the biological values, processes, and potential threats to all of the watershed's threatened natural communities. The study resulted in a strategic plan that addresses ecology and sustainability throughout much of the area. As of 1998, the plan covers 14,000 acres.

The 1992 strategic plan identified a range of species, communities, processes, and patterns as conservation priorities. Among other criteria, priority species and communities were selected on the basis of their levels of rarity, ecological function, quality, and vulnerability. Hydrologic processes, including flooding, are considered critical to the biodiversity of the whole river system. Other processes, such as fire, herbivory, and predation, maintain the ecology of individual communities. The plan also notes patterns of vegetation and land uses that affect specific wildlife species.

The 1992 plan designated six focused planning areas in which conservation efforts would be concentrated. These units were based on similarities in biotic communities, ecological threats, protection strategies, and regulatory jurisdictions. A detailed plan is being developed for each focused planning area that outlines specific priorities and threats, additional studies required, and strategies to achieve plan goals for that area. Preferred land uses and management prescriptions are stated for core areas of the highest biological value, for buffer zones adjacent to the cores, and for transitional areas between the buffers and urbanization. The detailed plans have been developed in phases and prioritized based on the degree of threat to each area.

The scope and complexity of the project require a high level of ecological understanding. To address this need, TNC and its partner organizations created numerous ecological models and conducted surveys of the aquatic systems and selected communities and species. They developed a set of natural community relationships matrices to highlight associations among species, communities, processes, and land uses along transects throughout the watershed. A migration model shows potential wildlife routes through varied vegetation across an elevational gradient. A watershed hydrologic model, created with help from the U.S. Forest Service, the U.S. Geological Survey, and Bechtel Corporation, helps planners evaluate the impacts of potential water diversions from the river. Survey data will continue to improve the models, allowing greater understanding of key ecosystem attributes and their relationships.

The project's success to date stems in large part from the partnership of public and private organizations. In addition to TNC, Ducks Unlimited, the Wildlife Conservation Board, the California Department of Fish and Game, the U.S. Bureau of Land Management (BLM), Sacramento County, the American Farmland Trust, the California Department of Water Resources, and Living

Farms now participate jointly in the plan. The BLM in particular has played a key role in both land acquisition and preserve management; currently, a BLM employee serves as preserve manager, with a portion of that salary paid by TNC. The group shares a common vision, yet also benefits from the different expertise, data, and perspectives contributed by the nine members. For example, TNC's strengths include planning, rare and vulnerable species management, land acquisition, and an awareness of landscape processes and patterns. Ducks Unlimited, a nonprofit sportsmen's organization, adds extensive experience in managed wetlands. The resource agencies contribute technical expertise, data, and management. The participation of water and planning agencies is essential to implementing beneficial conservation policies, while the farm organizations can help bridge ecological and agricultural interests. A 1993 memorandum of understanding defines the role of each partner. Together, the group can accomplish more objectives on a much larger scale than any member could achieve on its own.

The long-term goal of the project is to create a sustainable mosaic of communities along the Cosumnes River. To this end, a primary objective is to develop strategic alliances with local government, industry, and the community. These alliances help resolve conflicts, increase appreciation for ecological values, and promote involvement in conservation activities. TNC and its partners are working actively with county planning departments to establish policies that protect conservation priorities and provide economic growth. Through landowner outreach and partnerships with farming and ranching associations, the project seeks to determine and promote ecologically compatible management practices. To ensure that the project is an asset to the community, it has offered environmental education in the schools, created a visitors' center, and built self-guided trails. Demonstration projects to showcase appropriate conservation, management, and development will build on these community links.

Approximately $35 million has been spent on the Cosumnes River Project to date. Of these funds, $10 million was obtained from private donations through TNC, and $25 million was received from federal and state government sources. The latter public sources include the BLM, the EPA, the federal Intermodal Surface Transportation Efficiency Act (ISTEA), State of California bond acts, and annual appropriations from the California legislature. Some funds have also been received as mitigation for private development.

The Cosumnes River Project is impressive in its approach to ecological conservation. The strategic plan encompasses multiple attributes of biodiversity by targeting key species, communities, patterns, and processes. These priorities and their interrelationships have been determined though a series of studies, surveys and models. By establishing the nine-member partnership, the project has been able to consider aspects of ecosystems ranging from the watershed scale to individual sites. Long-term sustainability is being addressed by encouraging the involvement and interests of local organizations and landowners. The Nature Conservancy expects plan development and implementation, already a decade in operation, to continue for another ten years. The Cosumnes River Project is an inspirational multiscale biodiversity plan.

FOR FURTHER INFORMATION CONTACT:

The Nature Conservancy
Cosumnes River Project
13501 Franklin Boulevard
Galt, CA 95632
916-684-2816

Chapter 2

Developing Conservation Priorities

Most people live near a special natural area where they have wandered familiar trails, picnicked, listened to the birds, or simply sat and thought. Following the framework introduced in chapter 1, they could probably characterize much of the biodiversity of this familiar open space. With enough research, they could identify biotic communities and species, locate them on a map, and describe distinctive patterns in the vegetation. They could pinpoint changes in certain communities and populations. Yet, if they were also responsible for conserving the area, such a portrayal would be just the first stage of a more complex process. Having described biodiversity, they would now have to translate this broad, unwieldy array of attributes into a conservation plan.

This chapter is designed to help planners develop a focus for a plan. It presents potential priorities that have been suggested by ecologists and conservationists over the past few decades. The priorities include aspects of biodiversity that might be especially influential in a natural area, as well as those that could easily be lost. Focusing on these types of attributes helps preserve a greater range of biodiversity.

The targets of a conservation plan will likely include a combination of components, patterns, and processes at various spatial or biological scales. Within the literature, components at the community and landscape levels have been given the most attention. We have been primarily interested in preserving species, the components of communities, and an efficient way to do this is to preserve the diversity of communities in each landscape. Accordingly, scientists have sought to identify categories of species and ecosystems that are either ecologically valuable or vulnerable. As the understanding of biodiversity has progressed, however, additional targets have been proposed. For instance, key patterns and processes that sustain biodiversity might now also be priorities. Work on populations and genetics has led to further guidelines at these scales. Depending on the local situation, any group of these attributes might constitute an appropriate focus.

A planner's own goals, mandates, and opportunities will help determine which of these potential priorities are applicable. One important consideration is the size of the planning area. This will determine the general range of attributes that might be addressed. Responsibility for a regional park, for example, would indicate greater emphasis on landscapes and communities. In contrast, a plan to protect a particular species population would focus primarily on population and genetic-level concerns. Both cases, however, would still include biodiversity targets from several scales. In general, it is useful to start with the largest scale applicable, since the higher levels will cover many aspects of biodiversity that exist at lower scales. Where this broad approach does not suffice, planners can add population and genetic scale attributes for specific species types.

Other considerations include the landscape itself, and the social, economic, and political context of the plan. What types of communities and native species occur in the area? Which processes support them? What is the configuration of open space and land use? Are there any immediate or anticipated threats? The answers to these sorts of questions will also suggest certain priorities. The local climate may dictate additional targets, and will undoubtedly influence a group of targets chosen strictly from a biodiversity perspective. For example, funding available to the project, public attitudes toward conservation and planning, and the specific interests of politicians, resource agency personnel, and local activists will all play a role.

Landscape Scale

A former colleague of mine at the California Department of Forestry and Fire Protection had a very effective way of conveying concepts of landscape conservation to the public.[1] He would begin a presentation with a slide of Vincent Van Gogh's familiar painting, *Starry Night*. After the audience had studied the colors, brushstrokes, and vibrant energy of the work, he would ask them how he might remove some of its values, yet still have it remain recognizable. One option would be to "save" patches of the painting, while blackening the rest. Although certain areas stayed pristine, it was obvious that the overall "landscape" of *Starry Night* was gone. Another alternative was to dim all the hues throughout the painting. Now every part of the landscape was modified, but you could still make out the painting. The analogy was the perfect lead-in to a discussion on the values, objectives, and approaches to landscape conservation.

As the *Starry Night* demonstration shows, there are different ways to approach landscape conservation, and different balances that can be achieved between biodiversity and human land uses. There is no correct answer; the objective from a biodiversity standpoint is simply to make choices which best preserve the "picture" of the landscape. To arrive at these choices, one has to determine which aspects of biodiversity are most significant. At the landscape scale, the major components include the biotic communities and abiotic factors such as soils and hydrologic features. Added to these components will be key spatial patterns and ecological processes that maintain the communities and selected species populations. As a group, the landscape priorities include:

• Community representation,
• Community types (species-rich, "natural," vulnerable, endemic, rare, sensitive),
• Unusual abiotic features (soils, substrates, perrenial water sources, springs),
• Functional associations of communities,
• Abiotic gradients,
• Extensive blocks of open space,
• Connections between natural areas,
• Migratory species' routes,
• Overall landscape pattern,
• Disturbance processes, and
• Hydrologic processes.

Within the set of potential landscape priorities, one of the most common is to protect representative samples of each major community. Community representation, with an emphasis on rare and threatened types, is the "coarse filter" approach developed by The Nature Conservancy.[2] Conserving examples of each community is a direct method of maintaining landscape diversity. Because many organisms are associated with specific communities, the approach should also preserve a majority of species. In addition, it is one of the few methods available for protecting the multitude of species yet undiscovered.

Among this range of communities, scientists have recommended certain categories for special attention. High among these are systems that are "species rich," or used by a great number of species. For conservation purposes, the species considered are only native species. In desert regions, for example, the majority of species are found in riparian zones. Riparian ecosystems offer water, shade, and other habitat features not found in the surrounding environment. While there is no single explanation for species richness, it has been correlated with such factors as lower latitudes, lower altitudes, the productivity of the ecosystem (the volume of biotic material it generates), the structural complexity of vegetation, higher year-round temperatures, water availability, and patterns in competition and predation.[3]

Communities that are essentially "natural" or considered viable over time are also ecologically valuable. A more "natural" community would be one that is only slightly modified, contains primarily native species, and requires less human input to maintain system function.[4] Among other values, these high quality examples provide a reference point against which we can compare other sites, and should better support biodiversity. The Nature Conservancy currently targets viable native communities as part of its conservation program.[5] To establish viability, ecologists assess the condition of the community and the ability of the surrounding landscape to sustain community processes. The assessment is used to determine if conservation of the site is feasible and worth a major expenditure of resources.

Vulnerable communities are also important planning targets. In California, for example, the coastal sage scrub is the focus of a state-level conservation program, since up to 90 percent of its historic distribution has been eliminated due to development.[6] Throughout the western United States, numerous freshwater communities are also threatened as a result of dams, water diversions, and other waterway modifications. In California alone, 72 percent of the native freshwater fish are either extinct, listed, or candidates for listing as endangered or threatened.[7] Such communities require immediate protection if they and their associated species are to survive.

Communities that occur in a limited geographic area may also be at risk. They are termed "endemic," as are the species within them, meaning that they are native to the region and exist nowhere else in the world. Different endemic communities and species are often found in the same region, since they develop as a result of certain environmental conditions. Islands are typically hotspots of endemism. On Hawaii, for instance, the original colonizing plants and animals are thought to have evolved into new species to take advantage of unoccupied habitats.[8] Most remained endemic since they had few opportunities to disperse. California has a large number of endemic species and communities due to its varied environment, and because its mountains and deserts have restricted dispersal. In the United States, California has the most endemics, followed by Hawaii, Florida, and Texas.[9]

Similar to endemics, rare communities are less secure because they exist in few locations; we have to be more careful with what we have. Those that occur on specialized soils, such as serpentine and limestone, are good examples. Old-growth forests are rare for two reasons: They require many centuries to develop, and they have been overexploited for commercial purposes. Other communities may be rare in one location, but relatively common in another. Because of the latter situation, scientists caution that rarity should be viewed at more than one spatial scale, for example, at a regional, state, or national scale in addition to the local level.[10] Communities that have become rare recently, for example, due to overharvesting or development, are usually at greater risk than those that have always been rare, because their species are not as adapted to the recent changes. They may, for example, now experience difficulty finding mates or become inbred. The Baraboo Hills Project, one of this chapter's case studies, prioritizes fifteen rare communities. Some relic stands of boreal forest have persisted on the hills' cool, north-facing cliffs since the last ice age, disappearing elsewhere as the climate warmed. One type of oak savanna, formerly distributed through four states, is now limited to the Baraboo Hills due to land use conversions to agriculture and development.

Communities that are inherently sensitive may also be planning targets. Jensen et al. (1993) note that desert habitats are particularly susceptible to degradation by virtue of their soil characteristics and overall harsh conditions.[11] Desert soils can be easily damaged, either by compaction or by erosion after the protective surface is broken. Recovery in this environment may take decades or even centuries.

A final category of priority components at the landscape scale is unusual abiotic features. Instead of targeting rare communities that grow on certain soils, one could approach the situation from the opposite direction, and focus on the rare soils and substrates that support these communities. In addition to wetlands and riparian zones, specific hydrologic features may be particularly valuable. Springs, for example, often harbor endemic or rare species, while perennial streams in arid landscapes are a precious ecological resource.

Although the components of a landscape, especially its biotic communities, are obvious starting points in establishing priorities, they cannot be the only ones. Species depend on many more types of interactions than occur within homogeneous community types. Moreover, the communities themselves developed and are maintained by a number of ecological processes. Thus our next step is to consider landscape patterns and processes.

One of the most important landscape patterns may be certain groupings of communities, the association of which enables valuable ecological processes to occur.[12] Estuaries and riparian zones are examples of this type of functional combination. Both result from aquatic and upland communities in close prox-imity. Estuaries also include both freshwater and saltwater habitats, and deposits of upstream nutrients, organic matter, and silt. The mix of elements from various communities produces the high productivity characteristic of these systems. Certain species also require multiple adjacent communities. Deer, for instance, move between wooded and open areas to feed and rest. Rap-tors roost in trees, yet often hunt in adjacent meadows or agricultural fields. Small animals such as aquatic insects and amphibians depend on a combina-tion of aquatic and terrestrial habitats for different stages in their life cycles. To preserve the functions of these areas, a site containing the entire grouping of communities would be an appropriate target.

A drive from sea level to the top of a coastal mountain demonstrates a sec-ond type of landscape pattern. In essence, the trip is a transect across an eleva-tional gradient. Along the way, other abiotic gradients are also evident. Differ-ences in elevation cause changes in temperature and precipitation. Landscape topography varies from flat plains to steep slopes. These abiotic gradients are important to biodiversity planning because they limit the distribution of species and communities. Due to their adaptations, organisms live within cer-tain ranges of climate and elevation. Some species, such as butterflies, use dif-ferent sides, or aspects, of a hillside at different points in their lives.[13] Preserv-ing the range of abiotic gradients in a region is therefore an indirect method of conserving species. Where gradients change quickly, for example in mountain-ous areas, this approach also may help organisms shift their ranges as the glob-al climate warms.[14]

The specific configuration of natural areas is a priority for conserving another group of animals. Extensive blocks of open space, for instance, provide the greater areas required by larger animals. They can support species not found in smaller spaces. Populations of the largest predators, however, need even more area than can be provided by a single park. For these organisms, vast interconnected networks of wilderness may be the only solution.[15] Migratory species depend on protection of their travel routes as well as their seasonal habitats. Since they move across multiple communities, such species are best addressed at the landscape scale.

Beyond these specific cases, the overall pattern of vegetation in the land-scape may be worth consideration. What are the ranges of patch size and shape? What is their position in relation to one another? Are there many vege-tation types close together, or is it all one homogenous stand? Together, the general characteristics of the pattern might constitute a target in their own right. Sometimes, we may know the implications of a certain type of landscape structure. For example, the vast, unfragmented forests of Wisconsin's Baraboo Hills are crucial to a range of sensitive species. (See case study, this chapter.) Often, however, we do not have the resources to understand how a given landscape might influence most aspects of biodiversity. In these latter situations, it may be appropriate to try to preserve the basic pattern, even if we do not yet know all the reasons why.

Disturbances are one of the most significant groups of processes at the landscape scale. As described in chapter 4, disturbances include such events as fire, flooding, extreme storms, and landslides. Since fires and flooding take place routinely in certain communities, resident species are often adapted to the characteristic patterns in which they have recurred over many centuries. The frequency, intensity, and seasons of these disturbances can affect reproduction and regeneration, as well as the diverse habitats that different species require. For these types of landscapes, maintaining or reinstituting disturbance patterns is a major priority.

A second set of significant landscape processes are those associated with hydrology. The hydrologic processes that directly affect biodiversity involve the flow of water, organisms, nutrients, and sediment across the landscape and along waterways. They primarily influence aquatic communities and terrestrial communities closely associated with water. Since streams and rivers are interconnected systems, these processes are best addressed at a broad, watershed scale.

One overall goal with regard to hydrologic processes is to maintain or restore the historic flow regime. Species in aquatic, riparian, and wetland communities are sustained by certain patterns of water flow: the volume and rate of flow (including occasional flooding), and the variations in these factors according to season and over the years. For watersheds where the historic flow regime still exists, protection of the entire site is a clear priority. (See the Cosumnes River Project case study, chapter 1.) In most cases, however, planners will encounter systems that have been substantially modified. The priorities in these latter situations will likely be limited to restoration of certain areas of watersheds and/or aspects of the hydrologic regime.

Community Scale

At the community scale, planners can focus on specific attributes of communities or ecosystems and the various forms in which these systems occur. This level of detail would be missed in a broad landscape-scale assessment. Chief among the attributes are categories of species that are especially valuable and vulnerable. Also included are patterns and processes that affect habitat quality within a community. Priorities at the community scale are:

- Species types (keystone, vulnerable, rare, endemic, specialist, migratory, exotic),
- Vegetation structure (vertical layers, vegetation density, canopy closure),
- Habitat resources, (water sources, breeding and roosting sites, snags, dead branches, leaf litter) and their availability and distribution, and
- Disturbances.

Depending on the size of a planning area, selected community-scale targets may be used to complement those at the landscape level, or they may be the primary focus. When planning a countywide open space, for example, only certain communities and species can be addressed at this degree of resolution. In contrast, a plan for a small park district might involve in-depth assessments of most communities.

Similar to the landscape scale, the community scale includes components considered particularly significant for maintaining diversity. The valuable components in this case are called *keystone species*, because they influence critical ecological processes. The elimination of a keystone species can result in significant ecosystem changes, including the loss of numerous other species. The concept is important in conservation because it demonstrates that organisms differ in their effects on ecosystem function. For example, the extinction of a common sparrow would likely have little or no impact on an ecosystem, especially if there were several other species of sparrows in the area. In contrast, the extinction of an oak species could have a great ecological influence, since oaks are dominant components of biotic communities and provide acorns and habitat to a variety of other species.

The term "keystone species" was first coined to describe the effects of predatory seastars in California tide pools.[16] The seastars maintain diversity by feeding primarily on one type of prey; when the seastar is removed, its prey population increases, forcing a number of other species from the system. Since 1969, scientists have sought to identify additional keystone species. Some of the candidates include beavers, whose activities modify stream and riparian systems,[17] and sea otters, which maintain kelp forests by reducing sea urchin populations, which otherwise decimate the kelp.[18] Groups of species have also been considered keystone, such as mycorrhizal fungi, critical to the growth and productivity of many trees, and nitrogen-fixing plants and their associated bacteria. Unfortunately, there is no clear definition of keystone species,[19] nor are we likely to find lists of which such organisms exist in our local areas. What is most useful is simply the idea that certain species are likely to be particularly influential in their ecosystems. Some of these may be recognized by ecologists, and should be accorded priority by conservation planners.

Vulnerable, rare, and endemic species are also potential targets at the community scale. Vulnerable species include many with which planners are already familiar: those identified on federal or state lists as endangered, threatened, or as candidates for listing. Beyond their legal status, such species clearly merit protection because they face an immediate threat. Native plant societies and other conservation organizations might suggest additional species that are approaching extinction or that are rare and thought to be at risk. As noted earlier, it is useful to assess rarity within broad scales, as well as at the local level. Endemic species, particularly plants, are often associated with certain regions or endemic communities, and so might already be covered under landscape-scale priorities.

Another type of priority species is a group termed *specialists*. Specialist species depend on a very narrow range of resources. Michigan's Kirtland's warbler, for example, breeds primarily in jack pine, a tree that requires fire for regeneration. After fire suppression policies caused a severe decline in jack pines, the warbler became endangered.[20] Insects are often specialists, requiring specific plants for feeding or on which to lay their eggs. This category of species is particularly vulnerable because its resources may constitute a small portion of a larger community. Planning or management to benefit other aspects of the community could eliminate them if they were not given special status.

Whereas the categories noted above are targets for protection, invasive exotic species may be targets for elimination. Exotic species have become established in numerous ecosystems across the United States. They comprise nearly 50 percent of the plants in coastal California, the majority of species in lowland Hawaii, and an estimated 30 to 60 percent of western fish species.[21] Such organisms are destructive to ecosystems because they displace native species and alter ecological processes. They possess characteristics that enable them to be superior competitors: They are hardy, adaptable, capable of dispersing long distances, and able to establish, spread, and persist in new environments. Exotic species have been known to affect such ecosystem properties as productivity, decomposition, nutrient cycling, water flows, soil fertility, and disturbance regimes.[22] The changes often favor exotics at the expense of native organisms. Examples of exotic species include bullfrogs in many western streams, zebra mussels in the Great Lakes, honeysuckle in eastern forests, cheatgrass in the Rocky Mountain region, and kudzu in the South.

Exotic species that have been identified as problems in local ecosystems require particular attention in planning and management. The most effective approach is to prevent their introduction, since eradication, aside from being costly, may be impossible. Disturbed areas, such as roadways, trailways, and recent burns are typical sites for exotic plants to establish. To avoid this occurrence, construction practices could include reseeding with local native species. Prescribed fires could also be monitored to ensure that they benefit native species, as opposed to opportunistic invaders. Nonnative animals introduced for fishing or hunting could be evaluated beforehand for their effects on native species and communities.

The patterns that are significant at the community level include varying structures of vegetation and the distribution of key habitat resources. Vegetation structure usually refers to the vertical layers, or height groups, that exist within a community. Grasses and small flowering plants might constitute one layer, while shrubs, small trees, and large conifers might make up other layers. Individual layers, or combinations of layers, provide habitat to different species. A second aspect of structure that affects habitat involves the density of vegetation, or the number of trees or plants in an area, and the space existing between them. Resources such as water sources, breeding and roosting sites, snags, dead branches, and leaf litter add additional habitat elements or may be habitats in their own right. Both vegetation structure and habitat resources can often be maintained or modified through management, thus influencing the species the community contains.

Community patterns are determined largely by ecological processes. Disturbances such as fire, flooding, storms, small animal burrows, and treefalls open up areas in the vegetation. These open areas are then colonized by new species adapted to greater amounts of sunlight, wind, or nutrients. Over time, the colonizing species may be replaced by others as environmental conditions slowly change. Whereas some degree of change is inevitable, certain types and regimes of disturbances are required to achieve specific community patterns. The two are linked; prioritizing a particular pattern necessitates implementing a particular disturbance regime. For example, in Montana's Beaverhead/Deerlodge National Forest (see case study in chapter 3) managers observed that aspen and ponderosa pine regenerated poorly in forests with dense understories. To promote these species, they reinstituted frequent, low-intensity controlled burns, which resulted in open forest stands.

Population Scale

Conserving a population of a target species requires consideration of attributes at several scales. At the landscape scale, the presence and spatial patterns of communities will be important. At the community scale, the species will need certain types of vegetation structures and habitat elements. At the population scale, attributes relating to population dynamics can be addressed. These population-scale priorities include:

• Minimum population sizes,
• Metapopulations (subpopulations and connections between subpopulations),
• Isolated populations,
• Dispersal, and
• Migration.

The implications of population-level processes for genetic diversity are highlighted by priorities at the genetic scale.

One of the most important priorities at the population level is maintaining adequate space, or habitat, to support a sufficiently large population over time. A second issue may be the spatial distribution of populations. For example, the population may actually consist of multiple, interconnected subpopulations, or it might occur in an unusual geographical location. The ability to carry out necessary movements, such as migration, dispersal, or searching for food, is also critical. Issues related to the population-scale priorities described below are explained further in chapter 4.

The concept of "minimum viable populations" has received particular emphasis in recent years. Small populations are liable to become extinct from a combination of chance events. These events include demographic factors, such as variations in sex ratios; environmental factors, such as droughts and storms; and genetic factors, such as inbreeding and the gradual loss of genetic diversity. Any one of these can reduce the size or fitness of a population, and several together can eliminate a small population altogether.

While environmental factors affect populations of any size, planners can minimize demographic factors and the immediate loss of genetic diversity by maintaining populations above a few hundred. Preserving long-term genetic diversity, however, may require animal populations of several thousand. Conserving genetic diversity in plant populations is more complex, due to their varied reproductive strategies. Many plants self-pollinate or reproduce through vegetative means such as sprouting. Thus they can occur naturally in small, inbred groups, and tolerate small population sizes better than organisms that interbreed.[23] Most populations with fewer than one hundred numbers can be considered a priority since they are immediately threatened. Others with fewer than five hundred or one thousand may still be planning targets if the goal is conservation over numerous centuries.

The patterns that may be priorities at the population scale include metapopulation configurations and the distribution of populations throughout a species' range. Metapopulations are groups of populations linked by individuals that travel occasionally among them. For example, birds nesting on islands and pikas, small rodents that live in patches of mountain rocks, exist by necessity in this type of structure. Scientists have found an increasing number of species that occur in metapopulations. The links among the subpopulations help maintain genetic diversity, because they allow interbreeding. They also help sustain a species in a region. If a population is eliminated in one area, it can be reestablished by individuals from an adjacent population. Populations at the edge of a species' range, or separate from other populations, may be targets because they are often genetically distinct. The ensatinas populations described in chapter 1, for example, vary significantly due to virtual geographic isolation. Preserving this diversity helps maintain the evolutionary opportunities of the species.

Among the processes that sustain populations, dispersal may be the most significant for planners, since it depends on the design of open space. Dispersal occurs when juvenile animals leave the area in which they were born to establish their own ranges as adults. Plant dispersal involves the distribution of seeds and spores to new locations in the landscape. Dispersal helps maintain the size of a population and allows it to shift locations during unfavorable environmental conditions. It also enables interbreeding among populations. Preserving a target population thus includes learning how that species disperses and protecting the appropriate configuration of open space to allow the process to occur.

Genetic Scale

Now distributed globally, the Monterey pine (*Pinus radiata*) is one of the most extensively harvested types of commercial trees. At the same time, it is a federal candidate for listing as a threatened species. This seeming contradiction stems from genetic diversity considerations. The native populations of Monterey pine have been reduced to three small stands on the California coast. While the species has been introduced worldwide, the range of genetic diversity that it contains is located in these three stands. From a genetic perspective, the native stands are the species; they hold all the ways it can exist, all its evolutionary potential, and all the genetic combinations that might increase its use as a commercial tree.

Genetic diversity refers to the variety of genes existing within an individual, population, or species. In planning, we are interested in the variations within a local population, and how these differences relate to the overall genetic diversity of the species, with the priorities being:

• Genetically distinct populations,
• Historic patterns of variations (within and among populations), and
• Historic patterns of dispersal and interbreeding.

Genetic diversity determines how a population responds to disturbances, and its potential to evolve. If a population is genetically diverse, it is more likely that some individuals will possess genes to withstand changes in environmental conditions. These individuals are adapted to their altered habitat and can survive. Through natural selection, the population evolves so that more individuals eventually possess the beneficial genes. Species are less likely to survive change or evolve if their populations are limited in genetic diversity.

Genetic diversity is distributed within species in many ways.[24] For example, incense-cedar trees in California contain a wide range of genes within each population, and their populations are genetically similar. This pattern is typical for many wind-pollinated plants and for animals that disperse across large distances. Due to their dispersal strategies, the populations of these species have more opportunities to interbreed and share genetic material. In contrast, a population of mountain frogs may evolve so that the individuals are genetically similar, but the population differs significantly from others of the same species. This diversity pattern is the result of restricted interbreeding and describes very isolated populations, as well as self-pollinating plants.

A general guideline for conserving genetic diversity is to retain the historic patterns of variation and dispersal. For species that vary gradually over a region, the priority would be to preserve interconnected populations throughout the geographic range. Maintaining opportunities for dispersal and interbreeding would be important to retain the gradient pattern. The opposite would be true for species that occur in small, isolated populations. Here, the priority would be to protect individual populations, especially those that are significantly different in genetic composition. Since interbreeding occurs rarely in such species, care should be taken to avoid mixing separate populations.

Ideally, genetic conservation is based on prior knowledge of the distribution of genetic material within a species. Scientists sample multiple populations to assess the range of genetic diversity both within and among the species' populations. Usually, however, planners do not have this type of information. Most genetic analysis has been conducted on endangered species, on animals in zoos, or where it is valuable for commercial applications, such as in forestry or agriculture. More data may be available for plants, since they are easier to sample.

Even without this information, genetic conservation is still possible. One strategy is to estimate the level of dispersal and interbreeding that may have existed historically among a species' populations. For example, we might assume that significant interbreeding occurred in a organism that was distributed evenly throughout a region. We could feel more secure if we knew that the species could disperse over great distances. Then again, a small group of endemic plants has probably had little interaction with other populations. Maintaining landscape links among populations would be important in the first case; in the second case, our focus would be to maintain the genetic integrity of the single population.

A second strategy is to avoid introductions from nonlocal populations.[25] This issue is particularly pertinent to restoration, where the plants used may be "native," but from populations located far from the area. Plant materials should be collected on or near the site, where environmental conditions are similar. From a practical standpoint, seeds or cuttings from other populations often lack site-specific adaptations and may not survive. For genetic conservation, the practice is detrimental because it weakens the local population. When the introduced and local individuals interbreed, the resulting offspring may also lack certain adaptations, so the population may decline.

A third approach, as suggested earlier, is to maintain populations above a certain minimum size. The slow, ongoing loss of genetic diversity that occurs in any isolated population has greater effects on small groups, since they have less to lose. A direct approach to maintaining the size of a population is to preserve the space that it requires. Additional habitat might be provided through certain management strategies, such as eliminating competitive exotics, or by choosing and timing management to support the target population.[26]

Combining Development with Biodiversity Conservation
Spring Island, South Carolina

Spring Island is a 3,000-acre sea island located on the South Carolina coast in Port Royal Sound. Until the mid-1990s the site remained virtually undeveloped. Used for limited farming, and then as a hunting preserve, it still retains many communities and species now rare in the Southeast. The Spring Island Company purchased the island in 1990. The developers' vision was to construct a private park, with housing, services, and a golf course, while maintaining the integrity of the island's ecological values. Prior to construction, they identified the range of communities and species and determined priorities for conservation. They sought to protect biodiversity by establishing nature preserves and policies for site design. To ensure long-term conservation, they founded a trust to manage the preserves and to foster environmental appreciation among the new residents. Spring Island demonstrates a promising model for combining development with ecological preservation.

Priorities at the landscape-scale guided the initial selection of sites for protection and development. One of the most important areas is the island's shoreline, since it is surrounded by salt marsh on all sides. Numerous species that feed in the marsh use these uplands for roosting and movement. Accordingly, no development was allowed within 100 feet of the shore or of any water feature. Development was also precluded from a ravine that supports rare plant species and habitat for neotropical songbirds. Communities that were protected include a large expanse of maritime forest and mature forested wetlands that also harbor endemic neotropical birds. Together, the preserves total more than 1,000 acres, approximately one-third of the island. New construction has been limited primarily to previously disturbed farming fields and old housing sites. New housing units were reduced to a maximum of five hundred, down from the 5,500 previously zoned for the island.

A major objective of the developers has been to maintain species diversity. Through surveys, they were able to determine which species occurred on the island. The habitat configurations and structures required by different types of organisms were then considered as part of the planning process. Highest priority was accorded to species that had declined elsewhere in their range, but still maintained significant populations on the island. Neotropical songbirds, bald eagles, and fox squirrels, for example, could either be harmed or protected by the Spring Island development. Bobcats and gray foxes were targeted because their numbers had been previously reduced by hunters. Amphibians as a group were given priority due to their relative sensitivity. The exotic brown-headed cowbird has also been monitored to determine potential impacts on native species.

The project has approached species conservation primarily through habitat management. Population-scale concerns are less relevant in this situation, since most species can disperse easily to the mainland. Their populations would therefore include individuals in other areas. In the event that these areas are eliminated, however, species with larger island populations have been given greater weight. Generally, however, the developers have protected species by maintaining the habitats that they require. Habitats for the most sensitive species have been included in the nature preserves. Others have been protected by retaining certain configurations of vegetation within the development itself.

Habitat around the homesites was protected by instituting setbacks and "nature curtains" (figure 2.1). In addition to the 100-foot setback for water features, no development was allowed within 150 feet of roads, or within 50 feet of the property boundaries. Within these setbacks, the 50 feet closest to the roads and 25 feet closest to the properties' side boundaries was designated as an undisturbed nature curtain. Laced throughout the development, the nature curtains provide habitat, link patches of vegetation, and support species movement.

One of the most valuable features of the project is the Spring Island Trust. The goal of the trust is to ensure long-term protection of the island's ecology. Its functions include conducting ecological surveys and monitoring, implementing beneficial management practices, and developing programs for residents and guests to increase environmental appreciation. It is a nonprofit organization funded by mandatory assessments of 1.5 percent on all homesites and 1 percent on all resale homes.

The Spring Island Trust is a significant concept among developments in that it assumes responsibility for preserve management, rather than leaving the job to homeowners, who may lack the necessary interest or expertise. At the same time, residents are recognized as vital components of conservation. To encourage a stewardship ethic, the trust employs two full-time naturalists to conduct tours, workshops, lectures, and seminars. They also advise homeowners on methods to maintain biodiversity on their properties. A Visiting Artist Program developed by the trust invites artists to stay on Spring Island, exhibit their work, and leave at least one piece inspired by the location. Researchers from nearby universities are also encouraged to conduct studies on the island. Their results increase environmental interest as well as baseline data. Each of these activities contributes to ongoing biodiversity conservation.

The developers feel that Spring Island has provided them with two types of

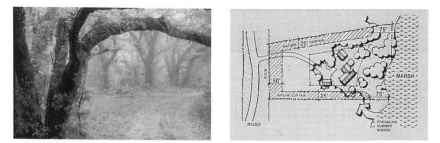

Figure 2.1. Live oak forest is a protected community at Spring Island (left); "nature curtains" designed along property boundaries provide habitat and connections between vegetation patches (right). (Photographs courtesy of the Spring Island Trust.)

reward. First, they are proud to have constructed a project which is environmentally sensitive. Second, they have achieved recognition in a small but unexploited market. They envision a growing demand for developments that preserve ecological values, and to date they have little competition. While they had initial difficulty securing funding, with time they were able to convince lenders of the concept's financial merit.

The Spring Island project contains several features which will help preserve the ecology of the island. By conducting surveys prior to construction, the developers obtained data to create the plan and against which they can monitor its success. The surveys also enabled them to identify target species, communities, and patterns of habitat. These priorities will be protected in nature preserves and through the design of individual homesites. The Spring Island Trust provides a vehicle for collecting additional data, for managing the preserves, and for encouraging ecological appreciation among the new residents. The project differs from some other developments in that the homes are expensive, and as such it has substantial funds for conservation. Since it is located on an island, issues such as landscape fragmentation and species dispersal were also less significant than they would be at other sites. Still, Spring Island demonstrates a variety of ways in which any development can protect biodiversity.

FOR FURTHER INFORMATION CONTACT:
> Bruce Lampright
> Spring Island Trust
> Route 6, Box 284
> Spring Island, SC 29910
> 803-986-2000

Protecting Landscapes and Communities

The Baraboo Hills Project, Baraboo, Wisconsin

LOCATION MAP

WISCONSIN

One of the finest examples of biological diversity in the upper Midwest lies in Wisconsin's Baraboo Hills. The 144,000 acre range encompasses the largest remaining upland deciduous forest in the state. It supports twenty-seven types of natural communities and provides habitat to seventy-seven rare or threatened species (figure 2.2). Yet now the unique ecology of the hills may be in jeopardy. A plan to widen Highway 12, which

Figure 2.2. The Baraboo Hills project includes measures to protect the large, unfragmented upland deciduous forest, and the many types of communities that occur in the landscape. It also targets many species, including the rare pickeral frog. (Photographs courtesy of The Nature Conservancy.)

bisects the range, is expected to attract new developments to house Madison commuters. Indiscriminate logging is also fragmenting the forest. Joining many other organizations and individuals, The Nature Conservancy has responded to the situation with a multipronged, community-based approach to conservation.

The diversity of the Baraboo Hills marks them as an ideal candidate for protection. Rising 500 feet from the surrounding plains, their varied topography and microclimates sustain a mix of natural communities found nowhere else in the region. Soils formed from the hills' unique quartzite support several taxa of rare plants and animals. Although the Baraboo hills cover less than 0.5 percent of the Midwest Savanna Ecoregion, they harbor 68 percent of the ecoregion's breeding bird species, and over 50 percent of Wisconsin's native vascular plant species. That such diversity still exists is also due in part to the topography and quartzite, which in the past have discouraged farming and development.

Extensive, continuous forests are one of the hill's most valuable features. Now scarce in the Midwest, these landscapes serve as a last refuge for many organisms, including songbirds dependent on deep forest interiors. They also provide unusually high water quality, essential for rare aquatic invertebrates. Having flourished in the hills, some populations appear to be recolonizing nearby lower-quality habitats.

The Nature Conservancy's aim is to preserve the hills' communities and species, as well as essential landscape patterns and processes. A fundamental part of this goal is landowner outreach, helping residents gain an appreciation for the hills' ecology and develop compatible management plans. To support the outreach, the diversity of the range has been documented in a comprehensive inventory and made available to the public upon request. In addition to the foregoing, The Nature Conservancy has contributed to county and township plans. The organization also continues to acquire key areas rich in biodiversity.

The inventory was performed by The Nature Conservancy in conjunction with the Wisconsin Department of Natural Resources. It resulted in a database and maps of the major vegetation types and rare and common species distributions. Specific surveys targeted birds, rare plants, natural communities, and individual forest stands. The work was funded primarily by private donations and the USDA Forest Service. Later, a grant from the Department of Defense enabled a second inventory of rare species at the Badger Army Ammunition Plant, located on the south-central edge of the range.

The data were entered into a geographic information system (GIS) with help from the University of Wisconsin's Land Information Computer Graphics Facility. The GIS allows project participants to analyze planning alternatives. For example, it was used to highlight concentrations of rare species and to determine where reforestation efforts could best reduce the effects of fragmentation. (See chapter 6 for further description of geographic information systems.)

Landowner outreach has focused on management planning and education. With additional funding from the Forest Stewardship Program, The Nature Conservancy and the Department of Natural Resources developed a forest ecologist position. The ecologist works with residents to design forest management plans that address their needs and preserve biodiversity in the larger Baraboo Hills ecosystem. Both on-site information and data from the GIS are used to develop management alternatives. In addition to individual consultations, The Nature Conservancy, the Department of Natural Resources, and the University of Wisconsin's Cooperative Extension have sponsored educational workshops for landowners. In one instance, the meetings evolved into the formation of a new land trust. The Nature Conservancy recently distributed "The Baraboo Bluff Forest Owners Handbook," a booklet that encourages landowners to recognize the economic and habitat values of their land and to develop appropriate management plans. Throughout the project, specific emphasis has been placed on creating partnerships between landowners and public and private organizations.

County and township land-use planning is a recent yet growing development in the Baraboo Hills region. The Nature Conservancy has been asked to provide data to planners on issues of biological significance. They were also invited to join county administrators and other nonprofit groups in an advisory steering committee to further the county effort. Among other activities, the committee worked with a University of Wisconsin class to identify the components and financial requirements of a countywide plan. Public support for conservation appears strong and will result in a countywide land-use plan in the near future.

The annual operating expenses of The Nature Conservancy's Baraboo office are approximately $250,000. Included in this figure are two full-time staff, several short-term and internship positions, as well as land management activities, grant projects, and property taxes. All of these expenses have been funded by charitable contributions, the majority of which have been local. In addition, the office has obtained grants from the Forest Service and the Department of Defense. The Forest Service's Forest Stewardship Program has been a particularly valuable funding source. Over a six-year period, the Forest Service gave more than $250,000 toward conservation projects in the Baraboo Hills, including landowner outreach, development of the GIS, and forest management workshops. In addition to The Nature Conservancy, the Wisconsin Department of Natural Resources and the Southwest Badger Resource Conservation District shared in the Forest Service grants.

The Nature Conservancy has sought to preserve the ecological values of the Baraboo Hills in several ways. They created an inventory to address key aspects of diversity, including community representation, forest fragmentation, and the locations of rare species. These landscape-scale issues were particularly relevant to the size of the hills. They have assisted landowners through educational programs and management planning advice and data. They have also supported public land-use planning and encouraged partnerships for conservation among community leaders. This broad approach is designed to address immediate threats to the range and build long-term appreciation for its diversity.

FOR FURTHER INFORMATION CONTACT:

Mary Jean Huston
The Nature Conservancy
107 Walnut Street
Baraboo, WI 53913
608-356-5300

Chapter 3

Change and Disturbance

Change is constant in nature. The landscapes viewed today represent a single point in a long evolutionary continuum. Landforms, climate patterns, communities, species, and adaptations exist now that were not present thousands of years ago, or perhaps even yesterday. Likewise, it is certain that change will continue to occur and that tomorrow's landscapes will differ in some way from those with which we are now familiar.

Environmental changes are fundamental to the distribution and responses of living organisms. Long-term climatic variations and geologic events have eliminated some species, while radically altering the ranges of others. On a shorter time scale, recurrent disturbances such as fire and flooding encourage species adaptations and enable new population configurations and the persistence of natural communities. A fallen tree or the burrowing of a small animal can help new seedlings to sprout.

Current landscapes also reflect the presence of humans. In most areas of the country, Native Americans managed vegetation and wildlife to improve hunting and gathering opportunities. These practices may have lasted for hundreds or thousands of years. Since the arrival of Europeans and the Industrial Age, much more extensive change has occurred. Intensive resource use has modified landscape patterns and affected the composition and dynamics of most communities. To accommodate population growth, many wildland areas continue to be developed, resulting in habitat reduction and fragmentation.

Because nature is dynamic, and because of our increasing potential for environmental impacts, change is an essential consideration in conservation planning. Goals should address the range of conditions possible in natural communities. These conditions are maintained by characteristic processes that fluctuate over time, such as regeneration, succession, and disturbance. Since not all ecological processes can be retained near developed areas, planners should assume that management will be necessary. These factors, combined with public concerns, will help determine a sustainable landscape.

Long-term Changes

Some environmental changes cannot be influenced by planners, yet are useful to consider since they have been instrumental in producing the landscapes we value. These are processes that usually occur over thousands or millions of years. Mountain uplift, erosion, soil development, and glacial movements continually create and alter land forms. Climate patterns also usually fluctuate on time scales of thousands of years. Both geologic and climatic processes affect the distribution and diversity of natural communities, as well as the evolution of new species.[1]

Climate is a primary determinant in the location of vegetation types, and changes in climate result in species extinctions and migrations. In North America, for example, we know from analyzing lake-bed sediments that a different mixture of vegetation exists today than was present during the last ice age.[2] Even an increase of a few degrees in temperature can have a substantial effect, since it may exceed the environmental tolerance of some species and can also alter fire and hydrologic patterns. Such long-term environmental changes are constantly occurring, and in a broad sense are responsible for the landscapes we see today.

Short-term Changes

In contrast to long-term variations, many landscape changes are either readily apparent or else familiar because they have occurred during the past few centuries. For instance, one could be aware of a high number of mosquitoes in a certain year, or that the 1988 Yellowstone fires reduced the pine forest and increased grasses and wildflowers. Similarly, it is known that the vegetation in the northeastern United States differs both from when European settlers first arrived and from when it was cleared for agriculture. These short-term changes tend to be most important to the public, and they are the ones over which planners and managers have the most effect.

Short-term changes are also significant because they determine specific attributes of ecological systems. While geology and climate regulate the general location of biotic communities, processes that vary over years, decades, or a few centuries affect their structure and dynamics. For example, depending on predators and food availability, the size of a bird population might fluctuate over a period of several years. The productivity of a grass species might vary within the same general timeframe. Community changes in composition, distribution, and structure are more obvious over several decades. On a broader scale, landscape patterns generally shift over the course of centuries due to slight climate variations or periodic widespread disturbances.

If nature is always changing, planners can assume that the targets of their conservation plan will too, whether they include single species, several communities, or entire landscapes. Not only are such changes inevitable, but they are often necessary for retaining diverse ecological systems. Thus it is rarely useful or appropriate to base a plan on a single reference state, such as the current extent of a community or appearance of a landscape. It is more practical to assume and plan for a range of conditions.[3]

Preserving or restoring the ranges associated with various biodiversity attributes can be a plan goal. For example, rather than focus solely on the minimum size of an endangered species population, a planner could consider probable fluctuations in population size and growth rate. (This data would then allow a better assessment of population thresholds and viability.) Rather than assume a community will remain in its present state, he or she could plan for the different stages of vegetation that could be expected and accommodated in that community. Similarly, a range of potential changes in landscapes might also be addressed in the planning process. The various spatial patterns produced by different management and development strategies could be modeled and evaluated as part of a plan.

A complementary approach is to address the processes that cause a plan target to fluctuate. For example, if a primary objective is to conserve woodlands, one could focus on tree regeneration as a process to be preserved and monitored. Regeneration itself may be affected by other processes, such as fire patterns, the spread of exotic plant species, or the intensity of grazing. If the stand is located near water, maintaining a certain hydrologic regime would be important. The value of addressing these processes is that they influence how the woodlands change and persist.

How Communities and Landscapes Change

Planners who deal with open space are usually responsible for large tracts of wild or semi-wild lands, such as those that might comprise a regional park or open space district. For this reason, it is especially useful to acquire a sense of how these areas change at the community and landscape levels. Natural communities differ in their types, speed, and probabilities of change, and these variations then affect spatial patterns in the landscape. Such variations can also affect the ultimate success of a conservation plan.

Succession is one of the most familiar processes of change in natural communities (figure 3.1).[4] A conifer forest after a fire or clearcut provides an example. The area is first colonized by grasses and small, broad-leaved herbs. These plants might be replaced by shrubs, which might be followed by hardwood trees that in turn could be succeeded by the original coniferous forest. The concept implies a slow, linear change "forward," unless it is abruptly "reversed" by another fire or harvesting disturbance. At each stage, different resources and competition lead to dominance by a different set of vegetation in the following stage. The direction of succession varies according to the nature of the disturbance, to overall environmental conditions, and to characteristics of the species that make up the community.

It is important to recognize succession in natural communities because the various stages offer different types of habitats. Many plants and animals may be adapted to just one or a few of these phases. If species diversity is a conservation objective, the area must be managed to retain the full range of successional states inherent in the landscape's communities. Periodic disturbances,

Figure 3.1. Photographs taken over a 15-year period document vegetative succession following a clearcut. (Photographs courtesy of Beaverhead/Deerlodge National Forest, Montana.)

whether natural or introduced by management, will be required to preserve the different stages.

Communities do not always change in predictable ways. Very large, intense, or frequent disturbances can occur or new disturbances to which some species are not adapted. Environmental conditions can be altered such that certain plants and animals are no longer able to reproduce or compete. The community will then be transformed into a new system, with a different species composition and other pathways for change.[5] Extensive exotic species invasions, major modifications in hydrologic, fire, or flooding patterns, and habitat fragmentation are examples of this type of radical disturbance.

A system conversion results because certain species cannot tolerate the new conditions; thresholds have been crossed. Planners may be able to work with resource managers and researchers to estimate basic thresholds for different communities. They may also be able to identify factors that might result in such alteration. Since conditions are different after a community has changed in this manner, plans or management techniques that previously benefitted specific species may no longer work. The plan will require a fresh approach to preserve remnants of the original community within the new environment. Extensive system modifications may mean that restoration to a former preferred state would be essentially impossible.[6]

In addition to the expected types of change, the speed and probability of community change are also issues for planners. For example, it is useful to know how fast the transition from one successional stage to another is likely to occur. This is a particularly important consideration for small preserves, or for landscape corridors, where animals depend on certain types of vegetation to move among different areas. In these situations, an awareness of vegetation dynamics may be essential to achieving a plan's objectives. The speed of change also has social implications, especially when it is rapid. For instance, while disturbances may be ecologically appropriate, they may be difficult to sell to a public concerned with safety and familiar with a certain landscape aesthetic.

Disturbances

Disturbances are an important and primary way in which nature changes.[7] In contrast to a process like succession, they are relatively distinct, rapid events that disrupt communities, species, populations, or the availability of resources. Examples of physical disturbances include fire, flooding, severe storms, droughts, landslides, and volcanos (figure 3.2). Animals also create disturbances, as when a beaver builds a dam, bark beetles attack a pine forest, or a

Figure 3.2. Flooding along the Mississippi River is an essential ecological process for its aquatic and riparian communities. (Photograph by Jeffrey A. Janvrin.)

gopher burrows underneath the ground. Human-generated disturbances, such as grazing and controlled burns, can either mimic those caused by wild animals or physical factors, or introduce a range of new factors into the system.

The public reaction to natural disturbances is often negative, primarily due to a concern for human safety and the threat of economic loss. Droughts and floods destroy agricultural profits; forest fires consume board feet; a landslide might send a homeowner's belongings to the bottom of a hill. A third concern is for nature itself. A disturbance may appear to be a destructive, almost violent event that alters the "normal" state of a landscape. The combination of a drought and insect infestation, for instance, seemingly devastates thousands of acres of forest.

While the foregoing are legitimate concerns, they are only part of the picture. Not included are the many positive and essential roles that disturbances play in ecological systems. Disturbances create changes necessary for species to regenerate and evolve. They alter vegetation structure and competitive relationships within communities, allowing new species to thrive. They release nutrients in soil and water, and so increase plant growth. They alter habitats, and these changed conditions help maintain biodiversity.

When a tree falls, or a fire burns a woodland understory, or a flood scours a sandbar, the situation is ripe for new seedlings to grow. Many plants require a minimum of sunlight and nutrients, as well as bare ground in order to sprout. Disturbances can also benefit the reproduction of animals. For example, the 1993 midwestern floods greatly increased shallow water areas required by spawning fish.[8] In addition, some species are adapted to certain disturbances, and these events help them to successfully regenerate. Several pine species require the intense heat of fire to open their cones and release seeds, while root-crown sprouting following fire or harvesting is common in oaks.

Disturbances change environmental conditions within natural communities. A new habitat is created, which produces a new combination of species. Those that could not compete in the former environment may now become dominant. Thus disturbances that have developed in conjunction with a landscape's vegetation are often beneficial. They ensure that species adapted to varying conditions are able to survive.

Of particular importance are disturbances that occur habitually in certain natural communities. They are central to the ecology of these systems, and the species within them are adapted to a specific "disturbance regime." A disturbance regime can be described by the frequency, intensity, and extent of the events that recur in an area. In general, smaller, less destructive disturbances occur often, while the largest events are the most rare. If the regime is substantially altered, a community or landscape can change to a completely different system.

Fire and flooding are two types of disturbances that have characteristic regimes.[9] Fires are common in grasslands, brushlands, woodlands, and forests when conditions are dry and the combustible material reaches a particular level. In each ecosystem, fires typically recur within a certain period of time, within a range of heat and size, as well as in specific seasons. Species inhabiting these areas often persist due to adaptations to the regime. For example, fires usually occur in annual grasslands after the grasses have completed their growth and set their seeds.

Two ways in which fire regimes are routinely altered are through fire suppression, and through prescribed burning in patterns different from the regime (figure 3.3). While these practices can be justified for valid reasons (for example, short-term public safety and fuels reduction, legal liability, and air quality constraints), biodiversity conservation is not one of them. Fire suppression often changes the regime to larger, more intense, and less frequent burns. Following decades of suppression, the landscape will likely include a modified suite of species that are less tolerant of fire and more tolerant of shade.[10] Burning more frequently, or in seasons other than when fires habitually occur, will alter plant species composition. During the cool season, plants that are usually

Figure 3.3. A prescribed burn at Mount Diablo State Park, California, supports species adapted to periodic fire disturbances. (Photograph by Carl Nielson.)

well-adapted to fire may be growing or flowering, and so have diminished resources with which to resist the blaze.[11]

Floods also vary in the length of time between events, in their force, and in the amount of area that they cover. For this reason, bridges are built to such standards as a "fifty-year flood" or a larger, more rare "hundred-year flood." Floodplain species, such as willows and cottonwoods, survive highly saturated soils and shifting substrates with adaptations including short life spans, fast growth rates, or seeds that can be easily dispersed by wind or water.[12] Entire riparian or meadow communities are maintained by specific patterns of periodic flooding. These systems are very sensitive to structures that alter the disturbance regime, such as levees that eliminate small, frequent floods or diversion channels that reduce stream flows.

Although disturbances are destructive by definition, species and communities may recover from them over a period of time through succession. Recovery is influenced by the intensity and time elapsed since the last disturbance and by environmental factors such as climate, soil, topography, and nutrient reserves. For example, a community that has been burned would likely return to an area if the fire was not too severe, if there had been adequate time since the last fire, and if erosion after the burn was not extensive. Recovery also depends on characteristics of species within and adjacent to an area that has been disturbed. A community would be restored more quickly if species within it were adapted to the disturbance, and if native plants and animals that could serve as new colonizers still existed within dispersal limits.

Since disturbances occur sporadically in space and time, communities and species can differ in their ability to resist them and in their capacity to recover from them. Some plants are inherently more sensitive than others or may be more vulnerable in certain situations, such as if the disturbance occurred during their reproductive stage. If they are already rare or endemic to the area, these species will require greater attention.

There are a variety of ways in which disturbances can be addressed in conservation plans. The most important is that open-space networks be designed and managed so that they can occur. Ideally, these networks should be large enough to accommodate disturbance regimes historically characteristic of the area and to include the full range of successional stages or vegetation states. Alternatively (since such space is rarely available), plans can include strategies to mimic disturbances through management. If the disturbance regime is unknown, scientists might estimate it by analyzing the structure of vegetation, consulting historical records, or, in the case of fires, examining fire scars in tree rings. Species that are sensitive to or dependent on disturbances should be identified. It will be particularly helpful to include educational programs to address negative public perceptions of disturbances.

Specific land use decisions also affect disturbance processes. For example, development within areas that are susceptible to flooding or landslides creates conflicts between ecological and safety issues. Whenever possible, these lands should be reserved as open space. In addition, increasing settlement at the urban-wildland interface is a particular concern. In the fire-prone landscapes of the West, higher numbers of people tend to produce more wildfires. The development also reduces options for in-season controlled burns.[13] Plans that emphasize clustered rather than scattered housing would help reduce safety conflicts and maintain flooding and fire regimes.

Human Disturbances

Since most contemporary landscapes are affected in some way by human beings, human-induced disturbances are an additional source of environmental alteration. Technically, of course, we are also "natural" and part of a variety of ecosystems. Thus it is inevitable that we will influence the dynamics of these systems simply because we are a component. Viewed as a category, however, human impacts are often greater in size and intensity than other disturbances.[14] In addition, they can introduce completely new sources of change, and so push valued landscapes over sustainable thresholds.

Inside a reserve network, activities such as resource extraction, road building, excessive hunting, and recreation disrupt ecological processes and communities. These activities can also alter disturbance regimes. Fire, for example, burns and travels differently in various types and structures of vegetation or in forests that are fragmented to different degrees. The altered disturbances in turn alter habitats and nutrient cycles. Depending on the type and intensity of the disturbance, human activities in the surrounding landscape may have an even greater impact. Clearing land adjacent to the reserve can modify wind, humidity, and water-flow patterns at its edge.[15] Agricultural activities can add pesticides, eroded sediments, excessive organic nutrients, and exotic species.[16] Development produces additional exotic species, diseases, and pollutants, and typically results in larger landscape changes, such as habitat reduction and fragmentation, and the diversion of waterways. Due to the scale, reducing the impact of human disturbances will likely involve coordination among a variety of landowners in many jurisdictions.

Certain design features can be incorporated into an open-space system to provide extra protection to species or communities. These strategies will help guard against ongoing human disturbances, as well as unforeseeable accidents such as pollution spills (figure 3.4). Buffer zones of less valued habitat can be retained around areas considered more valuable, for example, breeding areas or

Figure 3.4. A train derailment resulted in the release of nearly 20,000 gallons of metam-sodium pesticide into the Sacramento River, July 14, 1991. Planners must develop strategies to guard against such unforeseeable accidents. (Photograph by Katy Raddatz, San Francisco Examiner, *July 16, 1991, p. A12.)*

communities that are sensitive or species rich. They form a spatial shield around these priority areas. In the Pinhook Swamp case study, chapter 5, a half-mile buffer of upland vegetation was included as protection for the more valuable wetland communities. A second design tool is to maintain replicate patches of each vegetation type, or multiple species populations, across a landscape or region. If a community or population was jeopardized at one site, it could still survive somewhere else.

Some human disturbances extend far beyond the local or regional level, yet should still be considered in landscape conservation planning. Global warming is an example. Many scientists expect world temperatures to rise by a few degrees over the next century.[17] As this change occurs, species adapted to a certain temperatures will survive only if they can migrate, and so remain within their temperature range. Open-space networks that span gradients in elevation or latitude may help mitigate this effect if it happens slowly.

Overall, it is less useful to focus on the origin of a single disturbance than to plan for the cumulative effects of all potential disturbances. While an ecosystem may be able to recover from recurrent fires or floods, it may not have the capacity to persist if it is additionally impacted by pollution or habitat limitations. The goal is to retain essential natural disturbances, while also reducing the total rate and intensity of change to a level at which local ecosystems can be maintained.

The Role of Management

Historically, planning and management have been considered distinct functions, performed by different people in separate professions. While this is still largely the case, it is also apparent that overlap exists, and that conservation would benefit from greater communication and coordination between these fields. One reason is the recognition that environmental planning is an extensive, ongoing effort. It is not limited to open space design or to identifying the impact of a specific project. It also involves overall landscape sustainability, management, monitoring, research, and a continual reassessment of conservation strategies. A second reason is that a range of individuals and organizations are now practicing conservation planning. Some of these—for example, landowners, community activists, and resource managers—will also manage lands they plan for conservation. A third reason relates specifically to landscape change. Increasingly, preserving ecological processes or protecting natural areas from human impact depends on proper land management.

If sufficient portions of our landscapes could be retained in huge, isolated preserve networks, management might not be a significant issue. However, this is not the case. Many of our largest public open spaces provide a variety of services and resources, among them recreation, timber, grazing, and mining. These additional uses add new disturbances, and limit the extent to which historical disturbance regimes can be allowed. For example, clearcutting and road building, practices associated with forestry, have been debated for decades due to their impact. "New Forestry" techniques are preferable in terms of forest ecology, since they are designed to emulate natural disturbance patterns.[18]

Management is especially necessary in areas near intensive development, where open spaces sustain a variety of impacts due to their heavy use (e.g., Keeley 1993).[19] These effects are seen primarily at the perimeters, along trails, and in sites designated specifically for recreation. Erosion, soil compaction, and the destruction of vegetation are common in these areas. These disturbances facilitate the spread of exotic plants, while humans themselves often introduce new animals and, through them, new diseases. Impacts resulting from use alter the ecosystems we try to preserve.

Management is also a key issue for open space systems dominated by private ownership. In these areas, the traditional model of publicly owned preserves does not apply. Instead, the conservation goal is to sustain ecological values across a landscape of separately controlled properties. One way to do this is to encourage each owner to use sustainable management techniques and to facilitate management coordination among groups of adjacent landowners.

Due to the numerous influences on biotic communities, disturbances imposed by management must be carefully designed and controlled. While mimicking what is estimated to be the natural disturbance regime, they must also be planned to ensure that the system changes in the way that is desired. In particular, managers should guard against new introductions or the expansion of exotic species. The objective of a designed disturbance may be to "move" the system to a different successional state and/or to initiate a new successional pathway.[20] To achieve the objective(s), considerable thought and experimentation are necessary in devising the disturbance, controlling species colonization, and managing species once they have been established. For example, a stream restorationist might decide to reintroduce flooding to encourage regeneration of native riparian vegetation. Flooding, however, might also support the spread of exotic species currently occupying the site. To prevent the latter situation, the restorationist would need to devise methods to remove the exotics and to control new invasions in the future.[21]

Whether or not they are actually involved in management, it is practical and appropriate for planners to consider management possibilities for the lands they intend to conserve. Without resources for management, or without effective management strategies, ecological values may be lost. Ongoing management is especially crucial near developed land to counter impacts from heavy use. Highly vulnerable areas such as breeding areas, sensitive habitats, and landscape corridors will require specific attention. Management is the primary conservation strategy for open-space systems consisting largely of private landowners. Disturbances introduced by management should be designed and monitored to ensure that the intended changes actually occur.

Determining Ranges of Variability

One of the more problematic issues to address is the variability ranges for important biodiversity attributes. As suggested earlier, using a single baseline condition would be unworkable, since all organisms and communities change over time. By the same token, it would be unrealistic to select one "future condition" as a restoration goal. It is too difficult to predict the factors that will influence change, and then to limit these factors if that state ultimately is achieved. What is apparent is that any conservation target will fluctuate within a range and that determining a suitable range is a difficult and subjective process.[22]

One approach has been to attempt to determine "presettlement" or "pre-European" conditions. This seems generally appropriate, due to the environmental impacts that have occurred since that time. It makes sense that these earlier conditions would reflect patterns and processes necessary for landscape sustainability. However, this approach still cannot offer clear guidelines.[23] One reason is simply a lack of information. We do not necessarily know the composition and dynamics of communities that existed several hundred years ago. Second, these conditions may vary according to the period of time addressed. We could identify a different range if an entire millennium were addressed instead of a few centuries. A third issue is Native American management. It is generally impossible to separate the ways in which Native Americans modified processes and landscapes from those that may have been inherent or "natural." Lastly, some ecosystems have been so altered over the past few centuries that they can no longer return to prior conditions. For example, we cannot remove the annual grasses now dominant in Western rangelands and restore the native perennial species.

The foregoing discussion presents some of the complexity involved in determining ranges of variability from an ecological perspective. Yet conservation plans cannot be based solely on biodiversity values; they must also address social and economic concerns. Among the social issues will likely be public desire for maintaining the current state of the landscape. As stated earlier, many people perceive present conditions as "normal," and may not appreciate the need for change. Related to this issue is public support for certain species or processes. Popular opinion will influence whether future landscapes include specific endangered species, exotic species, predators, or natural disturbances. Economic concerns may include retaining certain natural communities or successional stages that support local resource-based industries. Also, the funding available for management will affect the ways in which change occurs. Open spaces associated with private developments, for example, often have little or no money set aside for management. Residents, unaware of the changing vegetation, assume that no management is necessary.

Inevitably, the ranges of variability we choose will be based on both ecological understanding and societal values (figure 3.5). As much as possible, planners should become familiar with the ways in which their conservation "targets" have changed or are likely to change, as well as with key processes that support these fluctuations. These estimated ranges will likely be modified by social and economic values. The goal is to determine a range of variability that is ecologically sustainable and addresses public concerns for each key biodiversity attribute.

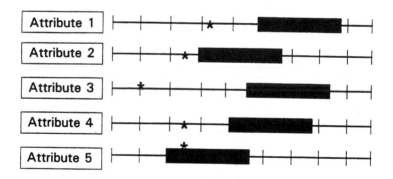

Figure 3.5. Ecosystem attributes vary within ranges, which may be determined by fluctuations over a time period and/or by societal values. The current state of an attribute can be assessed against this range. (Adapted from Caraher and Knapp (1995) and Hobbs and Norton (1996).)

Incorporating Historical Variations

Beaverhead/Deerlodge National Forest, Southwestern Montana

As with all national forests, Beaverhead/ Deerlodge National Forest is managed for multiple uses, including timber harvesting, grazing, recreation, and ecological protection. Providing for these uses requires data on forest ecology and the impacts it can withstand. In 1990, a new forest supervisor recognized significant gaps in this information. Resource managers lacked an understanding of historical conditions and processes and needed more knowledge of landscape-scale patterns and relationships. A broader approach was necessary to ensure the long-term maintenance of the forest ecosystems.

As a result, a multidisciplinary team was convened to perform a comprehensive ecological study of the national forest. Their objectives were to identify past and present patterns in vegetation structure, the processes that had shaped these patterns, as well as specific components and processes now absent from the forest. The findings of the study helped demonstrate how and why the forest has changed over time. They also suggested new directions for management. The analysis now guides the uses and vegetation treatments prescribed for Deerlodge.

The team started by dividing the forest into twenty-eight landscape units, since its area of over 3 million acres was too large to analyze at once. They limited the study to one of these units, called the North Flints, which included a range of ecological characteristics and land uses. While the results were derived solely from the North Flints, much of the information was applicable to the rest of the forest.

The analysis was based primarily on three vegetation maps designed to demonstrate conditions at different points in time (figure 3.6). They were created for 1991, showing the current structure; for 1950, before extensive timber harvesting; and for 1880, the time of the last large stand-replacing fire. The historical maps were reconstructed from old aerial photographs, stand data, and fire history analyses. The stand data included information on tree growth, succession, and management activity. Fire history was based on the dates and locations of stand-replacing fires and on tree fire scars, which indicated the frequency and intensity of understory burns. All of the data were entered into a geographic information system. (See chapter 6 for a description of this technology.)

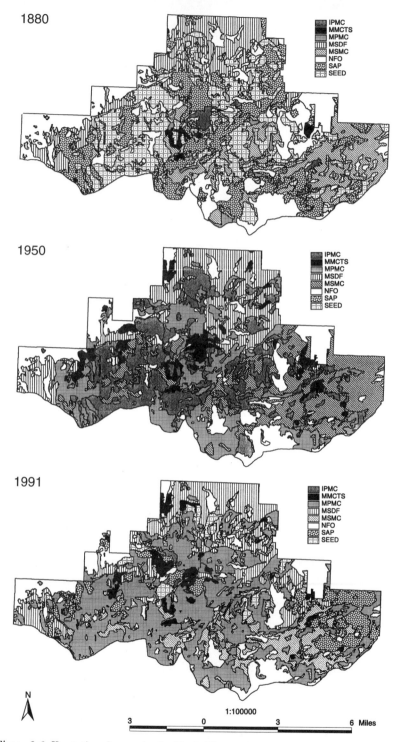

Figure 3.6. Vegetation changes in the North Flint Creek Range, Beaverhead/Deerlodge National Forest, from 1880 to 1991. (Maps courtesy of the Beaverhead/Deerlodge National Forest.)

The team compared the three maps and determined that significant changes in the forest had occurred. One of these changes was related to fire. In the lower elevation Douglas-fir community, for example, burns had often been low-intensity and had recurred at intervals of ten to forty years. Following fire suppression in the later part of the century, they tended to be less frequent and to consume a greater portion of the vegetation. The result was a different forest structure and composition. Whereas previous stands had been relatively open, they now included a dense understory. Species dependent on fire, such as ponderosa pine and aspen, had decreased. The team discovered an overall reduction in diversity, and also suggested that the changes in fire regime may have slowed decomposition and lowered soil productivity.

Other parts of the evaluation drew on ecological literature to describe expected changes in hydrology, fisheries, soils, and wildlife. For instance, riparian zones vary routinely due to flooding, soil organic matter fluctuates in response to specific conditions, and vegetation succession affects wildlife species and population sizes. The study also examined the effects of historical land uses. Among the human impacts were hydraulic mining, which had eliminated wetlands and fine sediments along many of the streams, and roads, which had increased erosion and threatened certain wildlife. Exotic species and the extermination of beavers had also changed the forest's fisheries.

This broad historical analysis enabled the team to identify varying patterns in the forest communities. Over time, different conditions had been produced due to processes associated with the forest and human uses of the land. These patterns clearly influenced the resources Deerlodge managers now sought to preserve. Both aspen and ponderosa pine, for example, depend on forest openings for regeneration, so maintaining these species would entail re-creating these openings.

The team attempted to determine a range of ecological variations within the forest, but eventually concluded that the objective was unrealistic. They could not identify all the ways in which vegetation might change, for instance, nor all the aspects of the fire regime. Even if theoretically possible, such an assessment would have required information from numerous dates over several centuries. In contrast, resources limited the study to an analysis of conditions at three points over 110 years. Instead of ranges of variation, therefore, the study showed highlighted differences in patterns and processes within the 110-year time frame. This information led to a greater understanding of potential landscape conditions, which could then be incorporated into planning.

Current management is based on a set of desired future conditions developed as part of the study. The future conditions reflect both the potential landscape variations and the values of forest managers and nearby residents. For example, they include reestablishing certain vegetation communities and successional stages, improving wildlife habitat, and allowing controlled burns. They also involve increasing aspen and ponderosa pine, species valued for aesthetic and commercial reasons, and continued resource use. They represent choices among different landscape conditions, with the goal of sustaining forest ecology and supporting multiple uses.

Beaverhead/Deerlodge National Forest has initiated several strategies to reach the desired future conditions. One of the most important is the careful design of timber harvests. In a recent operation, cuts were prescribed to spatially mimic a fire, including leaving areas of trees and woody debris. Both the harvest and subsequent controlled burn were planned to re-create an open stand structure. Another approach has been to close, recontour, and reseed many roads that are rarely used. Restoration of streams and abandoned mines has also begun. These are some of the ways in which a historical landscape analysis can be used to maintain ecosystems over time.

FOR FURTHER INFORMATION CONTACT:
Jina Mariani
USDA Forest Service
Beaverhead/Deerlodge National Forest
1820 Meadowlark Drive
Butte, MT 59701
406-494-2147

Determining Ecological Thresholds
Mono Lake, California

One of California's largest and most scenic bodies of water, Mono Lake has been the focus of an environmental controversy for nearly two decades. Part of the debate has centered on the impact caused by diverting water from the tributaries of this valuable public resource. Also involved has been the City of Los Angeles' right to the diverted water under California law and the potential consequences of reducing the allotment. At the core of the dispute was a fundamental disagreement over the specific ecological effects of continued diversions. In 1984, the California legislature commissioned an independent study to help resolve the impasse. Completed in 1988, the study assessed the impact of declining lake

Figure 3.7. Mono Lake's unique ecology offers important resources to a variety of migratory birds. (Photograph courtesy of the Mono Lake Committee.)

levels on the Mono Lake ecosystem. It identified thresholds at which specific parts of the ecosystem would be eliminated and suggested clear policy options. The information contributed to an agreement among all parties and to a creative solution that benefitted both Mono Lake and the City of Los Angeles.

Mono Lake is a rare biological resource (figure 3.7). It is estimated to be 750,000 to 1 million years old. Its chemistry is unusual in that it has no natural outlet, and evaporation over the years has resulted in water approximately three times as salty as the oceans. The ecosystem is simple yet highly productive. Algae are consumed by brine shrimp and brine flies, which in turn serve as food to millions of birds. Protected islands in the lake provide nesting sites for 90 percent of the state's population of California gulls. Mono Lake also offers important resources to many migratory shorebirds, such as eared grebes, and Wilson's and rednecked phalaropes.

While the lake's volume and salinity naturally fluctuate, recent changes due to human intervention have been especially dramatic. Los Angeles began diverting water from Mono Lake in 1941. These diversions averaged 90,000 acre-feet annually from 1941 to 1989 and comprised approximately 14 percent of the city's water supply. During this time, the level of Mono Lake fell by 45 feet, from an elevation of 6,417 feet to 6,372 feet. The volume of the lake decreased by one half, while its salinity doubled. With the decline in the lake level, nesting sites on the islands became exposed to coyote predation. The increased salinity threatened to exceed the tolerance of the brine shrimp and brine flies. In addition, dust from the exposed lake bottom began to create an air pollution hazard.

Researchers were charged with determining the impact of declining lake levels on various ecosystem components, including the effect of increased dust on human health. To do this, they compiled existing information and also used part of their funds to support the completion of selected key studies. The resulting Report of the Community and Organization Research Institute, or CORI Report, detailed events that might occur as the lake volume decreased.

The events were summarized at three potential lake levels. For example, if the lake were maintained at 6,382 feet, much of the existing ecosystem could be preserved. If it were lowered to 6,372 feet, breeding sites on several islands would be exposed, brine fly populations would be reduced, and the marshlands and streambeds would degrade. At 6,362 feet, the shrimp and fly populations would be severely threatened, and with them the birds they now support. The study also assessed effects on air quality standards at a range of lake levels. Lastly, the analysis recommended that an extra buffer level of 10 to 14 feet be maintained, since climate, in addition to the diversions, causes the lake's level to fluctuate. Then, even during periods of drought, the values stated for each of the levels would still be valid.

The CORI Report was the third independent scientific assessment of the impact of water diversions on Mono Lake. It was significant in that, at the time, it was the most comprehensive effort to identify ecological thresholds, and these thresholds were then tied to the policy choices facing decisionmakers. It formed the basis of a court decision in 1989, in which the City of Los Angeles was enjoined from further diversions, with the lake level temporarily maintained at 6,377 feet. The court then deferred to the State Water Resources Control Board to develop a binding solution. Responsible for California's water policy, the Water Board's mandate was to protect public trust values and ensure an adequate water supply for Los Angeles.

The resolution of the conflict required an innovative approach that would address the interests of all parties. Not only should Mono Lake be preserved, but another water source for Los Angeles would have to be secured without causing additional environmental damage. The Water Board received testimony from the range of agencies and environmental organizations involved in the Mono Lake basin. During the process, the groups agreed that the lake should be returned to 6,392 feet, higher than was suggested by the CORI Report, and that the streams and marshlands should also be restored. This level would still allow Los Angeles to divert 30,000 acre-feet of water per year.

The second part of the solution addressed the Los Angeles water supply. It resulted largely from the efforts of the Mono Lake Committee, the organization primarily responsible for protecting the lake and challenging the diversions. Through reclamation and conservation, the city could develop approximately 140,000 acre-feet per year. This would more than offset the amount lost from Mono Lake, would be a more reliable source during drought years, and would reduce pollution from sewage discharges. Yet the city lacked the necessary reclamation infrastructure. To this end, the Mono Lake Committee persuaded the State of California to make $36 million available in a 50 percent cost-share program, while the federal government agreed to a 25 percent cost-share program to develop 120,000 acre-feet. The State Water Resources Control Board released its final decision in 1994 with no dissent.

The controversy over Mono Lake has been long and has involved bitter disagreements and court battles. The CORI Report helped produce a breakthrough in that it was an independent scientific assessment of the impact of the water diversions. By identifying thresholds at which certain components of the ecosystem would be lost, it helped clarify policy options. Such information contributed to the development of a consensus. This type of study was possible in part because the Mono Lake system is simple, and the components and their relationships were relatively well known. For more complex systems, it is not yet clear which approach would be preferred or possible. In some instances, researchers might try to identify the most influential components and processes, and then gather data and estimate thresholds related to these factors. In other situations, they may be required to base their analysis solely on existing information.

FOR FURTHER INFORMATION CONTACT:
> Martha Davis
> Mono Lake Committee
> 1207 West Magnolia Blvd.
> Burbank, CA 91506
> 818-972-2025

Chapter 4

Area and Connectivity

Choose virtually any inhabited landscape: any nearby city or town and its surrounding hills, fields, or extended suburbs. Then examine how it has changed over the past few centuries, and you will recognize the twin processes of habitat reduction and fragmentation. In most areas, what were continuous wildlands have now been broken up and converted to agriculture, development, or some other type of human use. The total amount of open space has decreased, and individual patches have diminished and become more isolated from each other. This trend is considered one of the major causes of species extinctions today.[1]

Habitat reduction and fragmentation alter ecosystems by changing ecological processes. For example, when land is cleared next to a forest, species at the perimeter are exposed to a slightly harsher climate and new types of competition and predation. If the forest is fragmented into small stands, landscape-scale processes are also modified. Different kinds of vegetation, road networks, and development between the stands affect how water and other materials travel within the region. Fragmented landscapes also limit the movements of individual organisms and interactions among species populations. Populations within each forest remnant become smaller and more prone to extinction. The combination of these changes reduces native biodiversity.

Certain categories of species are especially vulnerable to habitat reduction and fragmentation. Habitat for rare and specialized organisms may simply no longer exist. Sensitive species may not be able to compete against others that are better adapted to the change. The new landscape pattern particularly affects animals requiring extensive areas for foraging, such as bears, or for migration, such as elk. Those that occur in low densities may have difficulty finding mates. Species that cannot cross the introduced vegetation or land uses will be confined to a single-habitat patch. Since organisms die out at different rates, depending on the length of their life spans, the impacts on a given species may not be apparent for decades.

The overall goal for planners is to maintain extensive, well-connected areas of open space. To achieve this goal, the best approach is to plan for the entire landscape: to consider and coordinate the whole range of land uses and jurisdictions. As there are no pat formulas to follow, the amount of area and degree of connectivity are best assessed relative to the species and processes at risk in each location. In some cases, planners will have opportunities to maintain or increase the size of a reserve network. They may be able to link disjointed open spaces, as was done along Interstate 75 in Florida (see case study at the end of this chapter). They can devise measures to mitigate some of the loss. In all situations, maintaining area and connectivity requires cooperation among multiple owners and decisionmakers.

Ecosystem Changes

Habitat reduction and fragmentation change the physical and biological conditions under which species live. The processes that alter these conditions occur at the edges of natural areas, within natural areas, and across the broader landscape. While the focus may be on biodiversity inside a reserve network, the pressures in this case generally stem from outside. They are caused by modifications in the overall landscape pattern, and designs and practices associated with various land uses.

Fragmentation increases "edge" habitat, and decreases "interior" habitat (figure 4.1). The edge of a biotic community or patch of vegetation is ecologically distinct from its interior. One way that it differs is in its microclimate. Plants and soils at the edge are exposed to greater sunlight, heat, and wind. This combination increases evapotranspiration, or water lost to the atmosphere. Essentially, the area becomes hotter and drier. Edge plants, especially trees, are also subject to more wind damage. In general, the edge of a vegetation patch has a more severe microclimate than its interior.[2] More edge habitat benefits species adapted to these harsher conditions.

A second way in which the edge differs from the interior of a patch is through its exposure to adjacent land uses. Clearing for purposes such as agriculture, forestry, or development creates new edges, and each use adds its own range of impacts. Remnant vegetation near agricultural fields usually receives higher levels of nutrients and pesticides.[3] Forestry practices often increase erosion,[4] while edges near urban areas are subject to more trampling, erosion, noise, light, and pollutants.[5]

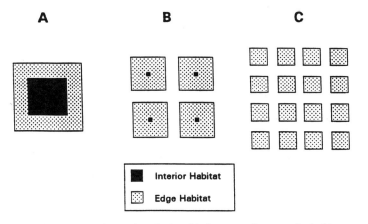

Figure 4.1. The diagram shows the relationship between the area of a habitat patch and the amount of interior habitat unaffected by edge effects. (From Soulé, 1991.)

Perhaps the most significant impact on reserves from adjacent land uses is the introduction of new species.[6] Plants and animals that thrive in human environments tend to be very adaptable, capable of dispersing long distances, and/or able to persist in a site for an extended time. These weedy "generalists," usually exotic species, spread into natural areas, where they often outcompete more sensitive native species. Exposed soils and the addition of nutrients help nonnative plants establish. Dogs, cats, and livestock also roam through open spaces, where they may feed on native species and introduce new diseases. One particularly destructive invader is the brown-headed cowbird. Fragmentation has enabled the cowbird to extend its range far beyond its original prairie habitat. By laying its eggs in other birds' nests, it displaces their chicks, and so has contributed to the decline of songbirds throughout eastern deciduous forests.[7]

The reduction and fragmentation of natural areas thus changes the ratio of edge to interior habitats. Habitat increases for edge species, organisms that are often the most adaptable, competitive, and likely to survive. In contrast, "interior" habitat free from edge effects is reduced. As interior habitats have decreased, so have the more sensitive and specialist native species.

Quantifying the amount of interior habitat remaining in an area first requires some knowledge of probable edge effects, as well as which "interior" species and communities are likely to be affected. Impacts associated with adjacent lands, human use of the open space, and exotic species will vary according to the location. Scientists have estimated the extent of some edge effects. For example, changes in microclimate may be evident two to three tree heights into a patch,[8] while the brown-headed cowbird has parasitized nests up to 600 meters inside a forest.[9] In most cases, however, generalizations are not useful, and it is best to assess each region according to its individual impacts and sensitivities.

In addition to creating new edges, fragmentation also influences ecological processes that operate across the larger landscape. One group of these processes is associated with hydrology.[10] The removal of vegetation results in fewer plants intercepting rainfall, thereby increasing soil saturation, runoff, and erosion. In developed regions, impermeable surfaces also contribute to more extreme runoff and erosion. In addition, drainage routes are typically altered to accommodate the new land uses. Each of these changes modifies the composition of communities and distribution of species.

Landscape-scale disturbances such as fires and floods are also likely to be affected.[11] Fragmentation influences how and where these events occur within a region. Fires, for example, burn differently in different types and structures of vegetation. Fragmentation can limit or redirect the spread of a fire. While this may be desirable for safety reasons, it also means that some natural areas may rarely receive a burn. In addition, the timing, intensity, and location of burns are often purposely changed. For species and communities that depend on specific disturbance patterns, fragmentation contributes to their decline.

Planning for entire landscapes can help minimize these changes in ecological conditions. By addressing land use and open-space requirements together, more effective reserve systems are likely to be conserved. This approach would require that open space planners communicate and coordinate with planners responsible for zoning, or transportation, for example. It would help ensure that ecological concerns are considered at the same time as these other issues. In particular, open-space planners can identify sensitive, interior species, and the types of landscape patterns they require. They can encourage management practices and institute regulations to reduce exotic species invasions. They can promote development designs to maintain at least some aspects of hydrologic and disturbance patterns. These types of measures will help support native biodiversity.

Connectivity and Species Movement

The landscape is constantly in motion. From the bobcat stalking a brush rabbit, to the mule deer migrating downslope from heavy snows, to pollen blown far on a windy day, movement is central to life. Species travel to satisfy basic life needs, and depend on flows of other organisms and materials to maintain their habitat. Preserving species therefore requires preserving their ability to move within the landscape.

The term *connectivity* refers to the capacity of a landscape to support the movements of organisms, materials, or energy.[12] Some large-scale processes influenced by connectivity include those associated with hydrology or disturbance regimes, as described above. Usually, however, the concept is related to species movement. For instance, a landscape with high connectivity for deer would allow a herd to move easily between its winter and summer habitats. In contrast, a more fragmented landscape could make passage difficult for deer, but retain high connectivity for birds, as long as the birds could fly from one area of vegetation to the next. Thus connectivity is a relative idea, depending on the process or species in question.

To assess landscape connectivity, it is useful to first consider the types of movements that species make. Animals, of course, are the organisms with the greatest requirements. Animals travel within a localized area to fulfill immediate needs and may also shift locations at specific points in their lives. The populations of both plants and animals expand, contract, and shift in response to their environment. For planners, the objective is to preserve or restore landscapes to support the greatest range of native species movement.

Animal movement can be separated into several predictable categories. Among these, daily movements are the most general, pertaining to all types of species. These activities include foraging for food, finding water, escaping predators, and moving to sheltered resting areas. They take place with a specific area of habitat, or home range, that is known to the animal and provides for its needs.

A home range is the amount of space an animal requires in a particular location (figure 4.2). Its dimensions vary according to the size of the animal, to the season, and to the quality of the habitat.[13] For example, the movements of a mouse can be measured in feet, while a mountain lion with its greater body and food requirements might roam over 50 or 100 square miles. Males generally need more space than females, and adults need more than juveniles. Both the size and location of home ranges can shift throughout the year due to the availability of resources. Habitats with fewer resources necessitate larger home ranges, since animals must travel greater distances to find sufficient food and water.

Migration is a second category of animal movement. Many species travel seasonally between their breeding grounds and primary feeding areas. In colder climates, they may also use a third location for hibernation. Birds are well known for their spectacular migrations, and most people are familiar with sites that serve as feeding or breeding areas or as stopover resting places. Dozens of songbird species, for example, breed and nest in the temperate forests of North America, and over winter in the Central or South American tropics. Salmon

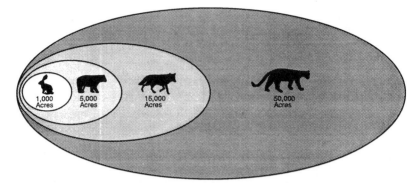

Figure 4.2. Home ranges for the jackrabbit, black bear, coyote, and mountain lion demonstrate common needs for movement among large predators as well as the different requirements of individual species. (Adapted from diagram in Mackintosh, 1989.)

and steelhead spend most of their lives at sea, but finally return upstream to their natal areas to spawn. Some monarch butterfly populations migrate all the way from the eastern United States or Canada to central Mexico and back.[14]

In addition to the foregoing are species that migrate over land. These animals include many ungulates, amphibians, and turtles. Ungulates such as deer and elk often move up and down elevational gradients, following their seasonal food supply. Many amphibians breed in permanent or seasonal water sources and journey a distance of yards or miles to areas where they will spend the remainder of the year. Turtles pass the majority of their lives in water, but require terrestrial sites in which to lay their eggs. Migratory species usually travel along predictable routes. Those of the larger, more noticeable species (for example, mammals and birds) are often known. There are comparatively few data on the migratory patterns of amphibians and turtles. Still, each of these animals depends on adequate protection of both their habitats and their travel routes.

Metamorphosis is another life history strategy that requires movement. Species that metamorphose move because their transformed bodies demand a different type of habitat. For example, certain aquatic insects live in water as larvae and later transfer to land as winged adults. Most amphibians migrate and metamorphose. As with migrating animals, species that undergo metamorphosis require at least two habitats and the ability to travel between them. Several countries in Europe have constructed amphibian underpasses to enable these slow-moving vertebrates to cross roadways; scientists in Amherst, Massachusetts also developed a underpass system for a population of spotted salamanders.[15]

Both animals and plants also disperse at certain points in their life cycles.[16] Many juvenile animals are forced to travel some distance from their natal areas to establish their own home ranges. A young red fox, for example, will disperse along a pathway equal to five diameters of its home range.[17] Plant dispersal occurs when seeds or spores are distributed throughout the landscape by water, wind, or animals. Dispersal limits competition between parents and offspring and curtails mating between close relatives. It may increase population viability by introducing new opportunities for interbreeding. Dispersal also allows a population to extend or shift its range. Under unfavorable conditions, even if most of the population dies, some individuals may survive in other locations.

Recently, the importance of dispersal has been underscored by advances in metapopulation theory. Metapopulations are groups of local populations connected by dispersing individuals (figure 4.3).[18] Although these smaller populations occasionally become extinct, the overall metapopulation is maintained within a region by dispersal. When conditions are suitable, individuals from the remaining populations can colonize the unoccupied habitats and establish new populations. Without dispersal, certain habitats may lose species permanently, or the entire metapopulation may disappear.

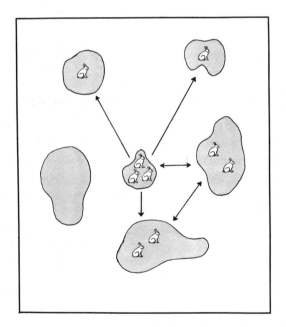

Figure 4.3. A metapopulation includes several subpopulations whose individuals are strengthened by occasional dispersal and interbreeding.

Although many species exist naturally in metapopulations, landscape fragmentation has increased the occurrence of these structures. As areas of vegetation have been broken into multiple patches, species populations have also been subdivided. These new metapopulations may be difficult to protect.[19] Maintaining such species in a region requires preserving at least some areas of optimal habitat where stronger populations can persist. Then, individuals from these habitats must be able to disperse to other areas, where they can either interbreed with existing populations or establish new ones. Fragmentation puts greater pressure on each subpopulation and limits opportunities for dispersal. Metapopulation models, with their emphasis on dispersal, have increasingly been used in the design of open-space networks. The management plan for the northern spotted owl, for example, is based on the bird's metapopulation structure.[20]

Preserving landscape connectivity entails recognition of these types of movements, and any barriers that could prevent them from occurring. Barriers to movement come in a variety of forms. Some barriers are natural, and so have always existed. For example, landscape features, such as ridges, water, soils, and vegetation, limit the distribution of species. Disturbances also function as barriers, since they alter vegetation and other factors necessary for habitat. In present-day landscapes, however, land-use conversions present the greatest restrictions. Numerous species depend on relatively natural biotic communities, and are not adapted to live in developed areas. Associated with development are additional obstructions, including noise, lighting, heat, and pollution. Physical barriers such as roads, dams, concrete stream channels, fences, and power line corridors further fragment the landscape.

Eliminating or minimizing movement barriers can be approached in several ways. The most basic strategy would be to plan landscapes with networks of open space, including some areas large enough to be relatively free from impacts. At a slightly more detailed level, open space can be designated where many species travel. Riparian zones, for example, are known movement corridors. To ensure protection of a particular species, however, connectivity should be assessed in relation to that species' needs. Animals with the most stringent movement requirements include those with large home ranges, those that migrate, and those whose distributions have been severely fragmented. Other organisms that would have difficulty dispersing across the new landscape might also be targeted. Once these species have been identified, removal or avoidance of designs and structures that would restrict their movements can be addressed.

One way in which modern landscapes particularly limit connectivity is through the proliferation of roads. Roads completely block the movements of small animals and serve as a primary source of mortality for wide-ranging mammals.[21] To reduce these effects, biodiversity concerns can be included in the original siting considerations, rather than being mitigated after the plans are finalized. Within open spaces, or sites where more species movement is anticipated, certain practices and designs may help reduce vehicle traffic. In Tilden Park in the San Francisco Bay Area, for example, one road is closed seasonally during the migration of the California newt.[22] Another option is to permanently close nonessential roads in natural areas. Where they must be retained, roads with two lanes instead of four, or with dirt instead paved surfaces, will present a barrier to fewer species.

Wildlife crossings are a recent development in road mitigation. Usually, they consist of a series of underpasses or overpasses designed to accommodate specific animals. Biologists and engineers have experimented with a variety of designs, ranging from amphibian underpasses to overpasses for mountain goats and underpasses for deer and large carnivores.[23] The most effective designs allow the target animals, as well as a range of other species, to use habitat on both sides of the road. Some crossings may also enhance landscape hydrologic processes. (See Interstate 75 Wildlife Crossings case study, this chapter.) Since the technologies are new, the performance of these structures should be monitored for several years.

Area and Population Size

The heath hen is a classic example of how multiple causes can drive a small population to extinction.[24] Originally common throughout much of the Northeast, hunting and habitat destruction reduced the species to just fifty individuals by 1908. Conditions improved with the establishment of a refuge, and the population increased to eight hundred over the next few years. Subsequently, however, several unpredictable factors caused the population to plummet. After a destructive fire, an unusually harsh winter, and heavy predation, the heath hen was down to 150 individuals by 1917. By chance, most of the 150 were males, resulting in even fewer breeding pairs. The population was then struck by disease. Numbering eleven in 1927, the heath hen became extinct in 1932.

Stories like this cause one to wonder how to best protect current species populations. Planners, for example, may ask how much habitat is sufficient to conserve a species. Implied in this question is a second question: What size does a population need to be to remain viable? Habitat reduction and fragmentation make these questions particularly relevant today. As the area of many open spaces has decreased, species populations have also decreased.

The smaller these populations become, the more prone they are to eventual extinction.

Over the past few decades, the concept of minimum viable populations has attracted considerable attention from conservation biologists. To get at the issue, scientists first sought to identify the major types of threats faced by small populations.[25] They then developed models that incorporated and evaluated these threats.[26] The populations of actual species have been assessed to estimate the size needed to keep the population below a certain level of risk, or alternatively, to estimate the risk faced by a population of a specified size. While this work cannot provide absolute answers, it offers planners an approach to questions of habitat and population size.

In addition to the more obvious threats, the models have shown that small populations are especially susceptible to unpredictable events. The heath hen, for example, was significantly impacted by fire, weather, predation, and demographic variations, none of which could have been foreseen. As we devise strategies to counter known causes of extinction, scientists stress that we must also maintain populations at sizes large enough to withstand unusual, unpredictable conditions. These unpredictable conditions include variations in demography, the environment, and genetic patterns.[27]

Demographic variations are a primary concern when populations are extremely small (less than one hundred), and especially when they also have slow growth rates. By chance, few offspring may survive in a given year or the majority may be of one sex. Such fluctuations in demography affect future breeding success. Their effects are inversely proportional to population size.[28] If a bird population numbered only twenty, for example, the failure of just five nests could be devastating.

Environmental variations affect a species' habitat. Among other factors, these include disturbances, a decreased food supply, and increased competition, predation, and disease. Environmental variations impact populations of all sizes. Since they often operate in concert with other influences, however, they increase the total pressure on small populations.[29] Again, the heath hen declined due to a combination of environmental events and an uneven sex ratio. Habitats with high environmental variability indicate the need for greater population sizes.[30] Since even the largest populations may not survive a catastrophe, the best strategy for these events is multiple reserves.

A third type of unpredictability is variation in genetic diversity. Genetic diversity is valuable because it helps a population or species adapt to changing environmental conditions. The broader the gene pool, the more opportunities there are for evolution. Maintaining the existing level of genetic diversity is thus assumed to be important for long-term persistence. Genetic diversity increases through mutation and through interbreeding with individuals from outside the population. For small populations, a sharp decline in genetic diversity poses an immediate threat. A drop in the gene pool can affect reproduction, and so lead to extinction.

Small populations lose genetic diversity when they are completely isolated.[31] One reason for this loss is a process called genetic drift. Due to random mating, as well as the arbitrary way in which DNA recombines, all the genes represented in one generation may not show up in the next. Over time, fewer possible genetic variations may exist for any given trait. A second reason for the decline is inbreeding. Mating between close relatives also reduces the variety of genetic material passed to the next generation. This practice can produce "inbreeding depression," or lower fertility and survival of offspring. Inbreeding depression typically follows a rapid increase in inbreeding, as occurs when formerly large populations are fragmented into multiple subpopulations. Both genetic drift and inbreeding depression disproportionately affect small populations. For example, after twenty generations, a population of one thousand would still have 99 percent of its original genetic diversity, whereas one of fifty would retain less than 82 percent.[32] To avoid genetic loss, critically low populations should be increased within a few generations,[33] or new breeding individuals should be introduced in each generation.[34]

Some scientists have tried to estimate the size a population must be to avoid extinction due to unpredictable events. These estimates are now considered by most to be very general and oversimplified, since species, habitat conditions, and the level of risk society is willing to assume can vary widely.[35] Some estimates are presented in terms of the census, or actual, population size, while others are offered for an "effective" population. The effective population is a genetic concept, and refers to the number of individuals actually involved in breeding and passing genetic material to the next generation.[36] As an approximation, the census size of a population can be considered to be three to four times its effective size.[37]

Based on the experience of animal breeders, Franklin (1980) and Soulé (1980) suggested that the effective size of a population would need to be at least fifty individuals to stem inbreeding depression. Franklin also estimated that a minimum effective population of five hundred might preserve long-term genetic diversity. Soulé and Simberloff (1986) advised that in most cases, an effective population of a few hundred and a census population of one thousand may be adequate for both concerns. Soulé (1987) later estimated a minimum boundary of a few thousand for a census population. Thomas (1990), referring to census population size, suggests that ten is too few, one hundred is usually inadequate, one thousand is adequate for species of normal variability, while ten thousand should be adequate for most birds and mammals.[38] For planners, the value of these numbers is simply to gain appreciation for the relative magnitude of populations that may be required. Lacking specific data on species, habitat, and risk, the estimates may have little relation to the requirements of any given situation.

A more precise method of determining minimum viable populations is through population viability analyses (PVAs).[39] PVAs are simulation models that incorporate extensive data on a species population. They include such parameters as birth and death rates, breeding behavior, habitat quantity and quality, home range size, spatial distribution, dispersal characteristics, and environmental variability. They are a form of risk assessment, assessing the likelihood of future, potentially catastrophic events based on current data and theory.[40] A PVA can be used to estimate the minimum number of individuals necessary for a population to persist for a specified amount of time, given a specified probability of survival. For example, a planner might use a PVA to estimate how many individuals would be needed for a population of black bears to survive, with 95 percent certainty, for five hundred years. Alternatively, if he or she had a population of one hundred bears, and wanted them to survive for five hundred years, that probability could also be estimated.

Due to the amount of data required, PVAs have been developed primarily for high-profile endangered species, such as the northern spotted owl, the grizzly bear, and California condor.[41] Even with all the necessary data, however, scientists emphasize that PVAs should not be assumed to be completely accurate. They focus on future, unknown events, and are best used as tools to assess probabilities.[42] In addition, the PVA process enhances understanding of the factors influencing a population, and so helps in comparing planning and management alternatives.[43]

Goldingay and Possingham (1995) conducted a population viability analysis on the yellow-bellied glider, an Australian marsupial that has experienced widespread habitat loss. The objective of the analysis was to determine minimum habitat areas needed to support populations with a 95 percent probability of persistence for one hundred years. The researchers obtained life history variable values from three detailed studies of the species. They also included an environmental parameter to simulate uncertainty in reproduction. They then varied the parameters to assess which were most sensitive and found that the adult mortality rate had the greatest influence on population viability. Each parameter set was simulated one hundred times for a two-hundred year period. The model predicted that at least 150 family groups were required for a viable population. The minimum habitat areas were estimated based on the size of the group home range and the proportion of forest in the area that could be occupied.[44]

Both the numbers and the concepts advanced by work on minimum viable populations are useful for planners. While they are extremely general, the population size estimates can at least help one assess magnitudes of risk. Suppose, for example, there was an isolated habitat area of 20,000 acres, and planners were concerned about a population in this area with an average home range of 800 acres. Assuming the species can use all of the 20,000 acres, the planners could divide the home range size into the total acreage and find that the reserve supports a population of roughly twenty-five individuals (20,000÷800 = 25). One does not need a lot of data to deduce that this is a high-risk population. The population-size estimates have also been used by ecologists to assess risks faced by certain animal groups. For example, they have related the spatial requirements of large carnivores to various public land assemblages and concluded that few areas in the country can support adequate populations of these species.[45]

Beyond the numbers, work in this field has produced several concepts that should help protect small populations. It is now apparent that variations in demography, environment, and genetics are important factors leading to population declines. The extent of anticipated fluctuations is one aspect of determining adequate safety margins. Maintaining links among populations is not only important for movement, but to stem losses in genetic diversity. For numerous reasons, small, isolated habitat patches cannot be expected to support many types of species over any extended period of time.

In summary, habitat reduction and fragmentation are leading contributors to native species extinctions. These incremental modifications in landscape pattern affect biodiversity by changing ecological processes and conditions. Among these changes are a loss in interior habitats and an increase in edge habitats. Edge habitats have a harsher microclimate and are more susceptible to influences from outside the reserve system, including exotic species. In addition, fragmentation modifies landscape-scale processes and inhibits a range of necessary species movements. The proliferation of small, isolated open spaces results in reduced populations that are more prone to extinction.

Since habitat reduction and fragmentation occur over extensive areas, they are best addressed at that scale through coordinated landscape planning. Ideally, open-space requirements should be considered in the same process as new land-use designations. This approach to planning necessarily involves cooperation among various jurisdictions, agencies, private landowners, and interests. It also entails planning at multiple biological scales. At the landscape level, a reserve network can be designed that incorporates and links a range of habitat types. At the community and population levels, the network can specifically address the needs of sensitive communities and species. Together, these strategies can help conserve native biodiversity.

Reducing Road Barriers for Large Carnivores
Interstate 75 Wildlife Crossings, Southwest Florida

When a two-lane road in southwest Florida was converted to Interstate 75, the Florida Department of Transportation worked with the U.S. Fish and Wildlife Service to design a series of wildlife crossings. The new highway would pass through a large portion of the range of the endangered Florida panther (*Felis concolor coryi*), increasing the prob-ability of panther roadkills. Thirteen bridges were retrofitted to augment the underneath crossing area, and twenty-three additional underpasses were constructed along the forty miles intersecting the panther range. In addition to serving as wildlife crossings, the structures also restored part of the natural sheetflow of the area's hydrology (figure 4.4).

Several considerations enter into the design of wildlife roadway crossings. First, the structures must be sited in areas where the target animals would naturally cross the road. The crossings must be located at sites adjacent to suitable habitat, and the substrate under the structures should be one that is preferred by the target species. To further encourage animals to use the crossings, the design of the underpasses should be high and wide, with a clear view through to the far side. Fencing the entire roadway will funnel animals to the structures, as well as prevent them from crossing in other areas. Maintenance of the fence is especially important so that animals will take advantage of openings and not become trapped along the highway corridor.

The Florida Department of Transportation was able to identify ten existing panther crossings using observational and roadkill information. Other suitable crossing sites were located by mapping vegetation on either side of the road and analyzing the area for the habitat and cover density preferred by the panthers. The structures were sited an average of one mile apart, a design close enough to ensure discovery by panthers moving toward them along the fence.

Looking through the new underpasses from an animal's viewpoint, each structure is 100-feet wide, 173-feet long, and 8-feet high. Each consists of two overhead two-lane bridges with an open central median to add an illusion of space. The entire 40-mile roadway section and the crossings are bordered by a chain link fence which is 10- to 12-feet high and topped with three strands of barbed wire.

Four wildlife crossings were mounted with infrared game counters and

Figure 4.4. Wildlife crossings under Interstate 75 in southwest Florida help preserve animal movements and waterflow.

cameras and monitored for periods of two, ten, fourteen, and sixteen months during and subsequent to construction. In addition to the panthers, bobcats (*Lynx rufus*), bears (*Ursus americanus*), deer (*Odocoileus virginiana*), raccoons (*Procyon lotor*), alligators (*Alligator mississipiensis*), and a variety of wading birds passed through the crossings. Species' use of the system varied according to location, season, and time of day. One of the primary factors determining use was the amount of standing water present. For example, panthers and bobcats preferred drier crossings, while raccoons and wading birds used those with more standing water.

Since roadkill data were not obtained prior to construction, it has not been possible to evaluate the degree to which the crossing system has prevented mortalities. In addition, the extent to which the system may have benefitted or restricted smaller animals, particularly those with a range of less than one mile, has not been clear. However, the monitoring did not demonstrate any panther roadkills on Interstate 75 since the system was installed.

Construction of the structures and fences on Interstate 75 cost approximately $13 million and was completed in four years. Since then, the Florida

Department of Transportation has also used the same crossings on another interstate, U.S. 1. In addition, the department installed a series of smaller, prefabricated structures on two 2-lane state roads. The latter crossings are 8-feet high, 20-feet wide, and measure 33-feet across the road. The state's Game and Freshwater Fish Commission has radiocollared panthers and bears along one of the roads. The animals' use of the system was monitored for one year prior to construction and will be assessed for two years afterward. If successful, the reduced expense associated with the smaller designs will enable more widespread application of this wildlife crossing system.

FOR FURTHER INFORMATION CONTACT:
> Gary Evink
> State of Florida Department of Transportation
> 605 Suwannee Street/M.S. 37
> Tallahassee, FL 32399-0450
> 904-487-2781

Protecting Populations in a Fragmented Environment
Black-Tailed Prairie Dog Habitat Conservation Plan,
Boulder, Colorado

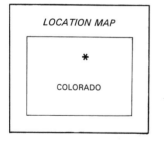

Less than one hundred years ago, black-tailed prairie dogs covered the grasslands of western North America with an estimated population of more than 5 billion. Viewed as a ranching and agricultural pest, they have been subject to extensive eradication campaigns. The species was reduced to near extinction in the 1970s, then recovered slightly and is considered rare today. Due to their ecological value, and ongoing threats to their habitat, the City of Boulder developed a plan to conserve the prairie dogs in its open-space system. The plan is based on a series of habitat conservation areas. It also contains provisions for public education, monitoring, and research. The Boulder Habitat Conservation Plan demonstrates an approach to conserving a threatened animal within a fragmented landscape (figure 4.5).

A primary reason for preserving prairie dogs is their role as a keystone species in short- and mixed-grass prairie communities. Prairie dogs forage near their burrows, and clip tall plants to enable them to spot predators at a distance. These activities alter the composition of grasses and forbs and increase

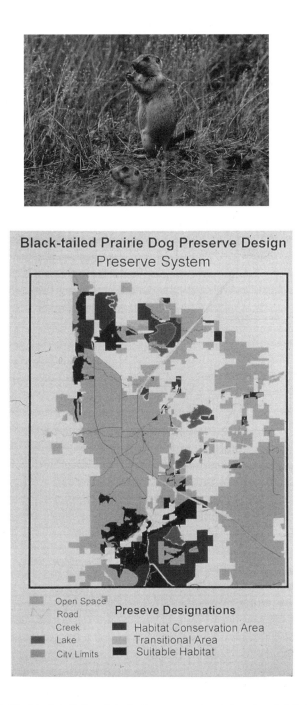

Figure 4.5. The black-tailed prairie dog preserve system is based on habitat conservation areas which are each capable of supporting a population. (Photograph of prairie dogs by David Jennings; preserve design map courtesy of the City of Boulder Open Space Department.)

nitrogen in the affected vegetation. Prairie dog colonies also attract numerous other animals. Up to 170 vertebrate species benefit in some way from their presence, including a variety of predators and other animals that live in the abandoned burrows. While many of these species are simply opportunistic, those that are more dependent have declined alongside the prairie dogs. The black-footed ferret, for example, is now endangered because it preys specifically on prairie dogs.

The goal of the Boulder Habitat Conservation Plan is to preserve black-tailed prairie dogs within suitable habitat areas. To do this, planners first identified locations within the open-space system where short- and mixed-grass prairie remained. They then refined this "coarse filter" with a "cultural filter." The cultural filter narrowed the potential habitat located by the coarse filter by eliminating areas that were unsuitable due to human uses. Irrigated croplands and pastures, for example, can alter grasslands to the point where they no longer support prairie dogs. These agricultural land uses are also valued and protected under another planning mandate. In the next step, planners evaluated the design of the potential reserves. They gave priority to sites that supported large habitat blocks and would also minimize conflicts with adjacent land uses.

Reducing conflicts with neighbors is an important objective of the plan. For prairie dogs, "edges" are a threat not because of altered ecological conditions, but because neighbors generally do not welcome them on their lands. Prairie dogs that move onto private property are likely to be exterminated. For this reason, planners preferred sites with low perimeter-to-area ratios. They also made use of natural barriers, such as wetlands and steep slopes, that would restrict movement out of the preserves. Where necessary, specially designed fences were also constructed as visual barriers, since prairie dogs will not travel beyond where they can see.

The analysis resulted in a series of habitat conservation areas (HCAs), transition areas, and removal areas. Several of the HCAs are located within existing large preserves. Multiple colonies could exist at each of these sites, within dispersal distance of each other. Five other HCAs are smaller and effectively isolated, but could still support populations of several hundred. The transitional areas are locations where colonies exist, but which also have characteristics unsuitable for a reserve. In time, planners intend to move these colonies to the HCAs. The removal areas include sites with low-quality habitat, or with significant neighbor conflicts, so colonies at these sites will also be relocated.

Community participation has been a fundamental part of the process. Before conducting the analysis, planners created a Prairie Dog Study Committee, comprising planners, researchers, nonprofits, resource agency personnel, neighbors, and open-space lessees. The committee helped develop the assumptions, goals, and objectives of the plan. They determined, for example, that prairie dogs and private property rights could both be protected by limiting the HCAs to public lands. To reach consensus, the committee identified issues that were important to each individual or interest group, developed alternative ways of addressing the issues, and evaluated the alternatives to create recommendations. The final system of HCAs represents tradeoffs made on all sides. The plan has undergone several revisions, with public comments incorporated in each successive draft.

Given past attitudes toward prairie dogs, outreach and education has also been important. Planners conducted a day-long symposium for land managers to discuss issues related to prairie dog management. They met individually with ranchers and farmers who lease open-space land. As a result of these efforts, most Boulder citizens accept prairie dog conservation as an appropriate goal for their municipal open space.

While the HCAs are able to support significant populations, the system as a whole remains fragmented. Prairie dogs from the smaller sites will not be able to breed with those from other colonies. In the absence of specific management, this could potentially affect genetic diversity. On the other hand, the fragmented design could also reduce the spread of sylvatic plague. Plague erupts in prairie dog colonies every ten to fifteen years and can eliminate whole colonies or reduce them to a few individuals. Links between colonies enable the dispersal of plague and juvenile prairie dogs. If an isolated colony is eliminated by plague, however, recolonization of the site will require human intervention.

The process by which the prairie dogs are relocated is another long-term issue. An essential part of the plan involves moving prairie dog colonies from unsuitable to suitable habitats. Successful relocations, however, may be difficult to achieve. Whereas juvenile prairie dogs are relatively easy to move, adults may try to return to their original sites. Planners will have to work with experienced ecologists to devise effective strategies.

The total cost of the plan, including management, monitoring, and overhead, is estimated at $70,000 to $90,000 per year. Funds will be obtained from the budget of the City of Boulder Open Space Department. Due to budget limitations, however, planners expect that only 50 to 75 percent of the funds may be available in any given year, meaning that only a proportion of the activities planned for the year will be implemented.

The Boulder Habitat Conservation Plan has resulted in a series of habitat conservation areas that are acceptable to the public. Each of the HCAs can support a prairie dog population of several hundred. Colonies in the larger existing preserves will have additional space to expand and will be within dis-

persal distance of each other. In the future, planners will implement sys-
temwide monitoring of the HCAs and census-selected areas for associated
species. Further research will help identify factors that affect biodiversity in
prairie dog colonies, characteristics of plague, and relationships between
prairie dogs and agriculture. Such work will be limited to an extent by available
funding. This multifaceted plan addresses prairie dog ecology, public attitudes,
viable populations, and long-term conservation issues within a fragmented
environment.

FOR FURTHER INFORMATION CONTACT:
    Mark Gershman
    Natural Resource Planner, City of Boulder
    Operations Center
    66 S. Cherryvale Road
    Boulder, CO 80303
    303-441-4142
    gershmanm@ci.boulder.co.us

Chapter 5

Reserve Design

Reserve design is one of the primary ways in which planners influence biodiversity preservation. Reserves can be sited to incorporate representative portions of the landscape or to conserve unique concentrations of biodiversity. Decisions about the size and configuration of a reserve determine how well specific species and ecosystems are protected. The precise location of a boundary can affect a range of ecological processes, including species movements and hydrology. Activities and land uses accommodated within and adjacent to the reserve greatly influence its conservation potential. Given the significance of these decisions, it is important to understand the ecological premises underlying reserve design.

Over the past two decades, the field of reserve design has advanced from basic guidelines to maximize species diversity to a recognition of the numerous types of factors that must be addressed to protect biodiversity as a whole. Some of these factors, such as population sizes and dispersal, were identified early on. More recently, scientists have realized that reserves must also support landscape dynamics within reserves and address ongoing external impacts. Since each landscape and social context is unique, there are no universal formulas to follow. Instead, reserve systems must be developed by considering the potential contribution of different design elements, which are themselves shaped by local ecology and opportunities.

The elements of reserve design include core areas, connections between these areas, the landscape matrix surrounding the system, and buffer zones between the system and the matrix (figure 5.1). The core areas are generally the bulk of the system, designed to incorporate the communities or populations most in need of protection. Landscape corridors can be sited to link the cores.

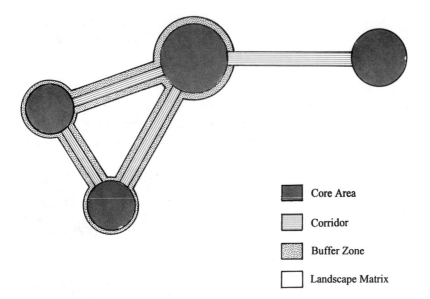

Core Area

Corridor

Buffer Zone

Landscape Matrix

Figure 5.1. The basic elements of reserve design include core areas, corridors to link the cores, buffer zones adjacent to the cores or corridors for added protection, and the landscape matrix in which the reserve is situated. This conceptual diagram shows a buffer zone around only parts of the reserve system.

The purpose of such connecting features is to support the movements of specific species, as well as other important ecological processes. The matrix is considered in reserve design since many interactions occur between a reserve and its surrounding landscape. Adjacent land uses influence the ecology of the reserve and can be planned to further a conservation strategy. Buffer zones are limited strips of the matrix adjacent to the reserve; their design, and the activities accommodated in them, are based on expected impacts from the external landscape.

Because knowledge of biodiversity is limited, the systems created to protect it can best be viewed as experiments. They are clearly valuable for conservation, but it is not always certain that they will meet specific goals. For example, since one can only estimate minimum viable populations, it is not possible to be sure how large a reserve should be to maintain a particular species. Also, relatively little is known about which animals might actually use a designated corridor. Therefore, it is prudent to err on the conservative side, that is, to leave more than the absolute minimum amount of space, or more than the minimum number of corridors. It will also be important to monitor these systems, and to be flexible enough to adapt them when they do not function as expected.

The Development of Reserve Design

The field of reserve design was greatly influenced by *The Theory of Island Bio-geography*, a book published in 1967 by Robert MacArthur and Edward Wilson.[1] The purpose of the book was to explain variations in species diversity on oceanic islands. According to MacArthur and Wilson, larger islands contain more species than smaller islands because they support larger species populations and thus experience fewer extinctions. Islands located closer to a mainland also contain more species, since they can be discovered and colonized by more organisms. All else being equal, large islands close to a source of colonization should exhibit the greatest species diversity.

The "theory" of island biogeography was soon applied to nature reserves. Noting the continuing fragmentation and degradation of wildlands, scientists began to view reserves as islands surrounded by inhospitable habitat. Concepts from island biogeography were used to develop principles for reserve design. In 1975, for example, Jared Diamond developed a series of design principles to minimize extinctions in nature reserves (figure 5.2). He agreed that a larger reserve "island" would hold more species than a smaller reserve. In addition, he suggested that a large reserve was preferable to several smaller reserves of the same total area. A system of smaller reserves would support fewer species, since some organisms would not be able to disperse among the open spaces. For the same reason, reserves located close together were better than those located far apart, and reserves connected by corridors were superior to those that were

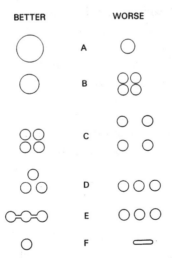

Figure 5.2. Principles for reserve design based on concepts from island biogeography. (From Diamond, 1975.)

disjunct. The best shape for a reserve would be circular, since it would minimize dispersal distance.[2]

While both the theory of island biogeography and its applications were later criticized, they were an important step in the development of the field. Diamond's principles identified several ideas that have proved fundamental for reserve design. For example, large reserves are clearly valuable for most reserve systems. His principles regarding the size and shape of reserves addressed the impact of edges and the importance of maintaining interior habitat for sensitive species. By advocating reserves located close together, or connected by corridors, he highlighted the value of connectivity for species dispersal.

Much of the criticism of principles such as Diamond's has been that they are too simplistic.[3] From a practical standpoint, they do not recognize the reality of creating a nature reserve. Rather than developing an ideal system based on such principles, planners are usually constrained by which lands are available for conservation and must plan and manage within these constraints. From a conservation standpoint, the principles have also proven limited. While they may be a good place to start, scientists now recognize that reserve design must address many additional concepts to effectively protect biodiversity.

Spatial issues—such as location, size, and connectivity—are one area in which reserve design now appears more complex. Developments in metapopulation theory confirm that the location of a reserve is important in relation to other open spaces. Location can also determine which attributes of biodiversity might be conserved at all. Reserves can be sited to protect a range of ecosystems or species, as well as areas of particularly high diversity. The size of the reserve influences biodiversity conservation in numerous ways. In addition to its value for wide-ranging and sensitive species, a large reserve can better sustain ecological processes, reduce management costs, and minimize external impacts. Small reserves can also be valuable for species that require less space and disperse over shorter distances. The degree of connectivity existing within landscapes or among reserves depends on the scale at which it is assessed and the needs of individual species.

Scientists also emphasize the importance of ecological processes operating within a reserve and across its boundaries. These processes are influenced by the design of the reserve, as well as by management and land use decisions. Disturbances are particularly important to maintain a varying mixture of habitat patches in the protected area. The landscape in which the reserve system is situated is an additional ecological consideration. Scientists no longer view reserves as habitat "islands." Reserves can be highly affected by external land and resource uses, and their boundaries can be crossed by species from both sides.

In summary, the field of reserve design has matured from simple principles to a complex series of considerations. Planners may already be familiar with some of the principles, since they have been around for some time and have been described in planning literature.[4] Recent studies and observations have confirmed some of these concepts and expanded them to include a range of additional concepts. Current approaches to design emphasize the importance of the specific landscape in which a reserve is located. Principles and guidelines are a useful start, but the complexity of each situation usually requires consideration of additional factors.

Initial Considerations

Imagine that you are in the position to establish a reserve or to augment an existing open-space system. Given a choice, where would you site the new protected area to further your conservation goals? Do you acquire lands or obtain easements to create one large open space? Would multiple reserves be appropriate? Is the shape of the reserves an important issue? These questions address some of the initial considerations in reserve design. They pertain to individual reserves, as well as to an extended reserve system.

Location

In practice, planners may have few options in the siting of reserves. There may be little open space remaining in the region. Public pressure to create the reserve may also be based on protecting certain landscapes or species habitats. To the extent that there is flexibility within the region, however, two approaches to reserve siting can be considered.

The first approach is to locate the reserve to maximize representation of biodiversity within protected areas. For example, if grassland and forested communities were already included in existing open spaces, it would be preferable to site the new reserve in an area of woodlands and shrubs. The entire system would then protect a greater range of regional communities. Representation can also address biodiversity at smaller scales. For instance, another option would be to evaluate the degree to which the diversity of habitats or species in a landscape was protected. However, representing biodiversity at more detailed levels generally requires conserving a greater area of land.[5] Since many existing reserves are located in areas of marginal human value, representation, at least at the community level, can be an important consideration.

A second and more common approach is to establish the reserve in a location of high ecological value. For example, it could include a river corridor and wetlands, or a region where the ranges of numerous species overlap, or an area supporting many endemic species. This approach enables planners to protect concentrations of biodiversity within a limited reserve area. Both approaches have value and both can be included in reserve design. At some point, however, the two will likely include tradeoffs. Protecting unique areas does not necessarily result in all or even most communities being conserved, nor does protecting representative areas guarantee preservation of other priorities. Thus the siting of reserves involves some consideration of which aspects of biodiversity are most in need of conservation.

Whichever of these strategies a planner follows, the reserve will likely be more effective if is located adjacent or near to existing open spaces. Adjoining reserves have the benefit of creating a larger natural area. Reserves sited close together will enable at least some species to travel between them. The values of increased size and connectivity to a conservation system are discussed below.

Size

The size of open spaces has always been important in reserve design. For numerous reasons, scientists have continued to urge planners to establish large reserves. A primary reason, as discussed in chapter 4, is that large open spaces are increasingly scarce due to habitat reduction and fragmentation. Habitat size affects the viability of species populations, particularly those of wide-ranging mammals. The extent of a reserve also influences the types of disturbances and successional vegetation that occur within the system. Lower habitat quality can effectively reduce the size of the reserve. Edge impacts also decrease interior habitat for sensitive species. While extensive reserves may not always be an option, planners can evaluate the probable success of a system in terms of its effect on these ecological factors.

The ability of a reserve to support specific species is a basic measure of its conservation value. Reserve size is fundamental to preserving viable species populations. In particular, it is the area of individual habitat types in relation to the spatial requirements of specific species that is the concern. For which organisms does the reserve contain sufficient habitat to maintain a population of several hundred individuals? Several thousand? For species that occur in metapopulations, larger reserves can also include more subpopulations, and so reduce dispersal risks.

Another way to assess the value of a reserve's size is to consider its effect on disturbances and successional vegetation. Different types of species depend on disturbances for the diverse habitats that they need. Size is related to disturbances in that extensive areas are required to maintain natural disturbance regimes. Shugart and West, for example, estimate this "minimum dynamic area" to be fifty to one hundred times the average habitat patch.[6] While this figure is only an estimate, common sense suggests that an area much greater than a single patch would be needed to provide a range of disturbance patch sizes and successional vegetation stages. Reserve size is also important because species need habitat as a refuge following a disturbance. Larger reserves are more likely to retain such habitat, as well as other populations to recolonize the disturbed area. In addition, certain organisms require specific types of disturbances for reproduction and regeneration. The reserve should be large enough to ensure a minimum probability that such disturbances will occur.

While natural disturbances are the ideal, most reserves will likely be too small to support a full regime. In these cases, preserving biodiversity will require controlled disturbances instituted through management. Here again, reserve size, as well as shape and adjacent land uses, is a consideration. Prescribed burns, for example, cannot be conducted within a certain distance of settlements for safety reasons. They may not be feasible in extremely small reserves or where development extends far into a protected area.

The size of a reserve may also affect the number of habitats and species it contains. All else being equal, large areas contain more diversity than small areas, since they can encompass a greater range of environmental conditions. In some instances, however, this generalization does not hold true. A small site may contain unusual soils or geology and foster high numbers of rare or endemic plants and invertebrates. In California, for example, serpentine soils support grassland communities rich in endemic species. Where dispersal, spatial requirements, and external impacts are not significant concerns, small reserves can be valuable additions to a conservation system.

Poor habitat quality can reduce the effective size of a reserve by reducing the populations it is able to support. Animal home ranges increase when individuals must travel greater distances to find food, water, shelter, or breeding areas. As home ranges increase, population sizes decrease. Factors affecting habitat quality include vegetation structure, prey species, competing species, water sources, and habitat elements such as leaf litter, dead snags and woody debris, and other breeding and roosting sites.

A final consideration for evaluating the size of a reserve is the probable influence of edge effects. Assuming that these impacts extend a constant distance into a reserve, reserve size will affect the amount of undisturbed habitat remaining for sensitive species. Large reserves may contain extensive areas free from external impacts, whereas small reserves may consist primarily of edge habitat. In addition to adjacent land uses, edge effects may also stem from uses and activities within the reserve. Roads, development, and intensively used trails create interior edges, fragment the reserve, and further limit undisturbed habitat area.

Shape

The shape of a reserve is a factor for small reserves, since it can effectively reduce the area of habitat left undisturbed. Elongated reserves may be entirely influenced by edge impacts, whereas circular reserves, with lower edge-area ratios, may retain central areas for sensitive species and communities. For larger reserves not dominated by edge impacts, shape is unimportant relative to other considerations. In most instances, it is more important to conserve an available parcel of land than to worry about its contribution to reserve shape.

Connectivity

In addition to promoting large reserves, awareness of the effects of habitat reduction and fragmentation has led scientists to consider strategies to maintain landscape connectivity. As described in chapter 4, fragmentation impedes ecological processes that operate at the landscape or regional scales. Some of these processes, such as flows of water, nutrients, and sediments, are abiotic. More commonly, however, concern for landscape connectivity is based on protecting animal movements and increasing available habitat.

The primary strategy for retaining connectivity is landscape corridors. Landscape corridors are intended to benefit species that require particular conditions for movement. They may support organisms limited to certain types and structures of vegetation or those that travel following specific landscape features. Corridors between reserves can also increase habitat area for large animals.

A landscape corridor is a linear landscape feature that differs from the surrounding vegetation, and links at least two patches that were historically connected.[7] With regard to reserve design, corridors are a design element distinct from the protected open spaces located at either end. Defined as a link between patches, they do not exist on their own, but rather as a part of a larger conservation system. They are assumed to contain habitat more conducive to a given species than the land outside their boundaries. To maintain genetic patterns, restored corridors are sited in areas where they once occurred, rather than introduced to link habitats and populations that historically had no connection.

Corridors can occur naturally in the landscape or exist as remnants of native vegetation. Naturally occurring corridors are places in the landscape where animals tend to travel. Riparian zones are well-known as movement areas for a variety of species. Some large predators, such as mountain lions, prefer to travel along canyon bottoms or ridgetops.[8] Migratory pathways can also be viewed as natural corridors. Often, however, conservationists are concerned with corridors as linear areas of vegetation remaining in a converted landscape. From a biodiversity perspective, such remnant corridors are important to the extent that they support the movements of species or abiotic elements. Hedgerows, for instance, help birds and small mammals travel across agricultural fields to a distant woodland. They offer protected habitat through an area that is considerably more risky to the species. Land set aside in a development can also serve as a habitat link to open spaces on either side.

A corridor need not always be a continuous strip of land. In some cases, a set of disjunct habitat patches will be adequate to support species movement. Certain birds, for example, can travel from patch to patch, over inhospitable habitat, as long as the patches are located within dispersal range. They can rest or feed in these areas on their way to a larger reserve or, if the areas are large enough, they can settle and breed. However, this type of corridor is limited to the relatively few species that can travel between the patches, and so is less preferable for biodiversity conservation.

The value of corridors lies in their expected ability to increase landscape connectivity and habitat. By connecting habitat patches, corridors can enable animals to conduct routine daily movements, to migrate, or to disperse. By enabling dispersal, corridors can increase the probability of interbreeding among populations and help retain genetic diversity. They can allow recolonization of habitats following a disturbance, and so maintain metapopulation structures. Riparian corridors can preserve hydrologic and geomorphologic processes. As protected open spaces, corridors also provide habitat. Even the narrowest corridors support plants and invertebrates, while increasingly wider corridors can provide habitat for more sensitive organisms and larger animals. One of the most important functions of corridors may be the way in which they support far-ranging species. Wide corridors connecting extensive reserves may greatly extend the total habitat area available to these animals and may be the only solution to protecting their populations. Pinhook Swamp (see case study at the end of this chapter), should provide such a connection for black bears between Florida's Osceola National Forest and the Okefenokee National Wildlife Refuge in Georgia.

To design a landscape corridor, planners must first consider the purposes for which it is intended. For example, if maintaining hydrologic processes is a priority, it would be helpful to protect waterways throughout a watershed, as well as addressing upstream land uses. If water quality and aquatic ecosystems are the target, the corridor must also provide an effective buffer to adjacent terrestrial impacts. When the goal is protecting species' movements, the corridor should be based on the needs and limitations of these organisms.

For animals, corridor design relates to habitat requirements, dispersal abilities, and sensitivity to impacts.[9] If the animal is to move from its habitat in one open space to a habitat in another, the corridor should also contain the same vegetation type and structure. The length of a corridor should be no longer than the distance the animal can disperse. Longer corridors should also be wider. Animals in corridors are more likely to encounter threatening situations traveling in corridors than they would in a reserve, and greater width can help decrease the level of risk. In addition, corridor width depends on the reaction of the organism to edge habitat and impacts. Sensitive interior species require corridors wide enough to retain a central strip of undisturbed habitat. If the target animal travels in a specific area of the landscape, the corridor should be sited in that location. Topographic variations might be considered in relation to the types of habitats included in the corridor or features that can serve as natural barriers between it and external land uses. Ideally, the reserve network would include different types of corridors to address the needs of a variety of species. It would also include multiple corridors, in case one or more are eliminated by disturbance.

As intuitive as the concept appears, the value of landscape corridors has been debated extensively in scientific circles. A primary reason for the debate is the lack of data. The most compelling studies have been conducted on small mammals, since the networks used by these species can be easily manipulated through experimentation.[10] Most studies, however, have been limited to descriptions, noting which animals have used corridors of a specific design in a specific location. As a result, it is still difficult to predict the value of a corridor for a given species.

A second reason is the inherent vulnerability of corridors. As linear features, corridors are subject to impacts along their length. They can be additionally affected by internal human uses. The combination of these impacts suggests that corridors may be most beneficial to edge and exotic species.

A third criticism relates to the types of species a corridor might benefit. Due to its design, a corridor will support some species and not others. It may also allow the passage of unwanted organisms, such as pathogens. For example, in the black-tailed prairie dog case study in chapter 4, planners needed to consider the potential spread of sylvatic plague among prairie dog colonies.

Lastly, scientists have noted instances in which conservation resources would be better spent on strategies other than corridors. Depending on the situation, it may be more effective to invest in augmenting existing reserves. In some cases, conservation goals may be better served by concentrating on the management of private lands, rather than establishing a reserve network at all.[11]

For example, more than eighty percent of California's extensive hardwood rangelands are in private ownership. Creating public reserves in this region would be extremely unpopular. To a large extent, it would also be unnecessary, since grazing, the predominant land use, is preferable to housing development, the primary threat to biodiversity. In this situation, landowner education and incentives are likely to be more practical and beneficial strategies than reserves.[12]

Because of their vulnerability, management and monitoring will be essential components of any plan involving corridors. Over time, the ecology of the narrow, linear landscape corridor will inevitably be altered by external and internal influences. Management will also be needed to control disturbances and to retain the successional vegetation stages required by various species. How these ecological changes will occur is often unpredictable, and the limited area of corridors leaves a small margin for error. In addition, since it is uncertain which species will successfully move along corridors, it is necessary to monitor their use. Monitoring will help ensure that a preserve network functions as intended and may also help other planners develop new designs.

The Landscape Matrix

While its design and content are often the focus, the landscape in which a reserve is located also has a significant influence on its biodiversity. Adjacent land uses create edge impacts along its boundaries and affect the degree to which species inside the system use external lands. Social and economic issues may create pressures for reserve uses incompatible with conservation. Regional land and resource uses affect biodiversity through the modification of large-scale ecological processes. To address edge effects, planners can create buffer zones, institute agreements with adjacent landowners, or manage affected ecosystems within the reserve. To counter regional impacts, they can help coordinate the policies and management practices of the agencies and landowners influencing the impacts.

The boundary of a reserve system is essentially a porous filter.[13] Passing across it from outside the reserve may be wild edge and exotic species, domestic livestock and pets, human recreationists, hunters, fishermen, and abiotic elements, such as wind, light, noise, and pollutants. In addition, reserve policies, for example fire suppression, can be dictated by adjacent land uses. Species inside a protected area may exit into residential or agricultural areas. Internal management may also affect neighboring landowners. Both sides are likely to feel the effects of management or land use across the boundary.

Border conflicts develop to the extent that internal and external values and uses differ. Yellowstone National Park, for example, has had problems with neighboring cattle ranchers since approximately 50 percent of its bison harbor a disease called brucellosis. Ranchers claim that their cattle can become infected from the bison, causing stillbirths or abortions. Unfortunately, 1997 was an extremely harsh winter in Yellowstone. The bison were forced to leave the park to find food, and when they did many hundreds were shot to prevent the transmission of brucellosis. This is an ongoing conflict that has not yet been resolved.

One effect of these varying pressures is that the functional boundary of a reserve may be different than its administrative boundary.[14] Dense housing sited next to the reserve, for instance, could effectively move the border back and reduce the area of protected lands. On the other hand, the Montana ranches mentioned above could allow many smaller animals to travel outside the national park. The functional boundary in this case might be extended into the ranch property. The location of the functional boundary depends on the intensity of pressures on both sides. Consideration of the concept may help planners evaluate which lands are adequately protected and where problems are likely to develop.

Buffer zones are a strategy designed to minimize conflicts between a reserve and its neighbors. Their purpose is to serve as transitional areas and to provide benefits both to the reserve and the local community. Buffer zones benefit the reserve by extending its functional boundary and minimizing edge impacts to sensitive species and ecosystems. They can also provide additional habitat and movement opportunities for large species and greater area for disturbances. Buffer zones serve neighbors because they require a lower degree of protection than the reserve and can accommodate multiple uses. For example, education, research, recreation, tourism, or low-impact grazing and forestry might occur in a buffer zone, as long as these uses did not impinge on conservation in the core area.[15]

The design of a buffer zone depends on the location and extent of impacts, the presence and location of biodiversity attributes requiring protection, and the ecology of the area. Much of the literature on buffer zones focuses on their use in maintaining water quality. In this case, the design would address the types of pollutants, indicators within the stream, and factors affecting the movement of pollutants, such as water flow, soils, topography, and buffer vegetation.[16] Buffer zones to protect biodiversity in a reserve would also address such site-specific variables. Instead of focusing on nitrogen, phosphorus, and sediment, however, we could consider the extent of edge effects from various land uses. Instead of stream indicators, we might consider which vulnerable habitats or species were located near the periphery of the reserve, and so could benefit from a buffer zone. The ecosystems within the proposed zone would be important to the extent that they enhanced or hindered movements across it.

Buffer zones are not applicable in all situations. The concept assumes adequate land for both a strictly protected area and a supplemental buffer. In landscapes with limited open space, buffer zones may not be appropriate. All of the natural areas might require a high level of protection or, if they are already significantly altered, all of them might be designated multiple use. In lieu of a buffer zone, planners can reduce edge effects through agreements with adjacent landowners or through reserve management. The purpose of an agreement would be to reduce impacts at the source, while management would reduce them after they were produced. Both strategies might be necessary and desirable whether or not buffer zones are used.

Beyond immediate edge effects, it is likely that biodiversity with a reserve system will be affected by broad-scale land and resource uses. The Everglades is a well-known example of this type of influence. Despite a 1.4 million acre park, and more than 100,000 acres in adjoining open spaces, many native species in the Everglades have continued to decline. Their decline is due in large part to changes in hydrology throughout southern Florida, a system of levees, canals, and water diversions that continues to alter the park's wetland ecosystems.[17] In southwest Australia, reserves are experiencing another type of impact from hydrological modifications. There, the clearing of more than 90 percent of the native woodlands has caused the water table to rise. The rising water table has brought salts to the surface of the soil, degrading lakes, streams, and native vegetation.[18] In addition to these hydrologic changes, most planners are familiar with the effects of widespread development, which can increase runoff, erosion, and the eutrophication of streams and rivers. Other examples of broad-scale impacts include air pollution, acid rain, and global climate change.

At a minimum, impacts that extend over large regions require coordination among multiple agencies and/or landowners. The extended Everglades ecosystem, for example, is managed by more than ten state and federal resource agencies.[19] Revegetation in southwest Australia is in the hands of numerous private farmers. Since planting native trees means reducing the acreage of their wheat farms, solutions to conserve biodiversity must also address the farmers' economic interests. While solving broad-scale conflicts is often beyond the scope of local planning, planners may still contribute to the process. When the impacts stem from land uses at the landscape or county level, planners can have a direct and significant influence.

Models for Reserve Design

When designing a reserve, planners should consider the influence of alternative configurations of design elements on regional biodiversity. Different combinations and designs of core reserves, corridors, and buffer zones can contribute to conservation in varying ways. Each proposed reserve system will also be affected by the surrounding landscape. Because the process is complex, it is useful to review the basic reserve models already developed. The designs of these models and the values they address can help planners decide which type of system might benefit their particular region.

One of the most influential models has been that of the biosphere reserves, a system developed by UNESCO's Man and the Biosphere Program (MAB). Launched in 1971, MAB's purpose was to provide information to solve practical management problems stemming from interactions between humans and the environment. The biosphere reserves were set up as a global network of protected areas for conservation, scientific research, and monitoring. Each reserve was selected to be representative of a specific type of biogeographic province. In addition to conservation, the reserves were intended to integrate a range of human activities and land uses. For example, a reserve could include areas for restoration, training and education, research, monitoring, housing, or agriculture. They were designed as holistic models of environmental protection and sustainable development, with a strong emphasis on local participation and indigenous management practices. The first biosphere reserve was established in 1976, and there are now approximately three hundred biosphere reserves existing throughout the world.[20]

The general model of a biosphere reserve consists of a strictly protected core area surrounded by one or more buffer or transition zones (figure 5.3). The core areas include examples of natural or minimally disturbed ecosystems occurring within the province. Since genetic conservation is an objective of the biosphere reserve program, centers of endemism and genetic richness are highly valued. Unusual natural features may also be included in the core areas. Human activities are accommodated in the buffer or transition zones. In these portions of the reserve, local communities may experiment with different types of sustainable land uses, scientists may perform research, or managers may conduct training and restoration programs. Activities within a biosphere reserve range from complete protection in the core areas to the most intensive uses in the outer transition zone.

For planners, the value of the biosphere reserve model lies in its use of environmental zoning. Central core areas are protected from external impacts by surrounding buffer zones. The outer zones are also designed to address the

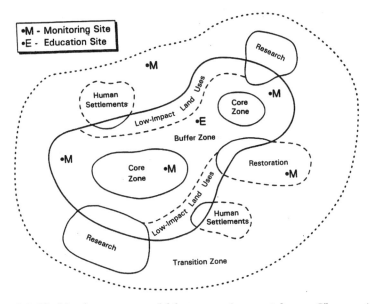

Figure 5.3. The biosphere reserve model features environmental zones. The zones integrate conservation and development by providing strict protection in the core areas, and allowing increased intensity of land uses in zones located progressively further from the cores. (Adapted from diagram in Noss and Cooperrider, 1994, based on Hough, 1988.)

economic and social needs of the local community. The community can use these areas in ways compatible with conservation. Demonstration projects can highlight useful indigenous practices, and stimulate new ideas. The zoning concept protects ecological values, and serves to showcase land uses that integrate conservation and development.

While the model is attractive, actual biosphere reserves have generally fallen short.[21] In developing countries, it has been difficult to limit resource extraction and settlements in both the core areas and the buffer zones. As a result, the conservation functions of the reserves have often been reduced. Also, local communities have not fully participated in the design and establishment of the systems.[22]

In the United States, biosphere reserves have usually been superimposed on existing protected areas, such as national parks. As such, they may lack buffer or transition zones and many of the functions intended for these areas. It should be noted, though, that these criticisms center on the implementation of the concept, rather than on the model itself. In the United States, at least, features of the reserve zones may be very useful to incorporate into new conservation systems. If developed locally, with the participation of affected agencies and landowners, the system could avoid some of the problems experienced by existing biosphere reserves.

An example of a second type of reserve is that developed by the Interagency Spotted Owl Scientific Committee to protect the northern spotted owl. The committee was convened as a result of congressional legislation, which directed the U.S. Fish and Wildlife Service, the USDA Forest Service, the National Park Service, and the U.S. Bureau of Land Management to develop a scientifically credible conservation strategy for the owl. The management plan is based on a series of separate habitat conservation areas, or HCAs, to support the spotted owl's metapopulation structure. The HCAs are designed to be within dispersal range of most juvenile owls (figure 5.4). They were developed from maps depicting the range of the owls, the distribution of their old-growth habitat, locations where they now occur, and lands suitable for the establishment of

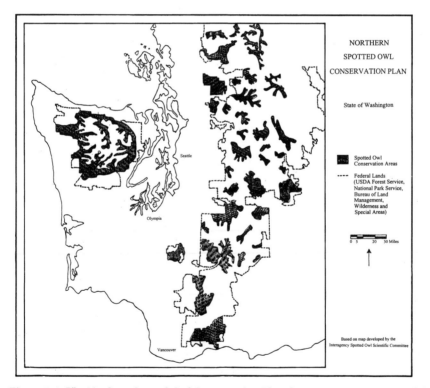

Figure 5.4. The Northern Spotted Owl Conservation Plan demonstrates a reserve model based on separated habitat conservation areas within a managed landscape matrix. (Based on a map developed by the Interagency Spotted Owl Scientific Committee.)

the HCAs. Population viability analysis suggested that each HCA be large enough to support at least twenty pairs of spotted owls. They were planned within 12 miles of each other, a distance the majority of the juvenile owls would be able to travel. While corridors are not necessary for owl dispersal, juveniles move more easily through certain structures of vegetation. Accordingly, the plan states that canopy closure in the matrix between protected areas be at least 40 percent, and that 50 percent of matrix trees average at least 11 inches in diameter.[23]

The northern spotted owl management plan demonstrates how reserve designs maintain certain landscape patterns and, in doing so, protect some aspects of biodiversity more than others. The HCA system is designed for a single type of animal. It could benefit species with habitat and dispersal requirements similar to the spotted owl or others that could also exist within the HCA or matrix habitats. It would not support large animals completely limited to old-growth, since they would require corridors between the HCAs. The biosphere reserve model is best suited to protect concentrations of biodiversity or unique landscape features. It is less appropriate for preserving the range of biodiversity within a region.

A reserve network is essentially an extension of a biosphere reserve. This third type of model connects individual protected areas with corridors. Buffer and transition zones may be included around the whole system (see figure 5.1). Reserve networks address the importance of landscape connectivity and, when extensive, can support the movements and habitat requirements of large animal species. The reserve network model has the fewest limitations of the three, but can also require the greatest amount of protected land.

Larry Harris, a wildlife ecologist at the University of Florida and leading advocate of landscape corridors, proposed such a network for Oregon old-growth forests in 1984. In this system, long-rotation forest islands are surrounded by buffers of successional vegetation and linked by a series of corridors that include small and medium-sized "nodes" of old-growth forest. Harris also introduced the concept of "multiple-use modules," or MUMs, as focal points for a network. Similar to a biosphere reserve, a MUM would be located in an area rich in biodiversity and would allow the greatest intensity of uses in zones furthest from the cores.[24]

The concept of reserve networks developed from the realization that isolated reserves are not sufficient to preserve biodiversity. By themselves, systems of disjunct protected areas cannot sustain remaining populations of large carnivores. Not surprisingly, the same ecologists who championed the use of landscape corridors have also been involved in the design of reserve networks. In addition to addressing connectivity issues, these ecologists have suggested certain uses best suited to a reserve system. For example, road densities should be kept low throughout a network and should be eliminated from the ecologically sensitive cores. While buffer zones may support a variety of species not limited to pristine areas, this function depends on low-impact practices of grazing, forestry, or agriculture. Some recreational activities, such as driving off-road vehicles, may be incompatible with conservation. Housing developments included in a buffer zone should also be designed to maintain ecological processes.[25]

While reserve networks can be designed at any scale, the Wildlands Project has taken the concept a step further by proposing a network of connected wildlands throughout North America. It was developed by a group of leading conservation biologists and environmental activists. Among others, they include Reed Noss, Michael Soulé, and Dave Foreman. The Wildlands Project presents a vision of an extensive system of wilderness areas large enough to include all ecosystem types, all species with large area requirements, and complete natural hydrologic and disturbance regimes. Rather than maximizing biodiversity protection within a limited area, it demonstrates what might be necessary to preserve the full range of diversity. Reserve networks created by local and regional planning groups would be connected across the continent. Recognizing the enormity of such a plan, those involved suggest that it may take a century or more to implement. In addition to changing our approach to land use, it would also involve reducing human population and resource consumption. The Wildlands Project represents an ideal; it was proposed to provide motivation and direction to those in the process of bioregional conservation planning.[26]

In addition to the United States, many other countries have shown interest in the reserve network concept. Reconstruction of the degraded southwest Australian landscape will follow this general model. Scientists, resource managers, and landowners plan protection of existing reserves and corridors, as well as revegetation to increase the area of these fragments and linkages among them.[27] Ecological networks have also been implemented or planned throughout Europe. They have been designed for regions and for entire countries. The Council of Europe is currently planning an extensive ecological network to span the European Union.[28]

Beyond Reserves

However well a reserve system is designed, it probably will protect just a portion of a region's biodiversity. Most of our landscape is dedicated to human settlements or to providing the materials, energy, and services that we require. As our population increases, this "domesticated" landscape also grows, creating pressures to further reduce the wildlands needed to support biodiversity. Accordingly, measures to preserve biodiversity must also address the other, larger area in which we live.

Reserves are an essential strategy for protecting valuable and threatened communities, species, and ecological processes. However, they may also be viewed as a limited, short-term approach to biodiversity conservation. They are limited in that much of biodiversity will inevitably exist outside reserves. They are short-term because they do not deal with the causes of biodiversity loss, causes that over time continue to impact species and ecological processes both inside and outside reserve systems. A comprehensive long-term solution would address the source of the problem as well as mitigate its effects.

While the causes of biodiversity loss are complex, they can largely be traced to the ways in which we provide for the needs of our society. We meet our needs through various types of systems. For example, we have systems to obtain food, water, and energy; to develop housing communities; to manufacture products; to transport ourselves; and to dispose of sewage and wastewater. Each of these systems requires inputs of resources and energy from the environment and each releases byproducts back to the environment. The designs of such systems have traditionally been based more on considerations of economics and convenience than on ecological impacts. As a result, they tend to be incongruous with ecological processes and create pressures on biodiversity. As our population grows, these pressures will increase.

Redesigning the systems that support our lives is a long-term solution to biodiversity loss. Here, the field of ecological design offers a promising approach. The goal of ecological design is to develop processes and products based on ecological criteria. It seeks to minimize the use of energy and original resources, as well as the generation of wastes and pollutants. It accomplishes this goal in part by linking systems; for example, the waste products of one process might be recycled and reused for another. Innovative systems have also been developed based on ecological processes. A marshland, for instance, can be used to treat sewage in lieu of a commercial plant. Each new system demonstrates methods to support communities in a more sustainable manner and may have the added benefit of increasing appreciation for biodiversity, elevating its relative value within our society.[29]

Sustainability and ecological design are broad subjects and beyond the scope of this book. They are noted here simply because a discussion of biodiversity conservation would be incomplete without mentioning approaches that address the causes of the problem. For the present, we can protect much of our native biodiversity by preserving, designing, restoring, and managing our open spaces based on ecological principles. Ultimately, however, conservation will require that we turn to the rest of the landscape and develop better ways to integrate biodiversity protection into the ways in which we live.

Preserving the Keystone
Pinhook Swamp Linkage, Northeastern Florida

LOCATION MAP

GEORGIA

FLORIDA

One of the largest wildlife reserves in the United States, the Okefenokee National Wildlife Refuge in Georgia is separated from Florida's Osceola National Forest by just 10 miles. The distinction has little meaning ecologically, however, because the entire area functions as an integrated swampland complex that offers undisturbed habitat to a wide diversity of plants and animals. The swamp is the headwaters of two major rivers: The St. Mary's River drains the eastern portion of the swamp and runs to the Atlantic Ocean, while to the west, the Suwannee River flows into the Gulf of Mexico. Pinhook Swamp is the area that lies between the two federally protected forested wetlands (figure 5.5). Although largely inaccessible, Pinhook has become increasingly threatened by roads, subdivisions, conversions of uplands to pine plantations, and potential mining and oil exploration. The Nature Conservancy (TNC) and the USDA Forest Service are now negotiating with landowners to acquire Pinhook Swamp for long-term protection.

Pinhook Swamp is an essential part of the conservation plan for the area because it serves as an ecological connection between the two adjoining reserves. Consisting of the same peat and mineral soils, it gives rise to vegetation communities and hydrological regimes that are similar to the federally protected areas. Topographical features, such as ridges, also link Pinhook to other parts of the swamp complex. Florida black bears, bobcats, and river otters migrate along densely wooded waterways which run throughout the ecosystem. Although Pinhook Swamp itself is 170,600 acres, the three preserved units together total 693,000 acres. The combined reserve will protect several existing threatened and endangered species, and could serve as a reintroduction site for others.

The Nature Conservancy's plan to purchase Pinhook Swamp followed studies of both the St. Mary's and Suwannee river systems and resulted in a list of potential acquisitions offering high conservation value. TNC and the Forest Service then jointly developed priorities for Pinhook Swamp. The parcels were

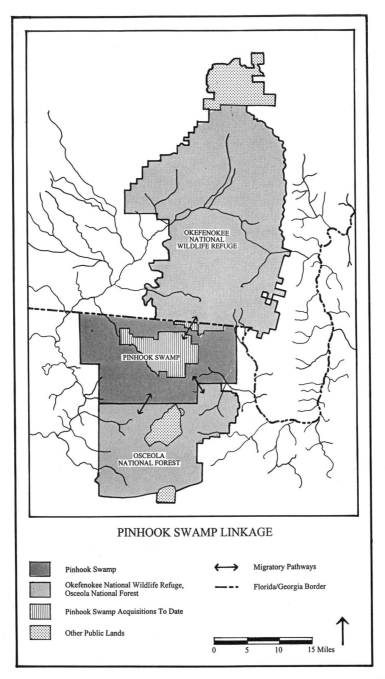

PINHOOK SWAMP LINKAGE

Pinhook Swamp		↔	Migratory Pathways
Okefenokee National Wildlife Refuge, Osceola National Forest		- - -	Florida/Georgia Border
Pinhook Swamp Acquisitions To Date			
Other Public Lands			

0   5   10   15 Miles

Figure 5.5. Pinhook Swamp provides connections between Okefenokee National Wildlife Refuge and Osceola National Forest, between the St. Mary's and Suwannee river systems, and between habitats for migrating species.

ranked by their contribution to the area's ecology. Available parcels receiving the highest priority have been purchased first. The boundaries of the Pinhook Swamp project were determined by the limits of the wetlands communities, with a buffer zone of upland habitat added along the perimeter. The buffer is a minimum of one-half mile, and it was increased in areas of high quality habitat or for specific management considerations. Particular emphasis was placed on the inclusion of three major migratory pathways which link the swamp to the Okefenokee Refuge and to Osceola National Forest.

Of the 170,600 acres, 38,855 have now been acquired. Both TNC and the Forest Service have negotiated with the landowners, which consist primarily of nine timber companies. The approach is to buy land only from willing sellers, and few substantial conflicts have arisen. At this point, the acquisitions are located in the center of the swamp. The objective for subsequent purchases is to create the first link between the Okefenokee Refuge and Osceola National Forest. While the process continues slowly, the level of threats to the area is also still relatively low.

A total of $13,280,000 has been spent to purchase the 38,855 acres. In the beginning, funds were obtained exclusively from the federal Land and Water Conservation Fund. When Congress recently limited appropriations to the Fund, TNC and the Forest Service began looking for additional monies. One likely source is another fund set up to mitigate phosphate mining in the region. Estimated at $20 million over twenty years, this fund is designed to support acquisitions, conservation easements, and restoration projects in riparian and upper watershed areas. It is overseen by TNC, although the projects are selected by an interagency team. A third possible source of money is Florida's Conservation and Recreational Lands Program, on whose Bargain Shared List Pinhook has been accorded high priority.

The Pinhook Swamp linkage exemplifies an approach to reserve design guided by landscape ecology. Conservation of the area is necessary to maintain the hydrology of the entire swamp complex and to accommodate numerous migrating and sensitive species. The swamp's location at the headwaters of two largely pristine rivers will also help to preserve these systems. Pinhook Swamp is the key link to retaining the high ecological value of this landscape.

FOR FURTHER INFORMATION CONTACT:

George Willson   Chris Zajicek
The Nature Conservancy   USDA Forest Service
625 North Adams Street   325 John Knox Road, Suite F-100
Tallahassee, FL 32301   Tallahassee, FL 32303
850-222-0199   850-942-9300

Conserving Regional Biodiversity Through Reserve Design
The Lower Rio Grande Valley National Wildlife Refuge, Southern Texas

The lower Rio Grande valley lies along the final stretch of the Rio Grande, in the southern tip of Texas across from Mexico. It is one of the most ecologically diverse regions of the United States. The valley is a crossroads, encompassing ecological conditions ranging from deserts to coastlands, species from North America and Latin America, and two major flyways for migratory birds. Fertile floodplain soils and a growing season of more than three hundred days a year also make it an important agricultural region. The mild climate and proximity to the border have led to increased residential and industrial uses, and population growth in recent decades from approximately 500,000 to 2 million. As a result of these changes, an estimated 95 percent of the valley's native vegetation has been cleared or altered (figure 5.6). The Lower Rio Grande Valley National Wildlife Refuge was established in 1982 to protect and

Figure 5.6. The Lower Rio Grande Valley National Wildlife Refuge consists primarily of the corridor of native vegetation still remaining along the river. (Photograph courtesy of the Frontera Audubon Society.)

restore the region's remaining natural ecosystems. Its goals are to preserve 132,500 acres, including portions of each of the major biotic communities, and one hundred endangered, threatened, rare, and peripheral wildlife species.

The refuge includes a rich mixture of communities and organisms. Variations in climate and drainage produce distinct biological changes across the valley. Dense thorn forests exist in the arid west, while palm forests occur near the river's mouth. Other unique species associations can be found in salt lakes and seasonal ponds, in oxbows and old river channels, and on clay dunes in the delta's coastal zone. For many species, the valley marks the extreme northern or southern end of their range. South Texas is the only location in the United States where sabal palms, endangered ocelots and jaguarundis, and more than four hundred types of birds occur. It is the wintering site for numerous North American waterfowl and songbirds, including 90 percent of the continent's redhead duck population. Hundreds of additional species of birds migrate through the valley on the Central and Mississippi flyways.

The refuge's 1982 Land Protection Plan is based on a multipronged approach to conservation. One of the most significant features of the plan is the establishment of a 275-mile river corridor. The corridor stretches from the woodlands below Falcon Dam, the western edge of the refuge, all the way to the Gulf of Mexico. It extends inland approximately 1 to 2 miles, depending on the location of levees, boundaries of individual parcels, and significant natural areas. Most of the valley's remaining native vegetation is located along the river, consequently, the corridor provides the best opportunity to protect habitat for many animals. The plan also proposes conservation of extensive areas of vegetation. The largest areas, the 24,000-acre Falcon woodlands and 17,000 acres of dunes and tidal flats at the mouth of the river, anchor the corridor on either end. Smaller "management units," including existing reserves and wildlife refuges, provide habitat nodes at intervals. In addition to the corridor, the plan calls for the preservation of other valuable ecosystems, such as the salt lakes and seasonal ponds to the north. By extending to the estuary, it connects to nearly 50,000 acres of open space located along the Gulf of Mexico. Perhaps most importantly, the plan is designed to encompass parts of each of the valley's eleven biotic communities.

While most of the conservation effort has been directed toward acquiring land or conservation easements, ecological restoration has also been a focus. Restoration is necessary in areas of the refuge where clearing has occurred for agriculture and ranching. The U.S. Fish and Wildlife Service currently restores approximately 1,000 acres annually through agreements with local farmers. The agency buys parcels from the farmers and allows them to continue working the lands for a limited period of time. In exchange, the farmers plant a portion of the land each year with native vegetation. In addition to the Fish and

Wildlife Service, The Nature Conservancy has provided volunteers and advice to landowners wishing to revegetate. The public has also become involved through Valley Proud, another highly visible local organization that promotes revegetation. Restoration efforts, and conservation in general, have been helped in part by the depressed agricultural economy. In many instances, farmers find it more profitable to participate in restoration programs, or to sell land or conservation easements, than to continue agricultural operations.

Numerous agencies, organizations, and individuals have contributed to the establishment of the refuge. The Frontera Audubon Society provided the initial impetus for its creation and continues to be a major participant. It maintains a part-time lobbyist in Washington, D.C., and has been instrumental in obtaining monies from the Land and Water Conservation Fund, the refuge's primary funding source. The U.S. Fish and Wildlife Service is the lead agency for the refuge and is responsible for acquiring, managing, and restoring most of the land. The Texas Parks and Wildlife Department also maintains parks and wildlife management units within the corridor, as do several counties and cities. The Nature Conservancy, the Sierra Club, and the National Aububon Society have participated in restoration or promotion. Local chambers of commerce have created birding and nature festivals in four cities. The Texas Historical Commission is working with many individuals in the valley to establish a "Heritage Corridor" along the river, which complements the conservation goals of the refuge. Schoolchildren have been involved in restoration and in planting native vegetation on school properties. Over the course of the project, an increasing number of contributing organizations have been formed, and grass-roots support has continued to develop.

While the Land Protection Plan is promising, the issues faced by the refuge are daunting. First, preserving the ecological integrity of any area that has lost 95 percent of its native vegetation is unrealistic. At best, the refuge will be able to protect and restore portions of the biotic communities, some of the ecological processes, and certain species populations. Second, some key properties may never be acquired. Title problems in the Falcon Woodlands, for example, have delayed the Fish and Wildlife Service's purchase of lands in much of this corridor anchor. Third, due to insufficient appropriations to the Land and Water Conservation Fund, progress on the project has been slow. Since 1982, 65,000 acres have been acquired, and approximately 50 miles, or 25 percent of the corridor, are now connected. The time required to complete the refuge may be too long for some of the species it was designed to protect. Longtime participants also note the difficulty of sustaining momentum for the project through multiple generations of staff at both the agencies and the nonprofit organizations.

One particular problem is the hydrologic regime of the Rio Grande. The water-flow patterns have been significantly modified and remain largely out of the control of refuge planners and managers. The Falcon Dam, located just west of the refuge, has precluded historic annual floods since it was constructed in 1953. Downstream levees also limit the river to a narrow portion of the floodplain. The floods that do occur are largely channeled via a flood control system directly to the Gulf of Mexico. The Fish and Wildlife Service can compensate to some degree for the lack of flooding by pumping large quantities of water into oxbows and other small channels. The practice helps maintain riparian plants and animals in limited areas. However, the scouring and silt deposition processes of the river no longer occur. Also, pumping is limited to periods of high water, such as after heavy rains or in peak irrigation season. At low water, the river is carrying less freshwater and is extremely polluted. As a result of the changes, ecosystems associated with the river have been altered; most notably, riparian vegetation has decreased.

The Lower Rio Grande Valley National Wildlife Refuge has developed a reserve design to protect regional biodiversity. Each major biotic community is represented in the refuge, and the reserve is located where most remnants of native vegetation occur. The combination of a corridor and larger habitat areas should support the region's larger animal species. Revegetation is included to restore corridor links that have been cleared. Many valuable features have been included in the plan and much has been accomplished to meet its goals. However, the refuge also demonstrates the challenges a reserve system may face. It is charged with preserving communities and species in a landscape where little native vegetation remains. Broad-scale hydrologic changes continue to alter the aquatic and riparian ecosystems. Funding constraints have forced the refuge to purchase parcels as resources become available, without analyses to determine which species the growing combination of acquisitions might best support. Due to the region's high biodiversity, almost any plot of land protected by the refuge is valuable. To fulfill the promise of the regional reserve, however, all those involved in the refuge must continue to work hard on several fronts.

FOR FURTHER INFORMATION CONTACT:

Larry Ditto (Project Leader)
U. S. Fish and Wildlife Service
Santa Ana/Lower Rio Grande Valley
    National Wildlife Refuges
Route 2, Box 202A
Alamo, TX 78516
210-787-3079

Cyndy Chapman
Frontera Audubon Society
1019 South Texas
P. O. Box 8124
Weslaco, TX 78596
210-968-3275

Chapter 6

Collecting Baseline Information

The planning area will become familiar following the preliminary scoping described in previous chapters. Planners will know the major ecosystem types, some of the species and ecological processes, and the issues that are likely to affect biodiversity. They will have identified initial priorities for conservation. The next step is to assemble more comprehensive scientific data to characterize the types and status of biodiversity in the landscape. These data will enable the development of a plan and provide a benchmark to assess its effects in the coming years.

There are several reasons for collecting this information. The immediate need is to gain sufficient knowledge to make planning recommendations and decisions. A second reason is to test current ecological models and hypotheses. The new data could either challenge or confirm the assumptions on which the selection of priorities is based. A third reason is to create baseline data for subsequent planning and monitoring. This is the beginning of a conservation process; future planners will require a basis against which the impacts of current actions can be evaluated. If the search indicates information gaps, or areas that require specific research, it will have served a fourth purpose. Lastly, the data will increase general understanding of area biodiversity.

Data collection can be long, expensive, and confusing. To focus the process, the priorities previously identified should guide the types of information that are acquired. The emphasis should be on data and data analyses that enable decisions and actions to protect these planning targets. Much of the information required for landscape-scale planning is already available. Here, the primary challenges are often locating the sources, and then reconciling differences between the data sets. (Contact information for federal agencies with useful planning resources is included in the appendix at the end of this chapter.) In some areas, however, the scale of existing information will be too broad, and planners will have to generate their own data. Information is less likely to exist for specific species or local communities. At these levels, planners may need to commission their own research or else adapt the results of studies conducted on similar species or in similar locations. Historical data, useful for estimating temporal changes, are generally scarce. Information on genetic diversity is similarly lacking and usually necessitates original research.

Due to the resources required, data collection might proceed in several phases. The first part of the process would be to identify the information necessary for immediate planning and to obtain it from the least expensive sources. Among these sources are public agencies, which provide a variety of data sets free or at minimal cost. A literature search and inquiries to researchers will reveal which studies have already been performed on target species or communities. In addition to these existing sources, some amount of new data is also likely to be necessary. In a subsequent phase, the baseline data could be supplemented with studies or analyses that require greater amounts of time or funding. For example, research spanning several years might be needed to understand the ecology of key species or to determine which aspects of biodiversity would be most beneficial to monitor. Monitoring, the subject of chapter 7, would constitute a third phase. Throughout the process, the efforts of planners, managers, and researchers should be coordinated to continually improve the knowledge base.

Preliminary Decisions

Before collecting data, planners must decide which types of information are most pertinent to their needs. In addition to the planning priorities, the purposes for which data are to be collected can serve as a guide. One common purpose is simply to describe the landscape. For example, it would be difficult to conduct environmental planning without knowing the location and distribution of key communities, where water flows, where and how growth is occurring, the extent of various land uses, and the topographical features of the landscape. In this case, it is sufficient to amass the relevant data sets. Another purpose is to answer specific questions. For example, planners may need detailed information on a rare or endangered species, on hydrologic or fire regimes, or on recent landscape fragmentation. In this case, the available data will likely be inadequate, and specific studies will need to be commissioned. Planners must then address issues relevant to study design, for example, the methodology of the study, the analyses to be used, and the types of data to be collected. All of these decisions are made prior to gathering the data.[1]

Other decisions involve the spatial and temporal scales over which the data are obtained. To establish the spatial scale, a planner determines the level of detail he or she needs to observe. For example, maps produced by the U.S. Geological Survey at a spatial scale of 1:24,000 show the locations of major vegetation types, settlements, rivers, and roads. In contrast, an aerial photograph at 1:2,000 scale could portray individual trees and the riffles, pools, and banks along a stream. In many cases, a planner would elect to acquire data at more than one spatial scale. While less detail might be sufficient for most areas, data with higher resolution, or more detail, might be required for biologically important communities such as wetlands or riparian zones.

Determining temporal scales is more difficult. Here, the issue is the time periods over which to assess variations in different attributes of biodiversity. These decisions are somewhat subjective, since change is always occurring; an assessment over a longer time period might always produce a different result. However, the time period selected reflects which changes are assumed to be the most important.[2]. For a community, it might extend through the range of successional stages. For a species population, it would be long enough to show changes in such factors as size and structure.

Another issue is the lack of historical data to evaluate temporal variations. For instance, while general changes in vegetation are often known, aerial photographs documenting patterns in landscape vegetation date only from the 1930s. Planners are also unlikely to uncover historical data on many species. Choosing temporal scales may therefore be a compromise between the period thought to be significant and that for which data are available. When historical data are lacking, planners may still be able to assess variations over time through modeling or new studies. For example, changes in vegetation patterns might be modeled if one could estimate such determining factors as climate, soils, succession, and the disturbance regime. A five- to ten-year monitoring study could show important variations in a population, and these results could be incorporated into the baseline data to describe the possible range of variability for that species.

Since collection information is expensive, planners might also consider ways to reduce costs at the outset. One way to do this is to strictly limit the search to data essential to the planning priorities and objectives. The use of existing data is another cost-saving measure. Sometimes, however, it may be less expensive to acquire new information. Buying and processing data from a satellite image, for example, may be cheaper in the long run than spending the time reconciling several existing maps. Those with very reduced budgets may be forced to limit plans to the landscape level, since addressing other scales usually entails costly field studies. When fieldwork is required, studies can be designed to minimize the cost of data collection and to use the data more than once.[3] A final measure to reduce costs is to coordinate with other jurisdictions, agencies, and organizations. Through such coordination, planners may discover ways to share resources for data collection, reconciliation, and storage, or to gather the information through comparable methodologies and scales.

Landscape Scale

In almost all cases, planners start the data-collection process by acquiring information at the landscape scale. The simplest place to begin is with data that describe the major components. Information pertaining to these components is consolidated in separate thematic maps, for example, a vegetation map, a soils map, a topography map, and so on. Usually, the data are entered into spatial databases called geographic information systems, or GISs (described later in this chapter). Additional data are then linked to areas delineated on the thematic maps. For instance, information on structure, depth, and area covered might be linked to each soil type in a soils map. This kind of organization allows planners not only to portray the components of a landscape, but to analyze patterns and model processes.

The most important data set to develop at the landscape scale is a vegetation map. Since most animals are associated with vegetation communities, this map can serve as a general indicator of the distribution of both plant and animal species. Different types of vegetation data are available from federal and state resource agencies. Unfortunately, collection efforts by these agencies are not well coordinated and tend to result in data that vary in spatial scale, in the dates and purposes for which they were collected, and in the emphasis placed on different vegetation types. Consequently, vegetation is one area in which planners may need to spend time reconciling several existing maps. Depending on the need, it may be more worthwhile to create an original map, to provide uniform coverage of the planning area at the desired date and scale. A new map would also ensure that the data are collected and classified for the planner's purposes. A map developed to assess the fire risks associated with different vegetation types, for instance, may not be suitable for biodiversity analysis.

Wildlife species distributions are mapped based on known geographic ranges and habitat preferences. Since habitat is such an important determinant for wildlife, however, this topic is primarily addressed later in this chapter, under the heading "Community Scale." Once the components and structure of a community have been identified, the potential occurrences of wildlife can be better predicted. These predicted distributions can then be analyzed back at the landscape scale. For example, the effects of patch size, roads, and development could be assessed for different animal species thought to occur in a community. One category of wildlife data that is useful to collect at the landscape level is the location of endangered, threatened, and rare species. National Heritage databases, developed originally by The Nature Conservancy, are now available in every state. In addition to wildlife, they show sites of imperiled and rare plant species and communities. National Heritage databases are usually located in state resource agencies, and are designed to overlay 1:24,000 topographical maps produced by the U.S. Geological Survey. These data can also be augmented by local sightings of the species.

The U.S. Geological Survey, or USGS, provides a wealth of data at the landscape scale. The most common are the topographical maps noted above. Topographical maps can usually be acquired in 7.5-minute quadrangles, where the data are approximately 1:24,000, a useful scale for planning. Geology maps in 7.5-minute quadrangles are available for a few selected areas.[4] The USGS also produces digital information, although the scale of the data is quite variable. Digital elevation models, which simulate topography, are available for most of the country at 1:24,000. Other categories, including transportation, hydrography, jurisdictional boundaries, and the public land survey, exist primarily at 1:100,000. Digital data on hydrologic units, which include the boundaries of river basins larger than 700 square miles, have been mapped at 1:250,000.

Additional abiotic information can be found by searching other national agencies. The USDA Natural Resources Conservation Service (formerly the Soil Conservation Service) develops soil maps at approximately 1:20,000 scale. For biodiversity purposes, useful data here would be the occurrences of rare soils, which can indicate rare or endemic species. Information on climate, including precipitation and temperature gradients, is available from the National Climatic Data Center and from state climatologists. Sites and facilities regulated by the Environmental Protection Agency, including Superfund sites, have been compiled in a computerized mapping package called Landview II. The program also includes census data, so planners can assess the characteristics of adjacent populations.[5]

Beyond these environmental categories, planners will need data that describe human uses of the land. Here, useful information would include roads, jurisdictional boundaries, and past, current, and projected land uses. Lands protected from development would comprise another map. As well as public lands, this data set could include private parcels with conservation easements and indicate the degree of protection provided by each area. This information may already be available in planning offices or through state or federal agencies.[6]

Much of the data collected at the landscape or regional scale is generated through remote sensing. Remote sensing involves processes through which instruments attached to airplanes or satellites obtain information about the landscape below. These instruments measure the intensity of radiation emitted or reflected from the earth at specified regions of the electromagnetic spectrum. In addition to the visible portion of the spectrum, they can measure radiation that we cannot see, such as infrared, ultraviolet, or radio frequencies. The information is then processed to produce landscape images.[7]

Aerial photographs are one type of remote sensing images (figure 6.1). Since photographs can be taken from airplanes flying at different altitudes, they are available at varying spatial scales. Typical scales for mapping vegetation range from 1:2,000 to approximately 1:62,500. They can also be acquired in different forms. The tones and textures of standard black and white photos are useful for distinguishing among vegetation types and land uses. Infrared photos, while less sharp, help differentiate deciduous and coniferous trees. Color film might be used in landscapes with highly contrasting colors, such as riparian zones in Southwest deserts. Variations in soil moisture and plant vigor can be determined from color infrared photos. The principal source for aerial pho-

Figure 6.1. Aerial photograph of the Low Nervion (Basque Country, Spain) used for a restoration study.

tographs is the USGS, but they can also be acquired from other federal agencies such as NASA, as well as from private companies (figure 6.2).

The second major category of remote sensing is satellite imagery.[8] Satellite sensors measure radiation at several bands of the electromagnetic spectrum. Measuring different bands together gives analysts more information to distinguish among areas of the landscape. A lake, for example, would exhibit a characteristic intensity of radiation at each of these bands, while a rock outcrop would produce a different characteristic pattern. The specific patterns associated with the lake and the outcrop are called "spectral signatures." Once these spectral signatures have been determined (with the help of additional data, such as aerial photos or field checks), other areas with the same patterns can also be classified. Recent images must be purchased from private companies;[9] older images (approximately ten or more years old) are available from the USGS.[10]

Satellite imagery and aerial photographs have different advantages and disadvantages for planners. Satellite imagery is more useful for mapping large regions. For example, a full-size Landsat TM image covers 31,450 square kilometers; using aerial photographs would entail piecing together many hundreds of pictures to cover the same area. Since satellite data are recorded digitally, they can also be input directly into geographic information systems (see section on GIS), and classified using computer-assisted methodologies. In contrast, aerial photographs require human interpretation and extensive labor to enter the resulting maps into a GIS. When mapping a smaller geographic area, however, aerial photos are usually preferred. Aerial photographs offer greater detail, accuracy, and precision. The smallest pixel, or area of resolution, in a satellite image ranges from 30 by 30 meters (Landsat TM) to 5 by 5 meters (India's new IRS satellite). Since each pixel is classified as a single type, details and varia-

Figure 6.2. Satellite image of Sunbury, Pennsylvania. A river, ridges, and valleys are evident. (Image acquired from the NASA website.)

tions within these areas are necessarily lost. Accuracy in satellite imagery may also be lower due to environmental variations. For example, a grassland saturated with water could produce a different spectral signature than one that was dry, and so receive a different classification.

While remote sensing is a primary source, some types of landscape-scale data are collected directly in the field. Water-flow information, for instance, is recorded by stream gauges operated by the USGS. Weather patterns are also tracked by instruments located at intervals across regions. The Forest Service's Forest Inventory and Analysis, a regional-scale inventory, is based on intensive sampling of regularly spaced forest sites.[11] The accuracy of remote sensing classifications is also assessed in part by field sampling.

Although much information exists, it is not always easy to locate. Planners might find useful data in federal agencies, in state agencies, in regional or county agencies, or in private organizations. They might purchase raw data from satellite imagery companies or preprocessed data from a consulting firm. With the right contacts, they might find exactly what they need from a researcher working on a study in their planning area. There is no one place to locate information and no one way to search for it. Instead, planners will need to learn which agencies or organizations are likely to have the data they require, and to search for it in different ways.

The above notwithstanding, the best place to start is with the federal agencies. Planners with Internet access will find it helpful to browse the web pages of the major agencies, for example, the USGS, the Fish and Wildlife Service, the Forest Service, and the Natural Resources Conservation Service. Given enough time, it is usually possible to identify the types of data available and how they can be acquired. After searching the federal agencies, the next step is to work one's way down the hierarchy and check state, regional, and county agencies. Then planners might contact environmental organizations and ecologists who have done work in the area.[12]

In the future, the process of locating useful data may be facilitated by digital libraries. Six digital libraries are currently being developed in the United States. Two of these libraries, the Berkeley Digital Library and the Alexandria Digital Library, focus on spatial environmental data. The Berkeley Library, however, is limited to California data sets. In time, planners may be able to locate the data they need more easily by searching a digital library using descriptive attributes (for example, the location, date, and scale of the data desired).[13]

Internet mailing lists are also a valuable source for all types of planning information. Since they focus on specific topics, mailing lists are an excellent tool to find colleagues working on similar issues or in similar types of environments. Planners can use these lists to find out which types of data are most valuable in a given situation, where they are found, or how they have been generated by others. They can share ideas, strategies, and methods. Mailing lists are a convenient way to network with the wide range of people now involved in biodiversity conservation. Since the field is new, there is great potential for researchers to learn from one another's experiences.[14]

As noted earlier, the challenge is not only to locate data, but to reconcile them once they have been acquired. Available data can vary in numerous ways. Two obvious differences are the date and spatial scale. Data may also differ in form; for example, raw data may exist as satellite imagery, aerial photographs, or tables. Some preprocessing will be necessary to create maps from these data and to alter them so that they conform to the same scale.

Other less obvious disparities also need to be addressed. The maps may be based on different geodetic coordinate systems or use different types of projections. A coordinate system is a way of referencing places on the Earth's surface. The most common system uses latitude and longitude; however, other coordinate systems, such as the Universal Transverse Mercator System (UTM), are also used. Map projections are representations of the Earth's spherical surface on a two-dimensional plane. Since this cannot be done without distortion, a variety of types of projections have been developed to minimize distortions in particular areas, while allowing greater distortions in others. To ensure that they match, maps need to be "rectified" to the same coordinate and projection systems.[15]

Other variations in maps that seem similar stem from the methods by which they were developed from the original data.[16] Aerial photographs, for example, contain distortions at their edges. Creating a map from aerial photographs (or from several separate maps) requires some "stretching" of geographic features that cross the edges to ensure that they meet. The resulting composite map may be slightly different from reality or from another map produced by another method. Maps produced from satellite imagery can vary from other maps because they are produced from pixel data. Since the entire pixel receives a single classification, they cannot show precise boundaries. These types of variations are corrected by "registering," or adjusting, the maps until the geographic features match.

The discussion above suggests that planners will benefit from obtaining not only maps, but the information that describes how the maps were developed. This type of information is called "metadata." Metadata include the type of original data used, its date and scale, the process by which it was collected, and the various steps taken to produce the map. Metadata helps planners assess the accuracy of a map and correct a series of maps so they can be analyzed together. Comparing maps without such information causes errors. This issue is particularly significant in change detection, where a current map is overlaid on an older map to assess changes that have occurred over the time period. Recognizing its importance, there is increasing demand for standardized types of metadata to accompany maps and data sets, particularly new ones produced by federal agencies. For older maps, however, metadata are often unavailable.

Once the data have been collected, they are typically entered into a geographic information system, or GIS. A GIS is a database for geographically referenced information. The geographic data are organized in thematic layers and linked to many other nonspatial data. GISs are an important technological development for planners, since they enable large quantities of information to be stored, retrieved, and analyzed. The data can be used in models to simulate ecological processes or conditions or to predict the outcome of policy alternatives (figure 6.3). Maps produced from a GIS can be tailored to present specific issues in an understandable format. While GIS programs have become increasingly user friendly, the systems still entail a significant investment in hardware, software, and staff training.[17]

One important value of a GIS is the ease with which landscape patterns can be discerned and analyzed. For example, if you wanted to determine if a certain vegetation type could support a wildlife population, you might create a frequency distribution of the vegetation patches by area. If you discovered that most of the patches were very small and were also isolated from each other, you would have cause for concern. In addition to analyzing a single map, different thematic maps in a GIS can be analyzed together. In gap analysis, for instance, maps of vegetation, predicted wildlife distributions, and protected lands are combined to assess which species are adequately protected and where the "gaps" still remain (see case study at the end of this chapter). Changes in spatial patterns can be ascertained by overlaying maps developed from data of different dates.

Ecological processes constitute the final category of data to obtain at the landscape level. Among others, these include processes relating to hydrology, fire regimes, and vegetation changes. The objective is to identify significant patterns and variations in the processes on which species in the area may depend. These historical patterns can then be compared to those that currently occur to help determine appropriate planning strategies. In addition, it will be important to collect information on recent and potential landscape processes resulting from human land uses. Fragmentation and growth, for example, are processes that continue to affect biodiversity across broad spatial scales.

Some of the most important characteristics of hydrology are the volume and seasons of flows. Variations in water flows both within and over many years

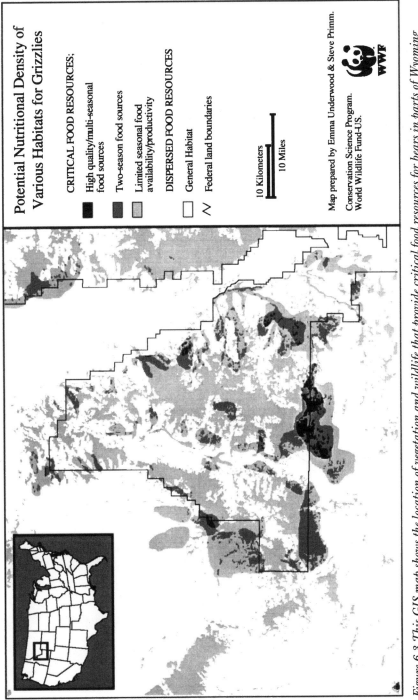

Figure 6.3 This GIS map shows the location of vegetation and wildlife that provide critical food resources for bears in parts of Wyoming and Montana. Courtesy of the World Wildlife Fund.

support diversity in aquatic and riparian communities. Not only minimum flows but occasional high water and flooding must occur. The primary ways to determine historical hydrologic patterns is with data from the USGS. Usually recorded over several decades, these data show the volume and rate of flows for most rivers and major streams.[18] Variations in discharges for small watersheds can be estimated using the watershed area, precipitation data, and standard "coefficients of runoff" developed for different vegetation types and land uses.[19] Development typically alters these patterns by limiting the channels where water flows, increasing and intensifying downstream flows and restricting infiltration to groundwater. Assessing these changes can help planners determine mitigation to counter their detrimental impacts.

Fire regimes are described by the size, intensity, recurrence interval, and seasons of burns over a period of time. The occurrence of fire supports species specifically adapted to it, as well as early successional communities. The variations in a fire regime allow different species and communities to occur across a landscape and over time. Unfortunately, planners are unlikely to find information on fire regimes readily available; instead, they may need to gather indications of patterns from several sources. Community ecologists, for example, might have information on the season and recurrence interval associated with burns in certain vegetation types. Fire ecologists and resource agencies might know the dates, sizes, and locations of major fires over the past few centuries. They may also be familiar with local management practices that include or preclude burning and former Native American customs. In certain instances, studies might be commissioned to assess tree scars on a site, enabling researchers to determine the date and extent of fires with greater precision. The data, while probably incomplete, may be sufficient to model an ecologically appropriate regime. Again, this model can be compared with the current fire regime to determine future management strategies.

At the landscape level, significant changes in vegetation might include the general amount of cover, the relative proportions of different communities, as well as new communities that develop from the introduction of exotic species. These changes are determined primarily by succession, disturbances, management, and land use. From a conservation perspective, the planning objective is to maintain the original range of vegetation types and successional stages, in amounts sufficient to support their associated species. (Small patches of exotic plants also might be targeted for elimination, though, if they extend across hillsides, they are nearly impossible to eradicate.) In most areas, local plant or community ecologists will have general knowledge of historic vegetation types and successional stages. Local extension offices and planning departments may have information on past management practices and land uses. More precise data on recent changes can be acquired from aerial photographs. Longer term data usually are nonexistent.[20] The available information can then be pieced together and used to guide management and land use planning, with the purpose of maintaining or re-creating the spectrum of vegetation communities.

As opposed to the processes noted above, data on fragmentation and growth are relatively easy to obtain. Fragmentation can be evaluated with maps created from older aerial photographs. Growth projections by county are available in most states.[21] Given the impact of habitat reduction and fragmentation on biodiversity, both types of data can be used to indicate priority areas for conservation planning.

Community Scale

The primary focus of conservation at the community level is to maintain species diversity. Rather than protecting myriad separate species, however, we usually approach this goal indirectly by preserving different types of habitat. It is impossible to identify and monitor all the organisms that exist in an area; it is more practical to maintain a range of habitat components and structures. Priority species, of course, do require specific surveys and studies to determine their locations and the status of their populations and habitats.

Habitat data that are not detectable by remote sensing are acquired through field sampling. The information required determines which type of field methodology is used. Random point samples, for example, would show the frequency and relative abundance of habitat features. Data collected along several line transects could additionally indicate the spatial arrangements of these features. By sampling randomly established plots in a community, researchers might learn which features occur there, as well as their density and spatial patterns. Plotless sampling techniques identify features that occur within a certain distance of a predetermined point, and are also used to discern spatial relationships. Whatever the procedure, it is likely that the study will require observations over several seasons, and perhaps several years. The researcher chooses the time period (assuming resources are available) to capture the variations in the habitat. Due to the expense, habitat sampling is usually limited to certain communities. Within these communities, the studies might focus on the most essential habitat attributes for target species or for different groups of animals, termed guilds, that use the habitat in similar ways.

A habitat consists of both biotic and abiotic attributes. Among others, the biotic components include snag size and density, litter depth and cover, tree cavities, and fruit and nut production. The vertical structure (layers of grasses and forbs, shrubs and trees), amount of cover, and spatial arrangement of vegetation and other habitat features are important patterns for wildlife. Abiotic, or nonliving, attributes might include rock size and cover, soil types and characteristics, water sources, and unique features such as caves, cliffs, sand dunes, or water sources. Topographical data, such as elevation, slope, and aspect, can be interpreted from aerial photographs or obtained from maps. Aquatic habitats are described by a different set of variables than terrestrial habitats. The significant attributes in this case might be the characteristics of stream flow, channels or shorelines, slope gradients, or water temperature, turbidity, and nutrients. Macroinvertebrates, such as insect larvae, are frequently used as indicators of aquatic habitats since many have strict ecological requirements.[22]

Once the habitat data are collected, they may be used in wildlife habitat relationship models to develop a species list. These models include the known geographic ranges of vertebrate species, and the habitat features on which they depend. They predict the occurrence of wildlife based on the location and habitat variables entered. By modifying the variables, they can also be used to assess how planning alternatives might impact different species. Long-term management effects have been forecast by linking these models with successional models. Since the results are just predictions, however, they should be verified in the field. The results may also differ in quality, because the quality of the data incorporated in the models usually varies. In addition, planners should be aware that such models typically lack a spatial component. Determining the effects of patch size, or proximity to other vegetation types or land uses, for example, would require a separate analysis.[23]

At some point, biologists will have to go into the field to survey particular species. Wildlife habitat models can only suggest a species list and still require field confirmation. Also, such models are limited to vertebrate wildlife; plant and invertebrate species, whose distribution is more influenced by microhabitat variables, are not included. In addition, existing information on most species is usually sketchy. One area may have been intensively sampled, while little information may be available for other areas. As a result, new field studies will probably be necessary to acquire current data on local species. Depending on the organisms and depth of information required, a number of sampling techniques might be used. As noted earlier, it is particularly important that studies be conducted over a sufficient number of seasons and years. A species may not be present during one observation period, but could return at a later time.

Species diversity is also determined by ecological processes operating at the community scale. The changes that occur in the composition and structure of a community over time are influenced by numerous processes, for example, succession, disturbances, regeneration, competition, predation, grazing, and timber harvesting. Scientists might study such dynamics in a forest by modeling the responses of various tree species to factors that affect reproduction and growth. Conditions such as disturbances, crowding, shading, and adequate or inadequate nutrients will affect the species that can exist in the forest and their spatial arrangement.[24] For planning purposes, however, one might simply sample the forest to ensure that the range of successional stages occur. Disturbance regimes associated with certain communities can also be incorporated into the baseline data. In addition, studies can be commissioned to assess the effects of key processes on a particular species.

Population Scale

The purpose of collecting data at this scale is to learn more about a population than whether it is present or absent. The value of the species is such that its local status and significant aspects of its ecology must be known. Some general information may be in the literature, and data in certain situations can be acquired from aerial photography. Usually, however, determining the circumstances of the population requires new field studies. The procedures noted earlier—points, transects, plots, or plotless techniques—are used to gather data for many types of questions. In addition, wildlife biologists often use mark-and-recapture techniques to estimate population size. With these methods, a sample of animals is marked and released, and the total population size is calculated as a function of marked and unmarked individuals captured in a subsequent sample. Information on wildlife movements, still relatively scarce, has increased in recent years due to sophisticated radio technologies.

What sorts of information are required for a plant or animal population? For small and threatened populations, planners typically need answers to demographic questions. One of the most common demographic concerns is the population's absolute or relative abundance, or its density (the number of individuals per unit area). This type of information can be required for a single population or for the subpopulations comprising a wildlife metapopulation. In addition to determining the current numbers, information on population size can be used to assess the probability of survival. For example, scientists might combine the population estimates with data on dispersal, patch size, and patch distribution to model the likelihood of metapopulation persistence.[25] Other demographic data used to evaluate population viability include the rates of reproduction, mortality, and regeneration, and the frequency distributions of age and sex.[26]

A second important category of information pertains to the movements of individual animals. Planners are likely to need the home range areas of various species. For many animals, home range estimates may be available in published literature. These figures, however, can vary tremendously due to differences in the ages and sexes of the animals studied, the geographic location, or habitat quality. Thus planners must be careful to use numbers, or to interpolate, from studies similar to their own situations. A more precise (and more expensive) option is to commission a new study employing radio telemetry. This procedure involves attaching radio transmitters to individual animals and tracking them over a period of time. Telemetry has been used on animals of all sizes, ranging from insects and turtles to mountain lions. In addition to home ranges, it has helped researchers understand which habitats are used by different species. It has also proved a valuable tool for studying dispersal and migration. Hand-held receivers are used to follow local movements, while satellite telemetry enables scientists to track animals over long distances and inhospitable terrain.

While the migratory routes of popular or game species may be known, those of other animals—perhaps most—still have not been studied. Information is available for species of particular interest, for example, monarch butterflies, and certain songbirds, hawks, and marine mammals. Resource agencies often have information on the migrations and wintering sites of large game species, such as elk and deer. For other types of species, planners may be on their own unless they have the means to initiate new research. Methodologies for collecting migratory data usually involve marking and tracking individual animals.[27] Bird banding, for example, is one way of marking; others include dabbing paint on the animals, clipping toes, or simply following individuals with unique distinguishing features. The transmitters used in telemetry are also essentially electronic markers. Once the markers are in place, the researchers either track the animals themselves, receive the data remotely (by way of telemetry), or else devise a system wherein they are contacted when the animals are found. For planners, studies of this type would most likely be limited to local migrations.

Genetic Scale

The genetic scale offers additional information on a population or species. Especially for endangered species, it may not be enough to ensure that a population is sufficiently large, that it is reproducing, or that individual animals are able to move. Planners may also want to assess the level and distribution of genetic diversity. The level of genetic diversity provides specific data to address the genetic threats facing small populations: inbreeding depression, destructive genes, and the further loss of the variety of gene forms. The distribution of genetic variations, whether they are uniform across a species' range or show distinctions among populations, will affect planning and management strategies. In the first case, one could focus on the species as a whole, without differentiating among populations. In the second case, it would be beneficial to preserve each genetically distinct population, to maintain the evolutionary potential of the species.

While both may address a single population or metapopulation, planning at the genetic scale adds to population-level approaches with a different type of data. DNA analysis allows researchers to discern distinctions and similarities among individuals, populations, and species. This information sheds new light on population processes that link groups of organisms, such as dispersal and interbreeding. Patterns in the data can suggest local adaptations and relationships among populations that should be preserved. Essentially, genetic data allows planners and managers to "fine-tune" strategies for population conservation.[28]

The field of genetic conservation is quite technical, as are the analytical methods usually employed. Therefore, before embarking on a description of the data, it is useful to explain some of the associated concepts. Genetic diversity deals fundamentally with the composition of DNA that exists within the cells of organisms. Each DNA strand, or chromosome, is comprised of myriad genes, which function as units of hereditary information. For the most part, genes are not distributed randomly along the chromosomes, but occur at identifiable sites, or "loci." Each gene may exist in alternative forms, which are called alleles. For example, blue eyes and brown eyes are different types of alleles that may occur at the locus for the eye color gene.

Genetic diversity itself may refer to different sorts of measurements. Two common indices of genetic diversity are polymorphism and heterozygosity (table 6.1).[29] Polymorphism measures the proportion of genes in a population that occur in alternative forms. If the population consists of individuals with blue, brown, and green eyes, then the gene for eye color is polymorphic, meaning that more than one type of allele exists for that gene. The total proportion of polymorphism in the population is calculated by dividing the number of polymorphic genes by the number of genes sampled. Heterozygosity measures the proportion of genes at which the average individual has two different alleles. While eye color may be a polymorphic gene, it is possible that only 45 percent of the population possesses different alleles at the eye color locus. The other 55 percent might have inherited two blue-eyed alleles, two green-eyed alleles, or two brown-eyed alleles from their parents. In this example, heterozygosity for the eye color gene would be 45 percent. Total heterozygosity for the

Table 6.1. Measures of Genetic Diversity

Polymorphism*

Gene Locus Sampled	Alleles Types in Population	Polymorphic
Eye color	Blue Brown Green	Yes
Hair color	Brown Red Blond	Yes
Hemophilia	Hemophilia No Hemophilia	No

* Based on three gene loci sampled, the proportion of polymorphism in the population equals 66 percent.

Heterozygosity

Genes	Alleles Inherited by Individual A	Alleles Inherited by Individual B	Alleles Inherited by Individual C	Heterozygosity for Gene
Eye color	Blue × Brown	Brown × Brown	Blue × Blue	33%
Hair color	Brown × Blond	Blond × Red	Brown × Brown	66%
Hemophilia	No Hemophilia × No Hemophilia	No Hemophilia × No Hemophilia	No Hemophilia × No Hemophilia	0%

population is calculated by averaging the proportions figured for all the sampled genes. Thus, the term "genetic diversity" might mean the relative amount of polymorphic gene loci in a population or species, and/or the average number of alleles that each individual has at these loci. To assess the distribution of genetic diversity in a species, scientists determine how much of the variation is contained within the populations, and how much is attributable to differences among populations.

A variety of methods exists to assess genetic diversity.[30] The oldest and simplest is evaluation based on physical differences. Before the advent of modern lab techniques, this was a primary approach to distinguishing among species and subspecies. The drawback of this method is that while some of the variations may have a genetic basis, others may be caused by environmental differences. To eliminate these environmental variations, researchers may perform additional breeding studies. Common garden experiments, for example, involve seeds collected throughout a species range and grown together under the same conditions. The differences in the resulting plants can then be assumed to be genetic. Such breeding studies generally require several years and are most practical for species with short life spans.

Recently, allozyme electrophoresis has been the predominant technique for assessing genetic diversity. Allozymes, or alternative forms of enzymes, are encoded by gene loci and associated with different types of alleles. The process of electrophoresis distinguishes among the allozymes. The allozymes are placed in a gel medium and subjected to an electronic current that causes them to move. Since different allozymes move different distances, scientists can determine which allozymes and thus which alleles are present in an individual.

In addition to allozyme studies, various techniques now exist to analyze DNA directly. Electrophoresis is still used, but instead of allozymes, sequences of DNA are passed through the electric current. The sequences also travel differing distances through the gel, allowing researchers to compare and contrast DNA samples. Such DNA analyses are the most powerful techniques available, but are currently too expensive and complicated for broad application. Allozyme electrophoresis is more common since it is cheaper and relatively easy to perform.

Genetics is a new and growing aspect of biodiversity conservation. Only in the past few decades have scientists developed the methods and equipment to analyze chromosomal variations. Similarities in the DNA show present and historical relationships among individuals, populations, and species. Distinctions in the DNA indicate the level and distribution of diversity. Continuing, rapid developments are expected in the field. One of the issues remaining is the accessibility of the techniques. Currently, genetic analysis as performed in laboratories requires such sophisticated equipment and expertise as to be outside of the realm of most planning efforts. A second issue is identifying the best approach to sampling genetic diversity. Scientists are still attempting to discover which techniques, and which portions of the DNA, best capture significant variations. As valuable and interesting as the information may be, however, genetic conservation remains secondary to biodiversity protection at other scales. Without landscapes, habitats, and sufficient populations, genetic diversity will have little meaning.

❖

The data collection process is an essential step in developing a conservation plan. Not only does it enable planners to make immediate decisions, but it allows them to test assumptions, to identify gaps in existing information, and to develop a baseline data set for subsequent monitoring. Usually, most of the data gathered will be at the landscape scale. Much is already available, especially from federal and state resource agencies. Depending on the planning priorities, however, many other types of information may be required. This may include newly commissioned remote sensing data at a particular spatial scale or more detailed data describing habitats, species populations, or genetic patterns and relationships. From such a broad range of possibilities, planners can focus on acquiring the types, dates, scales, and quality of information that best suit their needs.

Locating the Gaps in Biodiversity Protection
The National Gap Analysis Program

How can we determine if open spaces are situated to preserve the greatest number of communities and species? How can we prioritize the conservation of additional areas? The USGS Gap Analysis Program, assisted by many other public agencies and private organizations, is evaluating the current protection of biological diversity throughout the United States. It assesses the degree to which natural communities and vertebrate wildlife are represented in lands managed for conservation. Regional and local planners will benefit from the program through the identification of unprotected "gaps" in the conservation network and through access to extensive databases now being developed.

The Gap Analysis Program (GAP) is proceeding on a state-by-state basis. Forty-four states are participating to date; approximately half are expected to complete their analyses by the end of 1997. Each project is using a geographic information system (GIS) and will produce a series of data layers, maps, analyses, reports, and other products. Once a state has finished, the data are checked for accuracy and adjoining maps registered so that the edges match. The distributions of communities and species can thus be assessed not only within states, but across larger geographic regions.

The first step in a gap analysis is to develop a map of the dominant vegetation types. Vegetation maps are based on Landsat Thematic Mapper satellite images, with other technologies and field checks used to verify the data. A predicted vertebrate distribution map is then created using wildlife habitat relationship models. Categories of land management, ranked by varying levels of protection, form an additional layer. These three datasets comprise the basic elements of all gap analysis projects. GAP complements other site-specific information available at the state or local levels. For example, many states have used their Natural Heritage Program data on threatened and endangered species in conjunction with the GAP layers. Exotic plants and animals, native species well adapted to human disturbance, and occasional vagrant species are not addressed by the projects.

A variety of analyses can be performed after the data are collected. To assess risks to biodiversity, the states determine the proportions of natural communities and species distributions in each type of ownership. An organism that occurs primarily on lands managed for conservation would be more secure than one found predominately in areas open for development. A state might also delineate centers of species richness and rank these centers by contribution to state, regional, and continental biological diversity. Planners or managers can use the data to identify preliminary design options to conserve the majority of vertebrate species and vegetation types. When combined with higher resolution local information, the options can be developed into conservation plans. Each project operates semiautonomously and creates analyses, products, and partnerships according to its needs and resources.

For planners, one of the greatest values of GAP is that it provides context for local decisions. At a broad level, the data show where species and communities occur, and how well they are protected in different areas. This type of information offers planners a "big picture" and allows them to assess the impacts of plans and projects on a larger scale. Suppose, for example, that a project was expected to threaten a particular species population. Planners could use the GAP data to find out if the species was threatened in other parts of its range or whether it was well protected, meaning that the current impact could be relatively insignificant. Such a perspective can improve the quality of environmental impact assessments.

Due to the volume of data involved in the gap analyses, the resolution of the information used and represented was initially low. Maps for the first states were produced at a scale of 1:250,000, enabling researchers to work with less detail and to discern broad geographic patterns. The minimum mapping units, or the smallest areas represented on a map, were specified at 100 hectares (247 acres), although higher resolutions were often chosen for certain vegetation types. As the program progressed, however, later states opted to maintain and represent data in greater detail. Many current state projects have minimum mapping units of 30 square meters, the size of the satellite imagery pixels. This latter scale is considerably more useful for most planners. GAP staff are currently making the high-resolution data available in smaller packages for local jurisdictions. Those working at the state level will require workstations for the highest resolution data or, lacking such facitilies, may aggregate the information.

There are several ways in which regional and local planners can take advantage of GAP. First, the original data layers developed by the projects are valuable. Although broad in scale, for many states they are the first comprehensive information on vegetation and wildlife distributions. Second, planners can use the projects' analyses to identify potential issues within their areas. General patterns in natural community distribution, species richness, management, and existing conservation lands may suggest specific planning strategies. Third, planners can augment the data with local knowledge and plans and conduct their own analyses. At the county level, the results can be augmented with information from general plans and zoning, growth patterns, known species

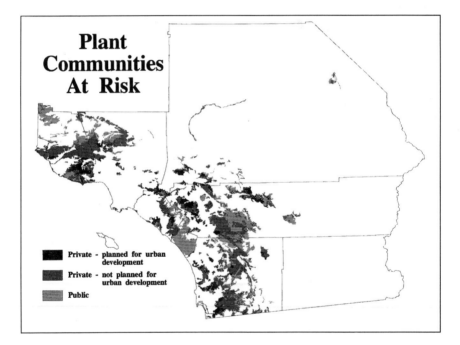

Figure 6.4. The Southern California Association of Governments used gap analysis data on threatened communities in conjunction with its own data on development trends to produce this map of plant communities at risk. Lands not planned for urban development may still include rural development. (Reproduced with permission, the American Society for Photogrammetry and Remote Sensing. J. Michael Scott, Timothy H. Tear, and Frank W. Davis, eds., Gap Analysis: A Landscape Approach to Biodiversity Planning, *1996, p. 230. Map produced by Richard E. Crowe.)*

distributions, and the management practices of local landowners. The data and products developed by the projects are in the public domain and, when completed, will be available through GAP home page, as well as on tape and CD-ROM.

One planning agency that has already applied gap analysis data is the Southern California Association of Governments (SCAG). SCAG used information from the California GAP project to identify plant communities at risk in its six-county area. The agency combined GAP information with its own data to create maps of jeopardized communities by management category, by county, and by SCAG subregion (figure 6.4). County and local plans were then evaluated to determine potential impacts on the communities. The analysis helped planners develop regional conservation strategies.

The national GAP is the first effort to evaluate the status of biodiversity protection throughout the United States. The approach is coarse by design, in that the objective is to broadly identify unprotected habitats. Regional and local plans are an essential complement to these projects, since they are a primary way in which the information will be used, and can also add data on the actual locations of species, habitat features, and local land uses. At this stage in the process, organizers are exploring ways to increase and improve the application of gap products. One approach is building partnerships with state agencies and nonprofit organizations. Another is the development of outreach and training programs. Several states are also creating new formats for the data to make it more readily usable for county planners. Whichever avenues states choose to follow, GAP will provide a valuable addition to biodiversity planning at all scales.

FOR FURTHER INFORMATION CONTACT:
http://www.gap.uidaho.edu/gap
(Virtually all information pertaining to the program, including the addresses of state gap projects, is available from this GAP home page.)

Patrick Crist
USGS Gap Analysis Program
530 S. Asbury Street, Suite 1
Moscow, ID 83843
208-885-3555
208-885-3618 (fax)
gap@uidaho.edu

Appendix: Planning Resources Available from Federal Agencies

Federal agencies can provide a wealth of maps, remote sensing images, software, and related data useful for planning. The agencies' Internet home pages describe the programs they administer and the types of information and tools they offer. Specific information pertaining to a given area is often located in regional, state, or local offices. To find other agencies, or other departments within the agencies listed below, start with the following: Federal Information Center, 800-688-9889, or http://www.yahoo.com/government/agencies.

U.S. Geological Survey
http://www.usgs.gov
USGS Earth Science Information Center
507 National Center
Reston, VA 20192
800-872-6277
703648-5548 (fax)
esicmail@usgs.gov

Resources available: geologic data, topographical maps, digital elevation model (DEM) data, digital line graph (DLG) data (including transportation, hydrography, jurisdictional boundaries, and public land survey), hydrologic unit data or maps, aerial photographs, and National Wetlands Inventory maps.

USGS EROS Data Center
Sioux Falls, SD 57198
605-594-6151
605-594-6589 (fax)
custserv@edcserver1.cr.usgs.gov

Resources available: older satellite images and aerial photographs.

USGS National Water Information Center
427 National Center
Reston, VA 20192
800-426-9000
h20info@usgs.gov

Resources available: data from stream and river gages, water observation wells, and ground and surface water quality stations.

USGS Biological Resources Division
National Program Manager
National Biological Information Infrastructure
12201 Sunrise Valley Drive
Mailstop 300
Reston, VA 20192
703-648-4205
703-648-4224 (fax)
http://www.nbs.gov

Resources available: The National Biological Information Infrastructure provides links to a variety of state and federal agencies that offer biological data from a variety of surveys and monitoring programs, including gap analysis (http://www.gap.uidaho.edu/gap), the North American Breeding Bird Survey, and the Nonindigenous Aquatic Species Program.

U.S. Bureau of the Census
ACSD Customer Service Branch
Washington, DC 20233
301-457-1128
301-457-3842 (fax)
http://www.census.gov

Resources available: the TIGER line files (including streets, rivers, railroads, jurisdictional boundaries, and census tracts).

U.S. Fish and Wildlife Service
1849 C Street NW
Washington, DC 20240
Attn: Ecological Services
202-208-4717
http://www.fws.gov

Resources available: data from a variety of programs, including endangered species, fisheries, coastal ecosystems, environmental contaminants, migratory bird management, and the National Wildlife Refuge System. National Wetlands Inventory maps are available from the USGS Earth Science Information Center.

USDA Natural Resources Conservation Service
National Cartography and Geospatial Center
501 Felix Street, Building 23
P.O. Mail 6567
Fort Worth, TX 76115
800-672-5559
817-334-5469 (fax)
http://ncg.nrcs.usda.gov

Resources available: soil maps and data.

USDA Forest Service
Ecosystem Management Coordination
P. O. Box 96090
Mailstop 1104
Washington, DC 20090-6090
202205-0895
http://www.fs.fed.us

Resources available: databases (forest inventory, insect pests and parasites, gypsy moths), software (visual analysis of forested landscapes, landscape spatial analysis, resource management models, land management decision support system), information (fire effects on species and communities, state and private forestry technical and financial assistance).

USDA Farm Service Agency
Aerial Photography Field Office, Sales Branch
P.O. Box 30010
Salt Lake City, UT 84130-0010
801-975-3503

Resources available: aerial photographs.

U.S. Bureau of Land Management
Planning, Assessment, and Community Support Group
Room 1001, LS Building
Department of the Interior
Washington, DC 20240
202-452-7793
http://www.blm.gov

Resources available: vegetation, timber, and habitat surveys; mineral surveys and claims; some aerial photographs and satellite imagery.

U.S. Environmental Protection Agency
Information Resources Center
401 M Street SW
Mailcode 3404
Washington, DC 20460
202-260-5922
http://www.epa.gov

Resources available: Landview III (software package of EPA regulated sites combined with 1990 census data); Envirofacts (relational database pertaining to toxics and hazardous waste sites, releases, permits, and facilities); SiteInfo (maps and reports related to EPA health and management concerns).

National Aeronautics and Space Administration (NASA)
http://www.nasa.gov

Resources available: satellite images and aerial photographs; http://www.hq.nasa.gov/office/pao/Library/prints.html offers a list of vendors that sell NASA images.

National Climatic Data Center
151 Patton Avenue, Room 120
Asheville, NC 28801-5001
704-271-4800
704-271-4876 (fax)
orders@ncdc.noaa.gov
http://www.ncdc.noaa.gov

Resources available: climate data. The names and addresses of state climatologists are listed at the web site.

Chapter 7

Monitoring and Adaptive Management

Natural areas are dynamic, comprising numerous interacting and evolving elements. The task for planners is to develop a working understanding of the system, and then to create a plan that best meets their goals. Yet this understanding is invariably limited and inaccurate to some degree. Inevitably, other unknown factors come into play and cause unexpected results. It is impossible to predict exactly how any ecosystem will develop; consequently, we cannot be confident that a plan established at one point in time will continue to be appropriate in the future. Faced with such uncertainty, how can anyone ensure the long-term integrity of open spaces? While there are no guarantees, one solution lies in the planning process. Rather than stop at the designation of a natural area, planners can coordinate with those responsible for future management and monitoring. They can incorporate mechanisms to assess the plan over time and to provide this information to those who need it. They can also encourage stakeholders to support an experimental approach to implementation and management. Planners can mitigate unavoidable uncertainties with a process emphasizing feedback, learning, and adaptability.

There are several reasons for planners to address the issue of uncertainty. First, everyone involved in a plan has an interest in learning which aspects succeed or fail, and why. There is no way to know a plan's value without monitoring its effects. Monitoring increases accountability and learning, and enables subsequent decisions to be made on more recent and complete data. Being able to show the need for it may be necessary to secure funding. Second, should monitoring uncover problems in the plan, the plan can be revised. Stakeholders, however, will be less likely to agree to such changes if they have not previ-

143

ously been alerted to the possibility. Third, there are risks and costs associated with uncertainty, and these can be incorporated into decision making. Information gaps and risk probabilities associated with certain actions or strategies may affect which alternatives are selected, and how they are implemented. Although it may seem counterproductive to acknowledge what one does not know, this position ultimately can be one of strength. When all parties recognize that some aspects of the environment are unknown, they can agree to an approach that is flexible and increases knowledge.

Monitoring and adaptive management are two related strategies for reducing uncertainty and improving ecological understanding. Monitoring usually involves tracking the effects of a plan or a management practice, or assessing the status of an area over time. It is accomplished by measuring ecological attributes associated with the monitoring objectives. For example, if the objective is to evaluate the effectiveness of a stream restoration project, researchers might measure changes in the stream channel, sedimentation rates, water characteristics, riparian vegetation, and fish and aquatic invertebrate populations. The data are then compared to predetermined ranges for each variable, and an assessment made as to whether the project is proceeding as planned.

Adaptive management is similar to monitoring in that it is designed to provide feedback on management and planning interventions over time. However, it differs from traditional monitoring in that its purpose is to increase ecological understanding more rapidly than would otherwise be the case. It is also a broader concept; adaptive management includes monitoring as one step in the process. Rather than implement a single best action or strategy, practitioners of "active" adaptive management devise and monitor several alternatives simultaneously. In addition to being a viable option in its own right, each is designed to teach managers more about the system. The combined results from several experiments increase the rate of learning and the likelihood of choosing a sustainable course of action. The CALFED Bay-Delta Program, one of the case studies in this chapter, has adopted adaptive management to implement a long-term water management plan in California. A range of actions will be tested for each management objective, since much is unknown about the ecosystems and many conflicting interests are involved.

While not all planners will be involved in monitoring or adaptive management, each strategy is relevant to biodiversity planning. Each can be used to assess different parts of a plan and to help determine alternative courses of action. Each may be facilitated by elements included in the plan and planning process. For example, a plan can be monitored as or after it is implemented to see which portions work effectively. The baseline data collected for the plan can be designed and organized for subsequent monitoring use. Planners can work with managers to establish and fund monitoring or adaptive management programs. By including stakeholders throughout the process, planners can support these programs long after their own jobs are finished. Thus it is useful to understand the need for monitoring and adaptive management, how they work, and their relationship to planning.

Uncertainty in Planning

Numerous unknown factors may influence the outcome of a conservation plan. Ecosystems can be very difficult to comprehend, particularly as one considers larger spatial scales and longer time periods. Their attributes also change, in many cases before the previous mix is understood. This complexity highlights the fact that it is impossible to know everything necessary to ensure the success of a plan in advance. Even the best developed plans can benefit from evaluation.

Before one can be convinced of the value of monitoring, however, it is necessary to understand why the outcome of a plan is uncertain.[1] Some causes are:

- Difficulty in delineating and understanding ecosystems (including ecological components and interactions, and social, economic, and political factors and influences),
- Constraints on data collection and analysis,
- Dependence on studies performed in other locations or on related species and communities,
- Unpredictable changes in ecosystems, and
- Errors in scientific studies.

One of the major reasons for uncertainty is lack of knowledge and understanding. In most instances, funding constrains both data collection and analysis. Even when data are not an issue, researchers can still have difficulty identifying key components or interactions in the system. Theories underlying various aspects of biodiversity are also limited. The concept of minimum viable populations, for example, is compelling, yet provides little practical guidance. In addition, most studies are conducted in specific areas containing specific species and communities, and it may be unclear if the results can be extrapolated to a different situation. Beyond strictly ecological factors, social, economic, and political concerns also impact natural areas. The influence and interactions among these issues can be similarly challenging to understand and at times impossible to predict.

Changes and variability in ecosystems add another level of uncertainty. Ecosystems and their attributes alter, fluctuate, or transform over time. Some of these changes, for example a planned modification in land use, may be known in advance. They can be figured into a plan, but their effects may still be difficult to anticipate. Other types of changes are predictable within a certain time frame. A wildfire, for instance, can be expected within a period of decades in flammable vegetation, but the specific year or any other influences occurring at that point will be unknown. Catastrophic events, such as a volcanic eruption or toxic spill, are essentially unpredictable, and therefore rarely incorporated into plans. Natural variability in ecosystems also makes it difficult to devise sampling designs for research. Errors can result from ill-conceived methods, and so lead to inaccurate conclusions.

Monitoring

Monitoring is performed to obtain information to make appropriate environmental decisions. Monitoring helps researchers evaluate past activities by indicating the status of key ecological attributes. One of the first steps is identifying the objectives for collecting information. These objectives guide the development of the program: which attributes will be measured; where, how often, and for how long they will be measured; and which types of analyses will be done on the results (figure 7.1). The product of a monitoring program is information that shows the extent and magnitude of change occurring in the ecosystem. The significance and causes of these changes are then assessed to determine a future direction.

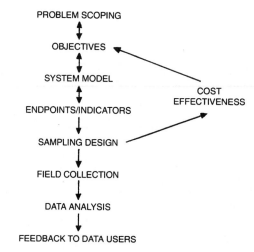

Figure 7.1. The monitoring process. (Adapted from Maher et al., 1994.)

Monitoring may be undertaken for a variety of reasons, each suggesting certain types of studies and required data.[2] Most familiar to planners are assessments of a specific project or plan. Here, a study might focus on whether the project was implemented as intended, on whether it had the expected effect, or on its overall impact. Related to these investigations are those that evaluate policies or management practices. For instance, monitoring in a national forest might address the effects of a recreational policy or whether a timber harvest plan complied with regulations.

In addition to the above, monitoring is also conducted for more general reasons. A long-term study might be initiated to increase understanding of local ecology. For example, researchers might be interested in determining the range of variability associated with an ecosystem component or in evaluating the significance of a particular type of process. Monitoring is also performed to detect ecological trends. In this case, a study would be designed to identify patterns of change distinct from natural fluctuations or random events. Such assessments may provide early warnings of ecological degradation or toxic impact. Examples of this type of investigation include the numerous climate change studies now underway. Another purpose of monitoring is to evaluate a model. Models form the basis of many planning decisions, yet we cannot judge their accuracy without feedback from actual events. Finally, the process of gathering baseline data is also sometimes considered as monitoring. While this usually does not involve measuring ecological attributes over time, it is often necessary to create a baseline as a first step in a monitoring project.

Given the scope of the biodiversity concept, it is not surprising that biodiversity monitoring requires a broad approach. Essentially, the goal of this type of monitoring, also termed ecosystem monitoring, is to ensure the continued integrity of ecosystems. Integrity is maintained by preserving all significant ecological attributes with their associated characteristics. Thus the approach involves evaluating components, patterns, and processes at various spatial, biological, and temporal scales. In almost every case, the system spans and is affected by various ownerships, constituencies, or jurisdictions. The efforts and interests of these different stakeholders must be addressed and coordinated. Even if the objectives are limited, it is usually necessary to contemplate a range of factors when framing a biodiversity monitoring program.

This broad approach is a recent development in monitoring and, as such, is not well formulated. The difficulty stems from the scope of the endeavor. In the past, a single agency might have assessed a population of sport fish or evaluated the effectiveness of a wetland mitigation project. Now, assuming the agency also has a mandate to conserve biodiversity, it has many more variables to consider. The fish interact with a variety of living and nonliving elements within an extended river and riparian ecosystem. The wetland can also be viewed as an interface between aquatic and upland systems. Which attributes, at which scales, should be assessed? Unfortunately, there are no set formulas to follow. Understanding of most ecosystems is limited, and in any case, each situation may have unique ecological, social, or economic characteristics. Funding available for monitoring also varies. In addition, now that the scope of consideration has widened, the agency usually will not be operating alone. It will need to coordinate, or develop a partnership, with a range of other agencies, nonprofit organizations, and/or private landowners who have jurisdiction or own property in that area. The group may benefit from others' experiences, but will likely need to develop its own program based on local considerations.

Certain aspects of monitoring can make it difficult to sustain as a program. One issue is that collecting data is usually less appealing than new projects in which something is actually constructed or accomplished. Thus decisionmakers and the public may be supportive of a project or plan, but not of a program to evaluate its effectiveness. Extended monitoring programs may also be less attractive to scientists and graduate students than focused, short-term studies. The latter offer more rewards, for example, greater professional recognition, more possibilities for publication, and more access to available funding.[3] A second issue is the time frame associated with monitoring. Long-term or ongoing programs must maintain funding sources, consistency and quality in their data, and relevancy with the public. The greater spatial and time scales associated with biodiversity monitoring make these concerns increasingly important.

Successful monitoring programs tend to include certain elements if they are to last for more than a few years. One of these elements is attention to data organization and management.[4] The program methods should be designed to ensure that the data are consistent and comparable among observers, collection periods, and, if applicable, between monitoring programs. The documentation of metadata is particularly important over longer time frames. A quality assurance plan to verify and record the quality of the data may also be incorporated.[5] Once gathered, the data must be entered and stored in a database in a form that is accessible and retrievable for the analyses and reports desired.

Another category of considerations is maintaining relevancy and links to the public and those who will use the data. Often, a monitoring program will be led by one or more extremely committed individuals. These "champions" can ensure that the program remains popular and visible.[6] It is also helpful to engage in organized public outreach. For example, a program might produce publications for different audiences, develop interpretive materials, or provide briefings for the community and policy makers.[7] In particular, the program should include feedback loops to ensure that decision makers receive the monitoring results in time to develop appropriate policies or to alter plans or management practices.

The use of volunteers in monitoring may be an especially valuable approach to sustaining political and financial support. Through participation in the program, citizens develop greater ecological awareness and may better appreciate the need for monitoring. Many volunteers enjoy the opportunity to be outdoors and to learn about their local landscape. In addition, their labor helps reduce program expenses. However, using volunteers is not cost-free. Volunteers must be trained, managed, and encouraged. Maintaining quality control procedures is particularly important, since volunteers are not professionally trained and their work may be challenged. The program will also be limited by the number of people that can be recruited, as well as by their interests. The Keeping Track case study in this chapter demonstrates several of these issues.

The Monitoring Process

The first step in monitoring is recognizing why it needs to be done.[8] This "problem-scoping" phase involves identifying issues and opportunities. Is the purpose to protect a resource, to comply with a legal mandate, or to help make a particular decision? Are there species or ecosystems known to be at risk? How badly is the information needed, how soon is it needed, and what are the consequences if it is wrong? What level of support might currently be expected from stakeholders or the public? The answers to such questions allow those developing the program to establish overall goals. Which goals are chosen depends in part on the groundwork previously laid by planners. The possibilities for the program might be greater, for example, if all concerned had been educated regarding the need for monitoring, if funding had already been obtained, or if other programs with which this one could coordinate had been identified.

The next task is to transform the general goals into specific objectives. To achieve this level of detail, it is necessary to collect and review any existing data. The objectives state what is to be done, when, where, and why it is to be done, and who will do it.[9] The results specified should be attainable and measurable. The accuracy and precision required from the project should also be included, based on the perceived environmental risk and the intended use of the data. For instance, an endangered species study, the results of which might be challenged in court, would require a high level of data accuracy to meet the challenge. If the purpose of monitoring is to detect a trend, the objectives should state the magnitude of change that will be considered significant, and what will happen if this degree of change is found. Evaluations of plans, policies, or management practices should include the criteria by which they will be assessed. Planners can assist future monitors by including criteria for monitoring as part of a plan.

Restoration planners can also facilitate monitoring of their projects by stating acceptable ranges of variation for each attribute to be assessed.[10] In addition, the objectives should state when the monitoring project will end or, if it is an ongoing or particularly long program, identify review points at which its current relevancy can be evaluated.

A conceptual model of the system must be created before the objectives can be implemented. It may be developed in conjunction with the objectives, since the two phases often influence each other. Assistance from researchers is helpful at this point. The model depicts the major components in the system, and shows how they are linked. The process of developing the model also helps clarify which parts are most significant and which may be useful to monitor. It is beneficial to include scientists from the different disciplines involved in the project. For a stream project, for example, these scientists might be aquatic ecologists, botanists, geologists, hydrologists, and wildlife ecologists. It is also valuable to involve nonscientists who can advocate issues important to the local community. Including a range of participants from the beginning increases the breadth of the discussion and may circumvent future conflicts.

Part of creating a model is determining the scale of the system. The monitoring boundaries are based on the extent of the issues that have been identified and the associated ecosystem attributes. To monitor an open space, for example, one would certainly measure attributes and ecological impacts occurring within the area. In addition, however, one could include factors influencing the area from outside the open space, such as exotic species or hydrological processes, and so end up with an expanded boundary. The scope of the program is also influenced by funding; larger areas are usually more variable than small areas, and so require more sampling to achieve the same accuracy of results. Once the boundary is established, monitors can determine which scales and types of data may be addressed. For instance, to monitor a riparian corridor at the scale of a whole river, one could assess such factors as the width and area of the riparian vegetation, its connectivity, and adjacent biotic communities and land uses. In contrast, monitoring the corridor along a section of stream might involve measuring the composition and structure of the vegetation, slope, or the percentage of cover on the streambank or floodplain.

After developing a general understanding of the system and issues, the next task is to decide what to measure. This step also influences the previous steps of establishing objectives and modeling. The factors that are assessed by monitoring are termed "endpoints." For a wetland, for example, useful endpoints to track would include variables associated with waterflow, slope, and soils, since they are fundamental to the functioning of the ecosystem. Biodiversity conservation requires monitoring a suite of endpoints, since no one variable can characterize the range of attributes and scales involved in a system. Different types of endpoints are particularly useful for monitoring impacts, since different parts of an ecosystem can be exposed at varying concentrations, times, or durations.[11] A table of potential ecosystem attributes useful for monitoring is included in chapter 1 of this book.[12]

Monitoring endpoints may be selected in much the same way as targets are chosen for planning. From numerous possible variables, one must determine priorities. As stated above, one group of priorities would be the monitoring criteria previously identified in a project or plan. Another category is priorities that are ecologically significant. In the paragraph above, the waterflow, slope, and soil variables suggested for a wetland would be in this group. Priorities that are particularly important to the public constitute another category. Among other concerns, these might include charismatic species, economically valuable resources, or pollutants and public health risks. Since these issues typically garner more support than those that are significant only for biodiversity, it is useful to link them in the same program. Any endpoint should be described to the public in terms about which they will care. In addition, monitoring programs should specifically target attributes or impacts to ecosystems that are most likely to change. To assess the effects of development, for example, one could measure the spread of urbanization, the reduction of biotic communities, or changes in fragmentation or connectivity. To evaluate the impacts of climate change, one could track the movements of ecotones, or the borders of biotic communities that tend to shift with variations in climate.[13]

Often, it is not possible to monitor an endpoint directly. Many ecological processes do not lend themselves to measurement. Other endpoints may be too difficult or expensive to monitor. In these cases, "indicators," or variables that can suggest the status of an endpoint, are selected as substitutes. For example, a manager may be interested in forest productivity, but productivity itself cannot be measured. In lieu of the endpoint, he or she might then monitor the growth rate, density, or diameter of the trees, all of which provide information pertaining to productivity. Having previously established the results that will be considered significant, the manager can determine whether or not a different course of action is warranted. Sometimes, the same variable may be both an endpoint and an indicator. This would be the case with an endangered species, where one of the purposes of monitoring is likely to protect the species, and it can be measured. Indicators are the actual variables measured by a monitoring program; these may or may not be the endpoints for which information is desired.

Several authors have offered criteria for selecting monitoring indicators.[14] One of the most basic is that the indicators be easy and economical to measure.

Low spatial and temporal variability are important, since greater variability creates "noise" in the data, making it more difficult to detect significant changes. If the indicators are abundant and distributed over a broad geographic area, data can be compared among regions or possibly among monitoring programs. Indicators that are linked to many other parts of the ecosystem are valuable to track since their decline can result in the declines of numerous species. Indicators of ecosystem stress should respond rapidly to the stress if they are to be used as early warnings. Other stress indicators may not respond as quickly, but may be useful if they accurately and clearly indicate the particular impact. Individual indicators typically include just some of the above criteria; by using multiple indicators, more of the criteria can be met.

Species are often used as monitoring indicators. Many types of plants and animals are effective indicators of water, air, or soil pollution.[15] Different plants have also been used to suggest information regarding abiotic ecosystem factors, such as light, temperature, or nitrogen availability.[16] Recently, there has been an increase in the use of vertebrates as indicators of habitat quality, or of the presence or absence of other species. This use of indicator species has been strongly criticized by some scientists.[17] They observe that a variety of factors affects the populations of species that use similar habitat and that many factors in addition to habitat may influence species populations. For example, the presence of the northern spotted owl may indicate that old-growth habitat of a certain size and configuration still exists. However, the components and structure of old-growth that support the owl may not be exactly the same as that needed to support another old-growth species. The other species may also be susceptible to disturbances that do not affect the owl. Thus the presence of the owl, even though it is strongly linked to old-growth habitat, does not guarantee the presence of other old-growth species. As with all indicators, indicator species should be correlated through research with their associated endpoint. In situations where this has not been done, monitoring programs may include studies to test the effectiveness of the indicators they use.

Perhaps as important as deciding what to monitor is determining how to monitor. The design of a study, project, or program defines the conclusions one is able to draw from the data. Before finalizing the design, it is helpful to consult a professional statistician. A statistician can help practitioners develop a sampling scheme to satisfy the monitoring objectives at the specified level of accuracy and precision. He or she can also help match statistical analyses with the required data types. In the process, monitors may discover that their objectives cannot be met with the resources they have available; this is useful information to know in advance.

Sampling design includes several basic steps. The first is to state the monitoring objectives in terms of testable hypotheses. Then the variability associated with the indicators must be established. The number and location of the samples, and the times, frequency, and period over which they are to be collected, can be determined from this spatial and temporal variability. For example, water flow measurements would likely be designed to capture differences between seasons, as well as flow variations caused by storms. The density and distribution of a bird population would affect where in the landscape they were sampled. In most cases, variability is not known in advance, but it can be estimated through statistical techniques, modeling, or pilot studies. Over time, these initial estimates can be checked through further monitoring. Among the samples, some must be "controls" that have not been influenced by the effect that is being monitored. For instance, to evaluate the impact of a stream diversion, monitors would measure indicators at other streams in addition to the one in question. This practice helps demonstrate which changes are due to the diversion and which may occur in any stream.

While a statistically valid sampling design is always desirable, in reality it is not always possible. It is particularly difficult to achieve at the landscape scale. Since landscapes are usually quite variable, large numbers of samples may be required to obtain statistically significant results, a situation beyond the means of most agencies and organizations. In corridor studies, researchers have generally settled for accumulating anecdotal and observational evidence, or modeling.[18] At the population scale, species with highly fluctuating populations also necessitate greater sample sizes. For rare or elusive species, it may not be possible to collect more than a few samples. Also, an extremely limited budget may preclude a rigorous sampling design. In such situations, it is important to compare the type of study that can be achieved by the project or program with the original monitoring objectives. If a high degree of accuracy and precision is required, it is unlikely that a study without a statistically valid design will be acceptable. On the other hand, the purpose of monitoring may be such that more ambiguous results will be acceptable. In certain cases, equivocal data may be the only option.

One monitoring situation to which sampling design does not apply is change detection. Change detection consists of comparing images produced at different points in time and measuring the changes caused by the variables of interest.[19] It does not include sampling, since an entire area is assessed. Usually, the procedure involves a comparison of two or more satellite images, in which case it is performed digitally according to computer algorithms. Maps can be used instead of imagery, but may introduce greater error due to differences in mapping techniques, accuracies, and classification and registration systems. Change detection is useful for landscape or regional scale monitoring.

For example, it is frequently used to distinguish variations in land use, vegetative cover, or the health and vigor of forests or crops. When comparing satellite images, monitors will be limited to assessing changes that have occurred just in the past few decades, the amount of time for which the imagery is available.

Once the data are collected, they are analyzed according to previously selected methods. The results are interpreted and significant changes identified. The next step is to communicate the information to those who need it for decision making and to those who are supporting the program. Managers or planners can then make necessary revisions, with the purpose of moving the indicator values back toward an acceptable range of variation. If still relevant to its supporters, the program can continue.

Adaptive Management

Monitoring is often used to track the effects of a particular environmental intervention, for example, a plan, project, policy, or management practice. Consider, however, a situation in which there is great uncertainty about which intervention to implement. Assume the situation is complex and contentious, but the stakeholders accept the uncertainty and also agree that some action still must be taken. Under these circumstances, it might be more appropriate to apply adaptive management,[20] rather than implement and monitor a single action. This approach enables practitioners to try several possible strategies at once, and thus learn about the system more rapidly. The strategies can represent diverse interests and ideas held by the stakeholders. Adaptive management is increasingly used in the management of natural areas and may also be applied to the implementation of a conservation plan.

To explain the need for adaptive management, proponents point to an overall lack of ecological understanding and to the added uncertainty resulting from rapid environmental changes.[21] The combination suggests that we cannot afford to continue to plan and manage simply by trial and error. The traditional strategy would be to develop one preferred model or action and either to proceed as if it were correct or to act very cautiously if too much is unknown. Barring unusual events, such as a large, unexpected disturbance, the learning from this approach can be too slow. Scientists are limited to studying the effects of the single conservative action; meanwhile, the surrounding ecosystem continues to be modified into new forms. In contrast, the adaptive management approach is to acknowledge uncertainty, and then to develop a range of viable actions, each of which is designed to probe a different aspect of the system. Ideally, this allows managers not only to learn about the existing system, but to keep up with ongoing changes. It also stimulates imaginative thinking and helps participants generate other options that have not yet been considered.

Adaptive management emphasizes a scientific, rational process. Practitioners first identify areas of uncertainty that currently prevent reliable decisions from being made. They then devise alternative interventions to help them understand these areas. The alternatives are developed using principles of experimental design. Each is proposed as an answer to a hypothesis. As much as possible, control and replicate samples are included in the design to strengthen the statistical significance of the results. Key indicators are monitored to assess the effects of the different interventions. The objectives, assumptions, decisions, and outcomes are documented, so that the knowledge and understanding gained in each phase of the operation will be passed on to those involved in later phases.

One tool frequently used in adaptive management is decision analysis. Decision analysis is a structured way to compare and contrast alternatives. To perform the analysis, managers identify possible alternatives, the potential outcomes of each alternative, and the probabilities, values, and costs associated with the outcomes. They use this information to construct a decision tree to calculate the overall value of each option. The overall value is determined by first multiplying the probability of each outcome by its individual value. The value of an outcome is a relative number reflecting the preference of the practitioner for that outcome. The various outcome products are then added for each alternative to compute the overall alternative values. Decision analysis helps managers clarify a problem, structure comparisons, and prioritize alternatives for implementation. It provides a method to incorporate risk and uncertainty into the decision-making process, and to identify the criteria by which the alternative outcomes will be assessed. It may also help managers decide whether it is worthwhile to pursue experimental alternatives or remain with the status quo. Figure 7.2 demonstrates how decision analysis might help a planner prioritize sites for a recreational trail.[22]

Adaptive management requires a long-term view. To assess the effects of a project on a species might necessitate studying that species for several of its generations. The design of adaptive management experiments may also span several years. In addition, it is assumed that some failures will occur, meaning that more time will be required while another alternative is implemented and evaluated. For management, the process may be an ongoing cycle of developing and implementing alternatives, evaluating the alternatives through monitoring and focused research, and then developing and implementing new or modified alternatives. In contrast to monitoring, these long time periods occur during as well as after the implementation of the plan or management practice.

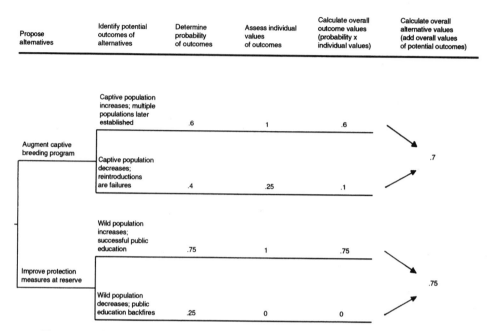

Propose alternatives	Identify potential outcomes of alternatives	Determine probability of outcomes	Assess individual values of outcomes	Calculate overall outcome values (probability x individual values)	Calculate overall alternative values (add overall values of potential outcomes)
Augment captive breeding program	Captive population increases; multiple populations later established	.6	1	.6	
	Captive population decreases; reintroductions are failures	.4	.25	.1	.7
Improve protection measures at reserve	Wild population increases; successful public education	.75	1	.75	
	Wild population decreases; public education backfires	.25	0	0	.75

Figure 7.2. The decision analysis process. (Adapted from Maguire, 1994.)

As a result, the CALFED Bay-Delta Program, described later in this chapter, will be implemented over twenty-five to thirty years. Since this interval is considerably longer than what is usually expected, it is important that the underlying reasons for its length be communicated to all concerned.

While it has a strong scientific bias, adaptive management is also a social and political process.[23] Because control over landscapes is usually fragmented, interaction among stakeholders is necessary. A balance among disparate interests must be created and maintained. Typically, all involved participate fully in the process, including planners, managers, monitors, researchers, and stakeholders. To achieve this participation, structures must be developed to foster trust. Trust is important both among the group members and between the members and the managers leading the process. Participants in adaptive management take risks in being open to new ideas and to the possibility of having their ideas and projects fail. In addition, the stakeholders must be certain that the agreements they work to develop will actually be implemented. As trust is created, participants are better able to negotiate an acceptable course of action.

Consensus building is a technique that can help create a climate conducive to negotiations. It refers to long-term, interactive group processes in which the participants search for commonalities. Such a group may not form unless the members feel that they have no other choice; for example, it may coalesce if the status quo is unsatisfactory, if they are convinced that they cannot accomplish their goals in any other way, or if they feel forced to participate to protect their interests. Once initiated, however, the process can benefit both the members and the subsequent negotiations. Consensus building helps develop trust and communication networks, provides a common basis for discussion, and can lead to new political alliances that promote the implementation of adaptive management.[24]

Taylor et al. (1997) outline four types of barriers to the effective implementation of adaptive management.[25] The categories include technical, economic, ecological, and social and institutional challenges. The technical challenges involve designing experiments to address ecological phenomena that operate at large spatial scales, long time periods, or have high levels of variability. As suggested earlier, these situations do not lend themselves well to traditional statistical methods, and there are presently no widely accepted alternatives. The economic challenges pertain primarily to the expense of experimentation, as well as to equity issues arising from the varying costs borne by different stakeholders. Assessing the costs and limiting the number of experiments can help in the first case; the latter may require institutional or legal guarantees. The ecological challenges involve the possibility that some experiments will cause irreversible ecological damage. Some solutions to this issue include foregoing adaptive management in pristine environments and, in other areas, assessing potential ecological benefits and costs before finalizing decisions on alternatives.

Of the four categories, it is the last one, social and institutional challenges, that will most affect planners. One of the main issues is that both individuals and institutions are averse to taking risks. For good reason, planners and managers may be reluctant to take on projects that might be perceived as failures. Some public agencies, politicians, and other stakeholders also may have a strong interest in preserving the status quo. They may work actively to scuttle the process or, in the case of agencies, simply not respond to monitoring results. Discussing the concept of uncertainty from the outset will help address these concerns. The risks of adaptive management may not appear so large if individuals understand the risks they are already undertaking. It may also be useful to negotiate the risks—and potential failures—that the project is willing to accept. In addition, those resistant to change may still be given certainty in some areas that are important to them. The CALFED Bay-Delta Program, for example, is developing a set of legal "assurances" which give stakeholders security that their interests will be upheld.

The discussion above suggests that adaptive management is most likely to succeed if certain institutional conditions are in place. The following examples of conditions were adapted from Lee (1993)[26]:

- There is a mandate to take action in the face of uncertainty,
- Decisionmakers are aware that any action is an experiment,
- Decisionmakers approach the process of adaptive management with a long-term view,
- Funding and institutional stability exist to conduct adaptive management experiments over a long time period,
- Organizational culture encourages learning from experience, and
- The area in question can no longer be preserved in a pristine state.

For example, decisionmakers must have a mandate to act in the face of uncertainty. Usually, this situation exists because a crisis has occurred or because the status quo is no longer acceptable. Another condition is that organizations encourage learning from experience. Learning may or may not be an important value, for organizations or the public. Lee also feels that adaptive management works best in environments that are no longer pristine and that are difficult for managers to understand. Not surprisingly, three large adaptive management programs currently in operation include the CALFED Bay-Delta Program, the Columbia River Basin Fish and Wildlife Program in the Pacific Northwest, and the Glen Canyon Dam Adaptive Management Program in the Southwest. All involve river systems that have been fundamentally altered by dams and other water projects; the current ecosystems require complex balancing of natural resources and competing human uses.[27]

Monitoring, Adaptive Management, and Planning

Planners need to know how well their plans work and that they will be implemented in the most effective manner. Monitoring and adaptive management are two strategies that address these concerns. Monitoring can be used to evaluate a plan while it is being implemented or over the years to come. Adaptive management can be a useful approach to implementing controversial strategies or strategies that deal with parts of ecosystems that are poorly understood.

Monitoring and adaptive management reduce the ecological uncertainty inherent in biodiversity planning. Rather than ignore the unknown, it is preferable to acknowledge it and devise methods to address it directly. One solution is to set up monitoring and/or adaptive management as part of a plan. In this case, planners will usually need to coordinate with those who will develop and operate the programs. If the programs are to be established at a later date, planners can still enact measures to facilitate their operation. One of the most important is to communicate the concept of uncertainty to all concerned with the plan. It is also valuable to ensure that the range of professionals and stakeholders participate fully in the plan from the beginning. Other useful measures include identifying gaps in data and understanding, current pressures on biodiversity, and the ecological attributes most likely to change. In addition, planners can establish measurable criteria for evaluation, what is to occur if the criteria are not met, and how the information will be communicated to those who need it.

Planners may expect some degree of controversy with both monitoring and adaptive management. Both require funding that might be used for other conservation priorities. Methods to study large-scale and highly variable attributes are still not well formulated. Conflicts may also arise with stakeholders who fear that information contrary to their interests may be uncovered. However, such concerns should not serve as permanent deterrents to the evaluation and careful implementation of conservation plans. Whatever the method, it is in the best interest of planners to continue to learn about their environment and to refine and improve the ways in which they preserve its biodiversity.

Monitoring Wildlife with Volunteers

Keeping Track,® Jericho, Vermont

Wildlife habitat information is a key element in open-space planning. It is especially useful to learn where large, wide-ranging mammals occur, since they are most vulnerable to habitat reduction and fragmentation. Protecting habitat for these animals also protects many other organisms in the process. Unfortunately, detailed data for such species usually are not available. Resource agencies lack the funding to conduct labor-intensive monitoring on most animals. Mammalian predators present the greatest challenge, because they are elusive and occur in low densities. To address this issue, Keeping Track,® a nonprofit corporation based in Vermont, was formed in 1994. Its purpose is to help local citizens' groups develop their own monitoring programs so they can use this information to influence local and regional planning. The organization trains volunteers to recognize animal tracks and signs, to set up monitoring transects, and to collect data on selected wide-ranging mammals (figure 7.3). The programs build enthusiasm and awareness for wildlife conservation and offer planners valuable habitat information.

Since its inception, Keeping Track has trained more than six hundred people from Vermont and New Hampshire to California and the Southwest. Most of the trainings are six-day workshops for established local groups. The groups range from watershed associations to conservation commissions appointed by municipal select boards; all are capable of administering a monitoring program for at least several years. In addition, Keeping Track has given shorter workshops for state and federal agency employees organizing citizen monitoring groups. The workshops help participants choose locally significant target species. In New England, for example, the program has emphasized black bear, otter, fisher, bobcat, mink, and moose. The Canada lynx and mountain lion have also been targets in states where they are endangered. The bulk of the training occurs in the field, where the group learns to identify tracks and other signs such as scat, claw marks on trees, and denning sites. Since a major focus of the program is on identifying habitat, evidence of resident animals is particularly important. Strict monitoring protocols are introduced to help ensure that the data will be credible and useful. The workshops also recommend books on habitat, tracking, and conservation biology. The fee is $400 per day for in-state clients, and $500 per day for those outside Vermont.

After the training, it is the group's responsibility to develop their own monitoring program. One task involves further tracking practice; volunteers may require several months to a few years to become confident in their abilities. The group also determines the location and number of the monitoring transects. Keeping Track suggests that the transects be 2.5 miles long and 60 feet wide. Usually, they are sited in habitats considered suitable for the target species and/or in areas potentially threatened by development, logging, or recreational activities. The number of transects is often limited by the number of volunteers available for monitoring. Once established, each transect is walked by three vol-

Figure 7.3. Keeping Track helps communities monitor the presence and habitats of large, wide-ranging mammals. (Photographs by Susan C. Morse.)

unteers four times per year. The monitors record the date and location of each track or sign observed. To reduce errors, Keeping Track suggests that all such observations be photographed and that the pictures include rulers to indicate size. Finally, the group must create a database to store the information and make it accessible to those who need it.

One of the most significant aspects of the Keeping Track approach is its reliance on volunteers. Without volunteers, the cost of monitoring is often prohibitive. The use of volunteers also offers several benefits. The monitors enjoy the opportunity to be outdoors and to learn about local wildlife, their habitats, and tracking. Their enthusiasm results in increased interest and support for conservation activities. The programs can also bring together people from diverse backgrounds, all sharing a goal of wildlife conservation. In addition to the benefits, though, volunteer programs face several challenges. A primary issue is simply maintaining a core group of volunteers over a number of years. In this case, Keeping Track estimates that a minimum of five years of monitoring is required before the data indicate significant patterns of habitat use. The longer the program can continue, the more useful the information becomes. Before being able to monitor, each volunteer also must be trained and spend additional time in field practice. Inexperienced participants need encouragement, and their work needs to be checked for errors. In addition, it can be difficult for such programs to perform necessary administrative and management functions, for example, overseeing the volunteers, and designing and managing the database.

As with all new organizations, Keeping Track is learning as it goes. At this point, its greatest strength lies in teaching and inspiring volunteers to initiate habitat monitoring programs. Areas that still need attention pertain primarily to the monitoring process and the development and maintenance of a monitoring program. For example, clients who come to Keeping Track are usually unfamiliar with the basic steps of monitoring, including identifying issues and objectives, and determining the different types of data and study designs that will best meet these needs. They also tend to lack understanding of the importance of statistical design, and so cannot judge whether or how it might be considered. They may not realize that the organization and administration of a volunteer monitoring program is very demanding in and of itself. Keeping Track has formed a Protocol Committee to investigate and help its clients with these types of issues. In Vermont, for example, the committee has been exploring the possibility of storing local groups' monitoring data with county planning agencies. Since it is a small nonprofit organization, however, Keeping Track's role in many instances may be limited to offering resources and information.

The founders of Keeping Track recognized the decline of wide-ranging mammals, and designed a program to monitor them and identify their needs. In the process, they tapped into an underutilized resource: citizen volunteers proud of their local areas, eager to learn about wildlife, and enthusiastic about conservation. The combination of monitoring with such volunteers is promising. Still, the development and operatation of a program requires considerable thought and effort. Before embarking on monitoring, local groups will benefit by identifying key conservation issues and objectives. This process helps determine which types of data and studies are necessary, and how the Keeping Track program can best meet their needs. Other issues might also be addressed at the beginning, for example, maintaining and overseeing a group of volunteers, and designing and managing a database. For the protection of our most elusive mammals, and of the habitats they require, these challenges are worth pursuing.

FOR FURTHER INFORMATION CONTACT:
    Sue Morse
    Keeping Track
    RD 1, Box 263
    Jericho, VT 05465
    802-899-2023

Implementing Ecological Restoration Through Adaptive Management

The CALFED Bay-Delta Program, California

LOCATION MAP

The 738,000-acre San Francisco Bay-Delta lies at the confluence of California's Sacramento and San Joaquin rivers. The hub of the state's water system, the Bay-Delta has been the focus of competing interests for decades. It supplies drinking water to more than 22 million residents, houses the largest wetland and estuary on the West Coast, and is key to California's strong agriculture, manufacturing, and fishing industries. Added to the current conflicts is a 150-year legacy of ecological degradation from hydraulic mining, dredging and channelization, flood control, diversions, pollution, and two statewide water supply projects. If allowed to continue, these water controversies will erode California's environmental quality and threaten its economic vitality. In 1995, a coalition of state and federal agencies launched the CALFED Bay-Delta Program as a comprehensive and innovative approach to the situation. The program addresses the entire Bay-Delta system—its ecological processes, its vast watersheds, and its numerous interest groups and stakeholders. The planning process is flexible, enabling new information to be incorporated as the program is implemented. The CALFED program offers new hope for ecological restoration and water management throughout the extended Bay-Delta ecosystem (figure 7.4).

The CALFED Bay-Delta Program is a large-scale solution to large-scale problems. Its geographic scope includes not only the Bay-Delta, but all the

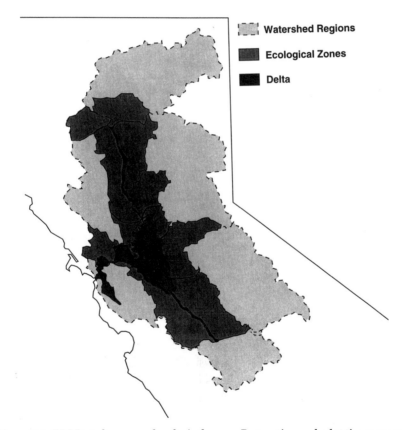

Figure 7.4. ERPP study area and ecological zones. Restoration and adaptive management actions performed by the CALFED Bay-Delta Program will be planned based on fourteen ecological zones. Additional watershed regions are also included in the project due to their influence on the ecological zones. (Map courtesy of the CALFED Bay-Delta Program.)

regions by which it is influenced: the Central Valley, the rivers and their tributary watersheds and, to a lesser extent, the higher mountain watersheds and the near-shore ocean. Recognizing the interests involved, the planners of the program ensured that all stakeholders, including the public, could participate. CALFED itself comprises all of the major state and federal water and natural resource agencies. Environmental, industry, agriculture, and urban groups are included as advisors, while the public has input through numerous meetings and workshops. Since the ecological problems have been occurring for over a century, the program planners envision a period of twenty-five to thirty years to restore ecosystem functions and secure protection for species and biotic communities. To accomplish its goals, the price tag of the program is expected to be $15 to $20 million per year. Funding to date includes $500 million from a California state bond, $430 million authorized by the federal government, and monies from existing restoration programs as well as water-user fees.

The CALFED program is organized around four major issues and is being implemented in three phases. The issues include water quality, ecosystem quality, water supply reliability, and water system integrity. Within the overall CALFED structure, four "common programs" have been developed to address each of the four issues. Of the three implementation phases, the first was completed in 1996. During this stage, planners defined the issues and developed three conceptual alternatives as potential solutions to the Bay-Delta problems. Each alternative includes elements from the four common programs. The alternatives differ primarily in their approaches to water conveyance and storage, areas that are particularly contentious with the public. Phase II, completed in 1997, involves preparing environmental impact reports and statements; analyzing the costs, benefits, and consequences of the alternatives; and choosing one preferred option out of the three. The remainder of the program, Phase III, will include the selection, analysis, and implementation of site-specific projects.

Due to the level of the conflicts, it was imperative that the main interest groups and general public be fully included in the planning process. The interest groups are involved through the Bay-Delta Advisory Council (BDAC). BDAC is federally chartered and consists of thirty-two members from a variety of industries, environmental organizations, and water interest groups. BDAC provides policy advice on the development of the program. A subcommittee of BDAC, the Ecosystem Roundtable, will help coordinate CALFED projects with existing restoration and management efforts, and help establish priorities for near-term restoration. Public comments are encouraged through regional discussions and workshops, through the environmental impact reporting process, and at the BDAC meetings. In addition, CALFED has given briefings to the media, legislature, interest groups, and organizations and developed educational materials.

The Ecosystem Restoration Program Plan (ERPP) is the plan for the ecosystem quality common program. The goal of the ERPP is to improve and increase aquatic and terrestrial habitats and improve ecological functions to support sustainable species populations. The plan focuses on the processes associated with streamflow, stream channels, watersheds, and floodplains. It includes such ambitious goals as restoring 75,000 to 120,000 acres of marsh and riverine habitat, 100 to 200 miles of riparian woodland, and 300,000 to 500,000 acre-feet per year of water during critical periods. The ERPP separates the area addressed by the CALFED program into fourteen ecological zones. A series of objectives has been developed for each region. The objectives are subdivided into targets and potential actions identified for each target. Which targets and actions are ultimately implemented by the program will be the focus of adaptive management.

Adaptive management is a logical approach to the implementation of the CALFED Bay-Delta Program. The extended Bay-Delta ecosystem is extremely complex, and many processes, habitats, and relationships associated with it are poorly understood. As a result, there is significant uncertainty in how to restore ecosystem health. While numerical targets have been developed for the ERPP, no one can know at this point if they are correct. In addition, the stakes and the costs are both high. What is required is a process that will increase the information base and have the flexibility to incorporate new data and public sentiments.

While adaptive management may be used in all four common programs, at this point it is envisioned primarily as an approach to ERPP implementation. Individual restoration projects, selected as program actions, will be implemented and compared to one another and prototypic models. To do this, ERPP staff have identified a series of indicators for each ecological zone. The indicators represent different spatial scales and will be tested for effectiveness during the course of the program. Those associated with each project will be monitored to evaluate ecosystem status and to assess progress toward the project goal. Adaptive management will also involve focused field research and pilot projects, and phased implementation according to priorities. To date, ERPP staff have developed the regional indicators and drafted a monitoring program. Still to be decided are the institution that will oversee the adaptive management and the role of the public.

The concepts of ecological uncertainty and adaptive management have been part of the public discussion from the beginning. Program planners felt that it was important to acknowledge gaps in understanding and the possibility of midcourse corrections. Some citizens applauded the admission, already aware of the lack of scientific data. Others have reacted more skeptically, feeling that uncertainty may simply be a justification for more research, greater costs, and avoiding responsibility. Overall, however, the public has been supportive of the adaptive management approach. This support does not mean that citizens are willing to compromise on the larger program objectives. While recognizing that the methods may change, the public still must trust that the program as a whole will meet their needs.

To address this requirement for certainty, the CALFED program is developing a set of assurances. Through the assurances, the CALFED program will commit to a package of performance contracts. For example, CALFED might commit to certain levels of spring runoff or to the exportation of a given volume of water from the Bay-Delta. However, they will not guarantee the means by which these objectives will be achieved. The assurances are a significant addition to adaptive management in that they allow different interest groups to work together and to participate in the program despite the ecological uncertainties. They will likely be in the form of a legal contract and will be under the auspices of an institution with the power and authority to ensure that they are enacted.

The CALFED Bay-Delta Program is an ambitious and novel approach to ecosystem restoration and water management. It is the largest restoration project to date in the United States. It involves a significant area of California, most of the state's residents as stakeholders, all of the major resource agencies, a decades-long time frame, and hundreds of millions of dollars. It is innovative in its use of adaptive management for program implementation. Since adaptive management is a recent concept, CALFED has found few models to follow. Much of their work, including the idea of assurances, is unprecedented. Californians will have a chance to see how the program and its methods play out over the next thirty years.

FOR MORE INFORMATION CONTACT:
Dick Daniel
CALFED Bay-Delta Program
1416 Ninth Street, Suite 1155
Sacramento, CA 95814
916-657-0199
916-654-9780 (fax)
ddaniel@water.ca.gov

Appendix

Planning Guidelines

Characterizing Biodiversity

1. Conceptualize biodiversity in the area in terms of a framework consisting of components, patterns, and processes. Different types of these attributes exist at different spatial scales and vary over some period of time.

2. Sketch out portions of the framework. Develop some preliminary estimates on:

   - Primary components, patterns and processes at the landscape level,

   - Areas that might require more detailed data, and consideration of community-scale attributes; for example, areas immediately threatened by land use change, or communities that are rare, sensitive, very productive, or high in species diversity,

   - Valuable and vulnerable species for which population or genetic-scale attributes may be important, and

   - The time periods over which these attributes vary.

Developing Conservation Priorities

1. Refine conservation priorities, starting with known threats to biodiversity and considering social, economic, and political issues important to the local community.

2. Identify landscape-scale priorities; for example, community representation, valuable and vulnerable communities, the configuration of communities in the landscape, and influential ecological processes.

3. Identify community-scale priorities for target communities; for example, valuable and vulnerable species, habitat structures and resources, and key disturbances.

4. Identify population-scale priorities for target species; for example, minimum population and habitat sizes, links to other nearby populations, and dispersal requirements.

5. Identify genetic-scale priorities for target populations; for example, patterns of genetic variation and patterns of dispersal.

Incorporating Change and Disturbance

1. Assess how different communities within the planning area are likely to change over time, including disturbances, successional stages, and human-induced changes. As possible, estimate potential thresholds for ongoing impacts.

2. Maintain historic disturbance regimes to the greatest extent possible.

3. Identify sensitive or vulnerable areas that would benefit from protective buffer zones. Retain multiple examples of target populations, communities, or resources.

4. Plan to manage the landscape to counter impacts from human use. Where natural disturbances cannot be allowed, imitate their effects through management.

5. Assume that the targets of a plan will fluctuate within ranges of variability. Establish acceptable, sustainable ranges based on historical ecological information and societal values.

Maintaining Area and Connectivity

1. Identify species and communities most likely to be affected by habitat reduction and fragmentation; for example, extensive tracts of forests, sensitive interior species, and wide-ranging animals. Determine probable sources of impacts and estimate species' requirements.

2. Identify landscape processes likely to be affected by habitat reduction and fragmentation; for example, fires, floods, and hydrologic processes.

3. Identify the most significant edge effects (invasive species, nutrients, pollutants, human usage, etc.) and where they occur.

4. Develop mechanisms (regular meetings, memorandum of understanding, etc.) to communicate and coordinate with other planners in the region

who influence land-use policies. Ensure that habitat reduction and fragmentation issues are also considered in their plans.

Reserve Design

1. Start the design process by identifying the core areas. Consider sites or regions that contain high concentrations of biodiversity and that contribute to its overall representation in the reserve system. Maintaining extensive areas of open space will be beneficial in almost all cases.

2. Evaluate the benefits and costs of including landscape corridors in the design. Benefits are usually related to improving connectivity and habitat for individual species and to maintaining other ecological processes in the landscape. Costs might include increased edge effects and management expenses or rejecting another design that could support a greater range of biodiversity.

3. As much as possible, estimate the types and extent of impacts on reserve biodiversity from the surrounding landscape. Identify strategies to reduce or eliminate these impacts, including buffer zones and management within the reserve and communicating and coordinating with neighbors and decisionmakers in agencies affecting the reserve.

4. Determine alternative strategies for areas where reserves would be unwelcome or impractical. For example, consider conservation easements and other financial incentives for private conservation, outreach and training for landowners, and public education.

Collecting Baseline Data

1. Determine the types of information required, based on the planning priorities, the spatial scale of the planning area, the time periods for which data are needed, and the level of data accuracy necessary to address conservation issues.

2. Identify existing information by search literature, resource agencies at all levels of government, environmental organizations, Internet mailing lists, and ecologists.

3. When possible, coordinate data collection with other jurisdictions, agencies, or organizations, to reduce costs and ensure comparable data.

4. Collect original data as necessary. Plans may require remote sensing data that is more current or of a more appropriate scale, or specific field studies to answer questions related to habitats or species populations.

Monitoring and Adaptive Management

1. Communicate the reasons for uncertainty in conservation planning to decisionmakers and the public, and the need for monitoring and/or adaptive management. Encourage active participation by all stakeholders.

2. Establish criteria by which the plan can be evaluated, thresholds to trigger alternative planning strategies, and feedback loops to ensure that those who need the information will receive it.

3. Identify gaps in data and ecological understanding, current pressures on biodiversity, and ecological attributes most likely to change.

4. Institute programs and funding strategies for monitoring and/or adaptive management, for assessing the plan as it is implemented, and for determining its long-term effects. Coordinate with other regional monitoring programs.

5. Work closely with planners or managers who will develop the monitoring or adaptive management programs.

Notes

Introduction

1. For example, P. R. Ehrlich and A. H. Ehrlich, "The Value of Biodiversity," *Ambio* 21, 3 (1992): 219–226; and D. B. Jensen, M. S. Torn, and J. Harte, *In Our Own Hands: A Strategy for Conserving California's Biological Diversity* (Berkeley: University of California Press, 1993).

2. I. L. McHarg, *Design with Nature* (Garden City, N.Y.: Natural History Press, 1969).

3. J. G. Fabos, *Planning the Total Landscape: A Guide to Intelligent Land Use* (Boulder, Colo.: Westview Press, 1978).

4. W. M. Marsh, *Landscape Planning: Environmental Applications* (New York: John Wiley & Sons, 1983).

5. F. Steiner, *The Living Landscape: An Ecological Approach to Landscape Planning* (New York: McGraw-Hill, 1991).

6. A. Spirn, *The Granite Garden: Urban Nature and Human Design* (New York: Basic Books, 1984).

7. M. Hough, *City Form and Natural Process: Toward a New Urban Vernacular* (New York: Van Nostrand Reinhold, 1984); M. Hough, "Nature and the City," *Landscape Architecture* 79, 7 (1989): 41–43; and M. Hough, *Cities and Natural Process* (New York: Routledge, 1995).

8. J. T. Lyle, *Design for Human Ecosystems: Landscape, Land Use, and Natural Resources* (New York: Van Nostrand Reinhold, 1985); J. T. Lyle, *Regenerative Design for Sustainable Development* (New York: John Wiley & Sons, 1994); and R. L. Thayer, Jr., *Gray World, Green Heart: Technology, Nature, and the Sustainable Landscape* (New York: John Wiley & Sons, 1994).

9. Jensen et al., *In Our Own Hands*, 1993.

10. Keystone Center, *Final Consensus Report on the Keystone Policy on Biological Diversity on Federal Lands* (Keystone, Colo.: Keystone Center, 1991).

11. M. E. Soulé, "What Is Conservation Biology?" *BioScience* 35, 11 (1985): 727–734.

12. P. F. Brussard, "The Current Status of Conservation Biology," *Bulletin of the Ecological Society of America* 66 (1985): 9–11.

13. For example, G. K. Meffe and C. R. Carroll, eds., *Principles of Conservation Biology* (Sunderland, Mass.: Sinauer Associates, 1994); P. L. Feidler and S. K. Jain, eds., *Conservation Biology: The Theory and Practice of Nature Preservation and Management* (New York: Chapman and Hall, 1992); and M. E. Soulé, ed., *Conservation Biology: The Science of Scarcity and Diversity* (Sunderland, Mass.: Sinauer Associates, 1986).

14. R. T. T. Forman, "Some General Principles of Landscape and Regional Ecology," *Landscape Ecology* 10, 3 (1995): 133–142; R. T. T. Forman and M. Godron, *Landscape Ecology* (New York: John Wiley & Sons, 1986); D. L. Urban, R. V. O'Neill, and H. H. Shugart, Jr., "Landscape Ecology: A Hierarchical Perspective Can Help Scientists Understand Spatial Patterns," *BioScience* 37, 2 (1987): 119–127; and I. S. Zonneveld and R. T. T. Forman, eds., *Changing Landscapes: An Ecological Perspective* (New York: Springer-Verlag, 1990).

15. C. D. Vos and P. Opdam, eds., *Landscape Ecology of a Stressed Environment* (New York: Chapman and Hall, 1993).

16. For example, D. S. Smith and P. Cawood Hellmund, eds., *Ecology of Greenways: Design and Function of Linear Conservation Areas* (Minneapolis: University of Minnesota Press, 1993).

17. R. T. T. Forman, "The Beginnings of Landscape Ecology in America," in Zonneveld and Forman, eds., *Changing Landscapes*, 35–41.

Chapter 1

1. R. F. Noss, "Indicators for Monitoring Biodiversity: A Hierarchical Approach," *Conservation Biology* 4, 4 (1990): 355–364. The framework presented in this chapter was first developed by Noss (1990) and draws substantially from his work.

2. For example, N. A. Campbell, *Biology* (Menlo Park, Calif.: Benjamin/Cummings Publishing, 1987); and E. P. Odum, *Fundamentals of Ecology* (Philadelphia: W. B. Saunders, 1971).

3. T. Hanes, "California Chaparral," in M. G. Barbour and J. Major, eds., *Terrestrial Vegetation of California* (Sacramento: California Native Plant Society, 1977).

4. R. C. Stebbins, *Natural History of the Salamanders of the Plethodontid Genus Ensatina* (Berkeley: University of California Publications in Zoology 54, 1954): 47–124.

5. Stebbins's figures address population density; for a rare or endangered population the actual size might be measured instead.

6. T. R. Jackman and D. B. Wake, "Evolutionary and Historical Analysis of Protein Variation in the Blotched Forms of Salamanders of the *Ensatina* Complex (Amphibia: Plethodontidae)," *Evolution* 48, 3 (1994): 876–897; and C. Moritz, C. J. Schneider, and D. B. Wake, "Evolutionary Relationships Within the *Ensatina eschscholtzii* Complex Confirm the Ring Species Interpretation," *Systematic Zoology* 41, 3 (1992): 273–291.

7. For example, R. V. O'Neill, D. L. DeAngelis, J. B. Waide, T. F. H. Allen, *A Hier-*

archical Concept of Ecosystems (Princeton: Princeton University Press, 1986); and D. L. Urban, R. V. O'Neill, and H. H. Shugart, Jr., "Landscape Ecology: A Hierarchical Perspective Can Help Scientists Understand Spatial Patterns," *BioScience* 37, 2 (1987): 119–127.

8. O'Neill et al., *A Hierarchical Concept of Ecosystems*, 1986; and T. F. H. Allen and T. W. Hoekstra, "The Confusion Between Scale-Defined Levels and Conventional Levels of Organization in Ecology," *Journal of Vegetation Science* 1 (1990): 5–12.

9. Campbell, *Biology*, 1987.

10. N. Frank, "Building Toward Disaster," address to the Eleventh Annual Symposium of the International Association of Landscape Ecology, Galveston, Texas, March 28, 1995.

11. W. H. Romme and D. G. Despain, "Historical Perspective on the Yellowstone Fires of 1988," *Bioscience* 39(10) (1989): 695–699; R. J. Hobbs and H. A. Mooney, "Spatial and Temporal Variability in California Annual Grassland: Results from a Long-Term Study," *Journal of Vegetation Science* 5 (1994): 1–13; and H. R. Delcourt, P. A. Delcourt, and T. Webb, III, "Dynamic Plant Ecology: The Spectrum of Vegetational Change in Space and Time," *Quaternary Science Review* 1 (1983): 153–175.

12. Romme and Despain, "Historical Perspective on the Yellowstone Fires of 1988," 1989.

13. W. H. Romme and D. H. Knight, "Landscape Diversity: The Concept Applied to Yellowstone Park," *BioScience* 32 (1982): 664–670.

14. Hobbs and Mooney, "Spatial and Temporal Variability in California Annual Grassland," 1994.

15. Urban et al., "Landscape Ecology: A Hierarchical Perspective," 1987.

Chapter 2

1. Greg Greenwood, California Department of Forestry and Fire Protection.

2. R. F. Noss, "From Plant Communities to Landscapes in Conservation Inventories: A Look at The Nature Conservancy (USA)," *Biological Conservation* 41 (1987): 11–37; and L. L. Master, "Assessing Threats and Setting Priorities for Conservation," *Conservation Biology* 5, 4 (1991): 559–563. This "coarse-filter" is combined with a "fine-filter" that targets vulnerable and rare species.

3. For general discussions of species richness, see M. Begon, J. L. Harper, and C. R. Townsend, eds., *Ecology: Individuals, Populations, and Communities*, 2nd ed. (Boston, Mass.: Blackwell Scientific Publications, 1990), 816–844; and G. K. Meffe and C. R. Carroll, eds., *Principles of Conservation Biology* (Sunderland, Mass.: Sinauer Associates, 1994), 97–103.

4. J. E. Anderson, "A Conceptual Framework for Evaluating and Quantifying Naturalness," *Conservation Biology* 5, 3 (1991): 347–352; and C. Margules and M. B. Usher, "Criteria Used in Assessing Wildlife Conservation Potential: A Review," *Biological Conservation* 21 (1981): 79–109.

5. The Nature Conservancy, *Conservation by Design: A Framework for Mission Success* (Arlington, Va: The Nature Conservancy, 1996).

6. M. A. Mantell, "The California Experiment," *National Wetlands Newsletter* 16, 5 (September/October 1994): 9–10.

7. P. B. Moyle, J. E. Williams, and E. D. Wikramanayake, "Fish Species of Special Concern in California," *Final Report Submitted to the California Department of Fish and Game* (Rancho Cordova: California Department of Fish and Game, Inland Fisheries Division, 1989).

8. E. O. Wilson, *The Diversity of Life* (Cambridge, Mass.: Harvard University Press, 1992), 94–112.

9. A. H. Gentry, "Endemism in Tropical versus Temperate Plant Communities," in M. E. Soulé, ed., *Conservation Biology: The Science of Scarcity and Diversity* (Sunderland, Mass.: Sinauer Associates, 1986), 153–181.

10. D. Rabinowitz, S. Cairns, and T. Dillon, "Seven Forms of Rarity and Their Frequency in the Flora of the British Isles," in Soulé, ed., *Conservation Biology*, 182–204; and C. Margules and M. B. Usher, "Criteria," 79–109.

11. D. B. Jensen, M. Torn, and J. Harte, *In Our Own Hands: A Strategy for Conserving California's Biological Diversity* (Berkeley: University of California Press, 1993).

12. Functional mosaics of ecosystems are discussed in Noss, "From Plant Communities to Landscapes," 11–37; and Jensen et al., *California's Biological Diversity*, 78.

13. P. R. Ehrlich and D. D. Murphy, "Monitoring Populations on Remnants of Native Vegetation," in D. A. Saunders, G. W. Arnold, A. A. Burbidge, and A. J. M. Hopkins, eds., *Nature Conservation: The Role of Remnants of Native Vegetation* (Chipping Norton, New South Wales, Australia: Surrey Beatty and Sons, 1987), 201–210.

14. M. L. Hunter, Jr., G. L. Jacobson, Jr., and T. Webb, III, "Paleoecology and the Coarse-Filter Approach to Maintaining Biological Diversity," *Conservation Biology* 2, 4 (1988): 375–385.

15. See "Special Section on Large Carnivore Conservation," *Conservation Biology* 10, 4 (August 1996).

16. R. T. Paine, "A Note on Trophic Complexity and Community Stability," *American Naturalist* 103 (1969): 91–93.

17. R. J. Naiman, C. A. Johnston, and J. C. Kelley, "Alteration of North American Streams by Beaver," *BioScience* 38, 11 (1988): 753–762.

18. J. A. Estes and J. F. Palmisano, "Sea Otters: Their Role in Structuring Near-Shore Communities," *Science* 185 (1974): 1058–1060.

19. L. S. Mills, M. E. Soulé, and D. F. Doak, "The Keystone-Species Concept in Ecology and Conservation," *BioScience* 43, 4 (1993): 219–224.

20. D. B. Botkin, D. A. Woodby, and R. A. Nisbet, "Kirtland's Warbler Habitats: A Possible Early Indicator of Climatic Warming," *Biological Conservation* 56 (1991): 63–78.

21. H. A. Mooney and J. A. Drake, eds., *Ecology of Biological Invasions of North America and Hawaii* (New York: Springer-Verlag, 1986).

22. P. M. Vitousek, "Biological Invasions and Ecosystem Properties: Can Species

Make a Difference?" in Mooney and Drake, eds., *Ecology of Biological Invasions of North America and Hawaii* (New York: Springer-Verlag, 1986), 163–176.

23. S. C. H. Barrett and J. R. Kohn, "Genetic and Evolutionary Consequences of Small Population Size in Plants: Implications for Conservation," in D. A. Falk and K. E. Holsinger, eds., *Genetics and Conservation of Rare Plants* (New York: Oxford University Press, 1991), 3–30; and E. S. Menges, "The Application of Minimum Viable Population Theory to Plants," in D. A. Falk and K. E. Holsinger, eds., *Genetics and Conservation of Rare Plants* (New York: Oxford University Press, 1991), 45–61.

24. C. I. Millar and W. J. Libby, "Strategies for Conserving Clinal, Ecotypic, and Disjunct Population Diversity in Widespread Species," in D. A. Falk and K. E. Holsinger, eds., *Genetics and Conservation of Rare Plants* (New York: Oxford University Press, 1991), 149–170.

25. C. I. Millar and W. J. Libby, "Restoration: Disneyland or a Native Ecosystem? A Question of Genetics," *Fremontia* 17, 2 (1989): 3–10.

26. Sycamore Associates, *Guidelines for Management of Genetic Resources in the California State Park System* (Lafayette, Calif.: Sycamore Associates, 1992).

Chapter 3

1. H. R. Delcourt, P. A. Delcourt, and T. Webb, "Dynamic Plant Ecology: The Spectrum of Vegetational Change in Space and Time," *Quaternary Science Reviews* 1 (1983): 153–175.

2. R. Byrne, S. Mensing, and E. Edlund, *Long-Term Changes in the Structure and Extent of California Oaks* (Sacramento: California Department of Forestry and Fire Protection, 1993).

3. R. J. Hobbs and D. A. Norton, "Toward a Conceptual Framework for Restoration Ecology," *Restoration Ecology* 4, 2 (1996): 93–110; and F. J. Swanson, J. A. Jones, D. O. Wallin, and J. H. Cissel, "Natural Variability—Implications for Ecosystem Management," in USDA Forest Service, *Eastside Forest Ecosystem Health Assessment*, vol. II, *Ecosystem Management: Principles and Applications* (Portland, Ore.: USDA Forest Service Pacific Northwest Experiment Station, 1993), 89–103.

4. J. O. Luken, *Directing Ecological Succession* (New York: Chapman and Hall, 1990).

5. R. J. Hobbs, "Dynamics of Vegetation Mosaics: Can We Predict Responses to Global Changes?" *Ecoscience* 1 (1994): 346–356.

6. Hobbs and Norton, "Towards a Conceptual Framework," 93–110; and J. Aronson, C. Floret, E. Le Floc'h, C. Ovalle, and R. Pontanier, "Restoration and Rehabilitation of Degraded Ecosystems in Arid and Semiarid Regions, I, A View from the South," *Restoration Ecology* 1 (1993): 8–17.

7. P. S. White, "Pattern, Process and Natural Disturbance in Vegetation," *The Botanical Review* 45, 3 (1979): 229–285; and S. T. A. Pickett and P. S. White, eds., *The Ecology of Natural Disturbance and Patch Dynamics* (New York: Academic Press, 1985).

8. W. A. Allen, "The Great Flood of 1993," *BioScience* 43, 11 (1983): 732–737.

9. For example, B. M. Kilgore, "Fire in Ecosystem Distribution and Structure: Western Forests and Scrublands," in H. A. Mooney et al., Technical Coordinators, *Proceedings of the Conference, Fire Regimes and Ecosystem Properties, December 11–15, 1978, Honolulu, Hawaii*, USDA Forest Service General Technical Report WO-26 (1981), 58–89; and M. L. Heinselman, "Fire Intensity and Frequency as Factors in the Distribution and Structure of Northern Ecosystems," in Mooney et al., *Proceedings of the Conference, Fire Regimes, and Ecosystem Properties*, 7–55.

10. Kilgore, "Fire in Ecosystem Distribution and Structure," 58–89; and R. A. Minnich, "Chaparral Fire History in San Diego County and Adjacent Northern Baja California: An Evaluation of Natural Fire Regimes and the Effects of Suppression Management," in S. C. Keeley, ed., *The California Chaparral: Paradigms Reexamined*, Publication 34 (Los Angeles: Los Angeles County Natural History Museum, 1989), 37–47.

11. V. T. Parker, "Effect of Wet-Season Management Burns on Chaparral Regeneration: Implications for Rare Species," in T. E. Elias, ed., *Proceedings of a Conference on the Conservation and Management of Rare and Endangered Plants* (Sacramento: California Native Plant Society, 1987), 233–237; and R. J. Hobbs, "Disturbance Regimes in Remnants of Natural Vegetation," in D. A. Saunders, G. W. Arnold, A. A. Burbridge, and A. J. M. Hopkins, eds., *Nature Conservation: The Role of Remnants of Native Vegetation* (Chipping Norton, New South Wales, Australia: Surrey Beatty and Sons, 1987), 233–240.

12. White, "Pattern, Process and Natural Disturbance in Vegetation," 229–285.

13. D. R. Weise and R. E. Martin, Technical Coordinators, *The Biswell Symposium: Fire Issues and Solutions in Urban Interface and Wildland Ecosystems, February 15–17, 1994, Walnut Creek, California*, General Technical Report PSW-GTR-158 (Albany, Calif.: USDA Forest Service Pacific Southwest Research Station, 1995).

14. White, "Pattern, Process, and Natural Disturbance in Vegetation," 229–285.

15. D. A. Saunders, R. J. Hobbs, and C. R. Margules, "Biological Consequences of Ecosystem Fragmentation: A Review," *Conservation Biology* 5, 1 (1991): 18–32.

16. Hobbs, "Disturbance Regimes," 233–240.

17. IPCC (International Panel on Climate Change), *Climate Change, the IPCC Scientific Assessment* (Cambridge, Mass.: Cambridge University Press, 1990).

18. J. F. Franklin, "Scientific Basis for New Perspectives in Forests and Streams," in R. J. Naiman, ed., *Watershed Management: Balancing Sustainability and Environmental Change* (New York: Springer-Verlag, 1992), 25–72.

19. J. E. Keeley, ed., *Interface Between Ecology and Land Development in California* (Los Angeles: Southern California Academy of Sciences, 1993).

20. M. Westoby, B. Walker, and I. Noy-Meir, "Opportunistic Management for Rangelands Not at Equilibrium," *Journal of Range Management* 42 (1989): 266–274; and Hobbs, "Dynamics of Vegetation Mosaics," 346–356.

21. Luken, *Directing Ecological Succession*, 1990.

22. Hobbs and Norton, "Towards a Conceptual Framework," 93–110; D. Caraher and W. H. Knapp, "Assessing Ecosystem Health in the Blue Mountains," in USDA For-

est Service, *Silviculture: From the Cradle of Forestry to Ecosystem Management*, General Technical Report SE-88 (Asheville, N.C.: USDA Forest Service Southeastern Forest Experiment Station, 1995), 34–41; and J. L. Walker and W. D. Boyer, "An Ecological Model and Information Needs Assessment for Longleaf Pine Ecosystem Restoration," in USDA Forest Service, *Silviculture*, General Technical Report SE-88 (Asheville, NC: USDA Forest Service Southeastern Forest Experiment Station, 1995), 138–147.

23. D. G. Sprugel, "Disturbance, Equilibrium, and Environmental Variability: What Is 'Natural' Vegetation in a Changing Environment?" *Biological Conservation* 58 (1991): 1–18.

Chapter 4

1. D. S. Wilcove, C. H. McLellan, and A. P. Dobson, "Habitat Fragmentation in the Temperate Zone," in M. E. Soulé, ed., *Conservation Biology: The Science of Scarcity and Diversity* (Sunderland, Mass.: Sinauer Associates, 1986), 237–256; and R. F. Noss, "Landscape Connectivity: Different Functions at Different Scales," in W. E. Hudson, ed., *Landscape Linkages and Biodiversity* (Washington, D.C.: Island Press, 1991), 27–39.

2. D. A. Saunders, R. J. Hobbs, and C. R. Margules, "Biological Consequences of Ecosystem Fragmentation: A Review," *Conservation Biology* 5, 1 (1991): 18–32; J. W. Ranney, M. C. Bruner, and J. B. Levenson, "The Importance of Edge in the Structure and Dynamics of Forest Islands," in R. L. Burgess and D. M. Sharpe, eds., *Forest Island Dynamics in Man-Dominated Landscapes* (New York: Springer-Verlag, 1981), 67–95; and R. Geiger, *The Climate Near the Ground* (Cambridge, Mass.: Harvard University Press, 1965).

3. Saunders et al., "Biological Consequences," 18–32; and R. Hobbs, "Disturbance Regimes in Remnants of Natural Vegetation," in D. A. Saunders, G. W. Arnold, A. A. Burbidge, and A. J. M. Hopkins, eds., *The Role of Remnants of Native Vegetation* (Chipping Norton, New South Wales, Australia: Surrey Beatty and Sons, 1987), 233–240.

4. L. D. Harris, *The Fragmented Forest: Island Biogeography Theory and the Preservation of Biotic Diversity* (Chicago: University of Chicago Press), 1984.

5. L. M. Hoehne, "The Groundlayer Vegetation of Forest Islands in an Urban-Suburban Matrix," in Burgess and Sharpe, eds., *Forest Island Dynamics in Man-Dominated Landscapes*, 41–54; and T. A. Scott, "Along the Wildland Urban Interface," in J. E. Keeley, ed., *Interface Between Ecology and Land Development in California* (Los Angeles: Southern California Academy of Sciences, 1993), 181–188.

6. For example, R. J. Hobbs and L. F. Huenneke, "Disturbance, Diversity, and Invasion: Implications for Conservation," *Conservation Biology* 6, 3 (1992): 324–333; and Hobbs, "Disturbance Regimes," 233–240.

7. M. Brittingham and S. Temple, "Have Cowbirds Caused Forest Songbirds to Decline?" *BioScience* 33, 1 (1983): 31–5; and D. S. Wilcove, "Nest Predation in Forest Tracts and the Decline of Migratory Songbirds," *Ecology* 66 (1985): 1211–1214.

8. Harris, *Fragmented Forest*, 1984.

9. Wilcove et al., "Habitat Fragmentation," 237–256.

10. Saunders et al., "Biological Consequences" 18–32; and R. J. Hobbs, "The

Effects of Landscape Fragmentation on Ecosystem Processes in the Western Australian Wheatbelt," *Biological Conservation* 64 (1993): 193–201.

11. Hobbs, "Disturbance Regimes," 233–240; and Hobbs and Huenneke, "Disturbance, Diversity, and Invasion," 324–333.

12. J. Baudry and H. G. Merriam, "Connectivity and Connectedness: Functional Versus Structural Patterns in Landscapes," in K. Schreiber, ed., *Connectivity in Landscape Ecology: Proceedings of the Second International Seminar of the International Association for Landscape Ecology, Munster, Germany, 1987* (Paderborn, Germany: Ferdinand Schoningh, 1988), 23–28.

13. A. S. Harestad and F. L. Bunnell, "Home Range and Body Weight—A Reevaluation," *Ecology* 60, 2 (1979): 389–402.

14. A. A. Mejia, L. T. de Alonso, L. Brower, and D. Murphy, "Maintaining Migratory Phenomena: The Mexican Monarch Butterfly Challenge," *Society for Conservation Biology Newsletter* 3 (1996): 1 and 17.

15. T. E. S. Langton, ed., *Amphibians and Roads: Proceedings of the Toad Tunnel Conference, Rendsburg, Federal Republic of Germany, 7–8 January 1989* (Shefford, England: ACO Polymer Products Ltd, 1989).

16. For example, D. W. Macdonald and H. Smith, "Dispersal, Dispersion, and Conservation in the Agricultural Ecosystem," in R. G. H. Bunce and D. C. Howards, eds., *Species Dispersal in Agricultural Habitats* (London: Belhaven Press, 1990), 18–64; and W. Z. Lidicker, "The Role of Dispersal in the Demography of Small Mammals, in E. B. Golley, D. Petrusewicz, and R. Ryskorski, eds., *Small Mammals: Their Productivity and Population Dynamics* (Cambridge, England: Cambridge University Press, 1975), 103–128.

17. Macdonald and Smith, "Dispersal, Dispersion, and Conservation," 18–64.

18. R. Levins, "Extinction" in M. Gerstenhaber, ed., *Some Mathematical Questions in Biology, Fifth Symposium on Mathematical Biology* (Providence, R.I.: American Mathematical Society, 1970), 77–107; and M. E. Gilpin, "The Genetic Effective Size of a Metapopulation," *Biological Journal of the Linnean Society* 42 (1991): 165–175.

19. P. Opdam, "Dispersal in Fragmented Populations: The Key to Survival," in Bunce and Howard, eds., *Species Dispersal in Agricultural Habitats,* 3–15; and Gilpin, "Genetic Effective Size of a Metapopulation," 165–175.

20. J. W. Thomas, E. D. Forsman, J. B. Lint, E. C. Meslow, B. R. Noon, and J. Verner, *A Conservation Strategy for the Northern Spotted Owl* (Portland, Ore.: United States Printing Office, 1990).

21. L. D. Harris and P. B. Gallagher, "New Initiatives for Wildlife Conservation: The Need for Movement Corridors," in G. Mackintosh, ed., *Preserving Communities and Corridors* (Washington, D.C.: Defenders of Wildlife, 1989), 11–34; and C. M. Schonewald-Cox and M. Buechner, "Park Protection and Public Roads," in P. L. Fiedler and S. K. Jain, eds., *Conservation Biology: The Theory and Practice of Nature Conservation and Management* (New York: Chapman and Hall, 1992), 373–395.

22. R. Russo, personal communication with chief naturalist, Charles Lee Tilden Regional Park, Calif., 1996.

23. T. E. S. Langton, ed., *Amphibians and Roads,* 1989; and M. L. Foster and S. R.

Humphrey, *Effectiveness of Wildlife Crossings in Reducing Animal/Auto Collisions on Interstate 75, Big Cypress Swamp, Florida* (Tallahassee: Florida Department of Transportation, 1992).

24. N. Simon and P. Geroudet, *Last Survivors* (New York: World Publishing Company, 1970).

25. M. L. Shaffer, "Minimum Population Sizes for Species Conservation," *BioScience* 31, 2 (1981): 131–134.

26. M. E. Gilpin and M. E. Soulé, "Minimum Viable Populations: Processes of Species Extinction," in *Conservation Biology: The Science of Scarcity and Diversity* (Sunderland, Mass.: Sinauer Associates, 1986), 19–34; and M. E. Soulé, ed., *Viable Populations for Conservation*, (New York: Cambridge University Press, 1987).

27. Shaffer, "Minimum Population Sizes," 131–134.

28. R. Lande, "Genetics and Demography in Biological Conservation," *Science* 241 (1988): 1455–1460.

29. Gilpin and Soulé, "Minimum Viable Populations," 19–34.

30. G. Caughley, "Directions in Conservation Biology," *Journal of Animal Ecology* 63 (1994): 215–244.

31. M. E. Soulé and B. A. Wilcox, eds., *Conservation Biology: An Evolutionary-Ecological Perspective* (Sunderland, Mass.: Sinauer Associates, 1980); O. H. Frankel and M. E. Soulé, *Conservation and Evolution* (New York: Cambridge University Press, 1981); and C. M. Schonewald-Cox, S. M. Chambers, B. MacBryde, and W. L. Thomas., eds., *Genetics and Conservation: A Reference for Managing Wild Animal and Plant Populations* (Menlo Park, Calif.: Benjamin/Cummings, 1983).

32. G. K. Meffe and C. R. Carroll, eds., *Principles of Conservation Biology* (Sunderland, Mass.: Sinauer Associates, 1994).

33. Caughley, "Directions in Conservation Biology," 215–244.

34. F. W. Allendorf, "Isolation, Gene Flow, and Genetic Differentiation Among Populations," in Schonewald-Cox et al., eds., *Genetics and Conservation*, 51–65.

35. For example, Shaffer, "Minimum Population Sizes," 131–134.

36. S. Wright, *Evolution and the Genetics of Populations*, vol. 3, *Experimental Results and Evolutionary Deductions* (Chicago: University of Chicago Press, 1977).

37. Caughley, "Directions in Conservation Biology," 215–244.

38. I. R. Franklin, "Evolutionary Change in Small Populations," in Soulé and Wilcox, eds., *Conservation Biology*, 135–150; M. E. Soulé, "Thresholds for Survival: Maintaining Fitness and Evolutionary Potential," in Soulé and Wilcox, eds., *Conservation Biology,*, 111–124; M. E. Soulé and D. Simberloff, "What Do Genetics and Ecology Tell Us About the Design of Nature Reserves?" *Biological Conservation* 35 (1986): 19–40; Soulé, *Viable Populations for Conservation*, 1987; and C. D. Thomas, "What Do Real Population Dynamics Tell Us About Minimum Viable Population Sizes?" *Conservation Biology* 4, 3 (1990): 324–327.

39. Soulé, *Viable Populations for Conservation*, 1987.

40. M. L. Shaffer, "Population Viability Analysis," *Conservation Biology* 4, 1 (1990): 39–40.

41. Thomas et al., *Northern Spotted Owl*, 1990; R. H. Lamberson, R. McKelvey, B. R. Noon, and C. Voss, "A Dynamic Analysis of Northern Spotted Owl Viability in a Fragmented Forest Landscape," *Conservation Biology* 6, 4 (1992): 505–512; M. L. Shaffer, "Determining Minimum Viable Population Sizes for the Grizzly Bear," in *International Conference on Bear Research and Management 5* (West Glacier Mont.: International Association for Bear Research and Management, 1983), 133–139; and Shaffer, "Population Viability Analysis," 39–40.

42. R. E. Grumbine, "Viable Populations, Reserve Size, and Federal Lands Management: A Critique," *Conservation Biology* 4, 2 (1990): 127–134; and J. L. Hunter, Jr., *Fundamentals of Conservation Biology* (Cambridge, Mass.: Blackwell Science, 1996).

43. H. P. Possingham, D. B. Lindenmayer, and T. W. Norton, "A Framework for the Improved Management of Threatened Species Based on Population Viability Analysis (PVA)," *Pacific Conservation Biology* 1 (1993): 39–45.

44. R. Goldingay and H. Possingham, "Area Requirements for Viable Populations of the Australian Gliding Marsupial *Petaurus australis*," *Biological Conservation* 73 (1995): 161–167.

45. W. D. Newmark, "A Land-Bridge Island Perspective on Mammalian Extinctions in Western North American Parks," *Nature* 325, 29 (1987): 430–432; and H. Salwasser, C. M. Schonewald-Cox, and R. Baker, "The Role of Interagency Cooperation in Managing Viable Populations," in Soulé, ed., *Viable Populations for Conservation*, 159–173.

Chapter 5

1. R. H. MacArthur and E. O. Wilson, *The Theory of Island Biogeography* (Princeton: Princeton University Press, 1967).

2. J. M. Diamond, "The Island Dilemma: Lessons of Modern Biogeographic Studies for the Design of Natural Reserves," *Biological Conservation* 7 (1975): 129–146. For additional guidelines based on the theory of island biogeography, see also, E. O. Wilson and E. O. Willis, "Applied Biogeography," in M. L. Cody and J. M. Diamond, eds., *Ecology and Evolution of Communities* (Cambridge, Mass.: Harvard University Press, 1975), 522–534.

3. For criticisms of the theory of island biogeography and its applications, see F. S. Gilbert, "The Equilibrium Theory of Island Biogeography: Fact of Fiction?" *Journal of Biogeography* 7 (1980): 209–235; C. Margules, A. J. Higgs, and R. W. Rafe, "Modern Biogeographic Theory: Are There Any Lessons for Nature Reserve Design?" *Biological Conservation* 24 (1982): 115–128; and D. Simberloff and L. G. Abele, "Conservation and Obfuscation: Subdivision of Reserves," *Oikos* 42, 3 (1984): 399–401.

4. M. E. Soulé, "Land Use Planning and Wildlife Maintenance: Guidelines for Conserving Wildlife in an Urban Landscape," *American Planning Association Journal* 57 (1991): 313–323.

5. C. R. Margules, A. O. Nicholls, and R. L. Pressey, "Selecting Networks of Reserves to Maximize Biological Diversity," *Biological Conservation* 43 (1988): 63–76.

6. H. H. Shugart and D. C. West, "Long-Term Dynamics of Forest Ecosystems," *American Scientist* 69 (1981): 647–652.

7. D. A. Saunders and R. J. Hobbs, "The Role of Corridors in Conservation: What Do We Know and Where Do We Go from Here?" in D. A. Saunders and R. J. Hobbs, eds., *Nature Conservation 2: The Role of Corridors* (Chipping Norton, New South Wales, Australia: Surrey Beatty and Sons, 1991), 421–427.

8. P. Beier, "Dispersal of Juvenile Cougars in Fragmented Habitat," *Journal of Wildlife Management* 59, 2 (1995): 228–237.

9. For an in-depth treatment of corridor design, see D. S. Smith and P. Cawood Hellmund, eds., *Ecology of Greenways: Design and Function of Linear Conservation Areas* (Minneapolis: University of Minnesota Press, 1993).

10. See for example, G. Merriam and A. Lanoue, "Corridor Use by Small Mammals: Field Measurement for Three Experimental Types of *Peromyscus leucopus*," *Landscape Ecology* 4, 2/3 (1990): 123–131; and A. F. Bennett, K. Henein, and G. Merriam, "Corridor Use and the Elements of Corridor Quality: Chipmunks and Fencerows in a Farmland Mosaic," *Biological Conservation* 68 (1994): 155–165.

11. Papers summarizing the potential benefits and costs of corridors include: D. Simberloff and J. Cox, "Consequences and Costs of Conservation Corridors," *Conservation Biology* 1, 1 (1987): 63–71; R. F. Noss, "Corridors in Real Landscapes: A Reply to Simberloff and Cox," *Conservation Biology* 1, 1 (1987): 159–164; D. Simberloff, J. A. Farr, J. Cox, and D. W. Mehlman, "Movement Corridors: Conservation Bargains or Poor Investments?" *Conservation Biology* 6, 4 (1992): 493–504; and R. J. Hobbs, "The Role of Corridors in Conservation: Solution or Bandwagon?" *Trends in Ecology and Evolution* 7, 11 (1992): 389–392.

12. C. L. Bolsinger, *The Hardwoods of California's Timberlands, Woodlands, and Savannas*, USDA Forest Service General Research Bulletin PNW-RB-148 (USDA Forest Service, 1988).

13. C. M. Schonewald-Cox and J. W. Bayless, "The Boundary Model: A Geographical Analysis of Design and Conservation of Nature Reserves," *Biological Conservation* 38 (1986): 305–322.

14. Ibid.

15. See for example, J. MacKinnon, K. MacKinnon, G. Child, and J. Thorsell, *Managing Protected Areas in the Tropics* (Gland, Switzerland: IUCN, 1986); and J. Sayer, *Rainforest Buffer Zones: Guidelines for Protected Area Managers* (Gland, Switzerland: IUCN, 1991).

16. J. D. Phillips, "An Evaluation of the Factors Determining the Effectiveness of Water Quality Buffer Zones," *Journal of Hydrology* 107 (1989): 133–145; and A. D. Muscutt, G. L. Harris, S. W. Bailey, and D. B. Davies, "Buffer Zones to Improve Water Quality: A Review of Their Potential Use in U.K. Agriculture," *Agriculture, Ecosystems and Environments* 45(1993): 59–77. For water quality, see also: R. D. Barling and I. Moore, "Role of Buffer Strips in Management of Waterway Pollution: A Review," *Environmental Management* 18, 4(1994): 543–558; and L. L. Osborne and D. A. Kovacic,

"Riparian Vegetated Buffer Strips in Water Quality Restoration and Stream Management," *Freshwater Biology* 29 (1993): 243–258.

17. R. F. Noss and A. Y. Cooperrider, *Saving Nature's Legacy* (Washington, D. C.: Island Press, 1994), 133–134.

18. R. J. George, D. J. McFarlane, and R. J. Speed, "The Consequences of a Changing Hydrologic Environment for Native Vegetation in South Western Australia," in D. A. Saunders, J. Craig, and L. Mattiske, eds., *Nature Conservation 4: The Role of Networks* (Chipping Norton, New South Wales, Australia: Surrey Beatty and Sons, 1995), 9–22.

19. L. D. Harris, "An Everglades Regional Biosphere Reserve," *Florida Fish and Wildlife News* 4, 2 (1990): 12–15.

20. UNESCO, *Task Force on Criteria and Guidelines for the Choice and Establishment of Biosphere Reserves, Man and the Biosphere Report No. 22* (Paris: UNESCO, 1974); and UNESCO, "Action Plan for Biosphere Reserves," *Nature and Resources* 20, 4 (1984): 11–22.

21. J. Hough, "Biosphere Reserves: Myth and Reality," *Endangered Species Update* 6, 1/2 (1988): 1–4.

22. M. P. Wells and K. E. Brandon, "The Principles and Practice of Buffer Zones and Local Participation in Biodiversity Conservation," *Ambio* 22, 2-3 (1993): 157–162.

23. J. W. Thomas, E. D. Forsman, J. B. Lint, E. C. Meslow, B. R. Noon, and J. Verner, *A Conservation Strategy for the Northern Spotted Owl* (Washington, D.C.: U. S. Government Printing Office, 1990).

24. L. D. Harris, *The Fragmented Forest: Island Biogeography Theory and the Preservation of Biotic Diversity* (Chicago: University of Chicago Press, 1984); R. F. Noss and L. D. Harris, "Nodes, Networks, and MUMs: Preserving Diversity at All Scales," *Environmental Management* 10, 3 (1986):299–309.

25. Noss and Cooperrider, *Saving Nature's Legacy,* 1994.

26. See *Wild Earth*, Special Issue on the Wildlands Project (1992).

27. R. J. Hobbs, "Can Revegetation Assist in the Conservation of Biodiversity in Agricultural Areas?" *Pacific Conservation Biology* 1 (1993): 29–38.

28. R. Jongman, "Ecological Networks in Europe: Congruent Developments," *Landschap*, Special Issue on the Planning of Ecological Networks (1995): 123–130.

29. S. Van der Ryn and S. Cowan, *Ecological Design* (Washington, D. C.: Island Press,1996).

Chapter 6

1. A. Y. Cooperrider, R. J. Boyd, and H. R. Stuart, eds., *Inventory and Monitoring of Wildlife Habitat* (Denver, Colo.: USDI Bureau of Land Management, Service Center, 1986). The first chapter provides clear overview of the inventory and monitoring process; the book as a whole is comprehensive resource for collecting wildlife habitat information.

2. J. C. Loftis, G. B. McBride, and J. C. Ellis, "Considerations of Scale in Water

Quality Monitoring and Data Analysis," *Water Resources Bulletin* 27, 2 (1991): 255–264.

3. M. P. Austin, "Vegetation: Data Collection and Analysis," in C. R. Margules and M. P. Austin, eds., *Nature Conservation: Cost Effective Biological Surveys and Data Analysis* (Australia: CSIRO, 1991), 37–41.

4. State resource agencies usually have better geologic information than the USGS; planners can locate these agencies by contacting the Earth Science Information Center noted below. State geologic agencies and professional geologic societies are also listed each year in the October issue of the journal *Geotimes*. In addition to geology information, ESIC provides topographical maps, digital elevation model (DEM) data, digital line graph (DLG) data (including transportation, hydrography, jurisdictional boundaries, and public land survey), hydrologic unit data or maps, and aerial photographs. ESIC's address is: U. S. Geologic Survey, Reston-ESIC, 507 National Center, Reston, VA 20192, 800-872-6277, 703/648-5548 (fax), esicmail@usgs.gov, http://www.usgs.gov.

5. Paper soil maps are available at offices of the USDA Natural Resources Conservation Service, located in most counties. Additional information on NRCS data can be found at their website: http://ncg.nrcs.usda.gov. Climate data can be acquired from: National Climatic Data Center, 151 Patton Avenue, Room 120, Asheville, NC 28801-5001, 704-271-4800, 704-271-4876 (fax), orders@ncdc.noaa.gov, http://www.ncdc.noaa.gov (the names and addresses of state climatologists are listed at this web site). Landview II is a joint project of the EPA and the U.S. Bureau of the Census and is available from the Bureau of the Census. (See following note.)

6. The TIGER line files were developed by the Bureau of the Census to provide computerized geographical support for the 1990 census. They include such useful planning data as streets, rivers, railroads, jurisdictional boundaries, and census tracts. (Some data duplicates that which is available from the USGS.) Contact: U.S. Bureau of the Census, ACSD Customer Service Branch, Washington, DC 20233, 301-457-1128, 301-457-3842 (fax), http://www.census.gov.

7. Robert N. Colwell, ed., *Manual of Remote Sensing*, 2nd ed. (Falls Church, Va: American Society of Photogrammetry, 1983).

8. Videography is another emerging remote sensing technology. The systems record data digitally and enable planners to focus exclusively on the landscape area in which they are interested. To date, however, they have not been used extensively due to poor spatial and spectral resolution. As the technology improves, their use will likely increase. See T. M. Airola, "Emerging Technologies: Digital Aerial Photography—An Overview," in J. M. Scott, T. H. Tear, and F. W. Davis, eds., *Gap Analysis: A Landscape Approach to Biodiversity Planning* (Bethesda, Md.: American Society for Photogrammetry and Remote Sensing, 1996), 269–277.

9. Recent satellite imagery can be acquired from two private companies, Space Imaging Eosat and SPOT Image Corporation. Space Imaging Eosat carries data from the Landsat satellites and India's IRS satellite, while SPOT Image Corporation features imagery from the French SPOT satellite. The data vary principally in resolution and in the number and type of electromagnetic bands sensed. Contact: Space Imaging

Eosat, 4300 Forbes Blvd., Landham, MD 20706, 800-232-9037 (customer service), 301/552-3762 (fax), http://www.eosat.com; and SPOT Image Corporation,1897 Preston White Drive, Reston, VA 20191-4368, 800-ASK-SPOT (customer service), 703-648-1813 (fax), http://www.spot.com.

10. Older satellite images are archived at: U.S. Geological Survey, EROS Data Center, Sioux Falls, SD 57198, 605-594-6151, 615-594-6589 (fax), custserv@edcserver1.cr.usgs.gov.

11. M. L. Morrison and B. G. Marcot, "An Evaluation of Resource Inventory and Monitoring Program Used in National Forest Planning," *Environmental Management* 19, 1 (1995): 147–156.

12. Personal communication, 1997, John Radke, associate professor of landscape architecture, University of California at Berkeley.

13. For further information about the digital library projects see *Communications of the ACM* 38, 4 (1995), entire issue. The URLs for the Berkeley and Alexandria Libraries respectively are, http://elib.cs.berkeley.edu; http://alexandria.sdc.ucsb.edu.

14. As of this writing some useful mailing lists include: bene@straylight.tamu.edu focusing on conservation biology; consbio@u.washington.edu, also conservation biology but with an international emphasis; pacific-biosnet@listproc.wsu.edu, for conservation and biological resource issues in the Northwest; bufferzone@listserv.vt.edu, on buffer zones; and tws-l@listserv.vt.edu, the Wildlife Society's list for wildlife management issues.

15. J. Mainwaring, *An Introduction to the Study of Map Projection* (New York: MacMillan, 1960); and J. Star and J. Estes, *Geographic Information Systems: An Introduction*, (Englewood Cliffs, N.J.: Prentice Hall, 1990), 76–125. The latter chapter covers the various ways that data are preprocessed prior to use in a geographic information system.

16. A. J. Cherrill, C. McClean, A. Lane, and R. M. Fuller, "A Comparison of Land Cover Types in an Ecological Field Survey in Northern England and a Remotely Sensed Land Cover Map of Great Britain," *Biological Conservation* 71 (1995); 313–323. This paper is an example of the differences that can be found in maps developed from different methodologies.

17. R. G. Congalton and K. Green, "The ABCs of GIS: An Introduction to Geographic Information Systems," *Journal of Forestry* 90, 11 (1992): 13–20.

18. Stream gage data can be found at the USGS web site or by contacting state water agencies. A list of these state agencies is also at the web site, or available from the National Water Information Clearinghouse at 800-426-9000. Stream gage data is published annually in Water Resource Data Books.

19. W. M. Marsh, *Landscape Planning: Environmental Applications* (Reading, Mass.: Addison-Wesley Publishing Company, 1983), 130–146.

20. Indications of vegetation composition hundreds or thousands of years ago can be obtained from fossil pollen, collected by coring lakebed soils. Older forest inventories may be available for the last hundred or so years. Some researchers have used witness trees, employed by early surveyors as boundary markers, as indicators of previous forest composition. See S. P. Hamburg and C. V. Cogbill, "Historic Decline of Red Spruce Populations and Climatic Warming," *Nature* 331, 4 (1988): 428–430.

21. P. R. Campbell, *Population Projections for States by Age, Race, and Sex, 1993–2020,* U.S. Bureau of the Census, Current Population Reports, P25-1111 (Washington, D.C.: U.S. Government Printing Office, 1994), B-1. State agencies that provide population projections by county are listed in the back of this publication.

22. Cooperrider et al., eds., *Inventory and Monitoring of Wildlife Habitat,* 587–612.

23. J. Verner, M. L. Morrison, and C. J. Ralph, eds., *Wildlife 2000: Modeling Habitat Relationships of Terrestrial Vertebrates* (Madison: The University of Wisconsin Press, 1986).

24. H. H. Shugart, Jr. and D. C. West, "Long-Term Dynamics of Forest Ecosystems," *American Scientist* 69 (1981): 647–651.

25. D. R. McCullough, ed., *Metapopulations and Wildlife Conservation* (Washington, D.C.: Island Press, 1996).

26. K. Bruce Jones, "Data Types," in A. Y. Cooperrider, R. J. Boyd, and H. R. Stuart, eds., *Inventory and Monitoring of Wildlife Habitat* (Denver, Colo.: USDI Bureau of Land Management, Service Center, 1986), 11–27; and T. H. Kunz, C. Wemmer, and V. Hayssen, "Sex, Age, and Reproductive Condition of Mammals," in D. E. Wilson, F. R. Cole, J. D. Nichols, R. Rudran, and M. S. Foster, eds., *Measuring and Monitoring Biological Diversity: Standard Methods for Mammals* (Washington, D. C.: Smithsonian Institution Press, 1996), 279–290.

27. H. Dingle, *Migration: The Biology of Life on the Move* (New York: Oxford University Press, 1996); and J. Behler, "Spying on Spotties," *Wildlife Conservation* (September/October 1996): 39–45.

28. G. K. Meffe and C. R. Carroll, eds., *Principles of Conservation Biology* (Sunderland, Mass.: Sinauer Associates, 1994), 143–179.

29. M. L. Hunter, Jr., *Fundamentals of Conservation Biology* (Cambridge, Mass.: Blackwell Science, 1996), 79–102.

30. B. A. Schaal, W. J. Leverich, and S. H. Rogstad, "Comparison of Methods for Assessing Genetic Variation in Plant Conservation Biology," in D. A. Falk, and K. E. Holsinger, eds., *Genetics and Conservation of Rare Plants* (New York: Oxford University Press, 1991), 123–134; J. L. Hambrick, M. J. W. Godt, D. A. Murawski, and M. D. Loveless, "Correlations Between Species Traits and Allozyme Diversity: Implications for Conservation Biology," in Falk and Holsinger, eds., *Genetics and Conservation of Rare Plants,* 75–86; B. Amos and A. Rus Hoelzel, "Applications of Molecular Genetic Techniques to the Conservation of Small Populations," *Biological Conservation* 61 (1992): 133–144; C. I. Millar and W. J. Libby, "Restoration: Disneyland or a Native Ecosystem?" *Fremontia* 17, 2 (1989): 3–10.

Chapter 7

1. Discussions of uncertainty appear throughout the adaptive management literature. See for example, C. Walters, *Adaptive Management of Renewable Resources,* (New York: MacMillan, 1986); and K. N. Lee, *Compass and Gyroscope: Integrating Science and Politics for the Environment,* (Washington, D.C.: Island Press, 1993). Some ideas

regarding uncertainty also stem from an e-mail conversation with J. R. Karr, professor of fisheries and zoology, University of Washington, 1997.

2. L. H. MacDonald, A. W. Smart, and R. C. Wissmar, *Monitoring Guidelines to Evaluate Effects of Forestry Activities on Streams in the Pacific Northwest and Alaska*, EPA 910/9-91-001 (Seattle, Wash.: U. S. Environmental Protection Agency, 1991).

3. T. J. Stohlgren, D. Binkley, T. T. Veblen, and W. L. Baker, "Attributes of Reliable Long-Term Landscape-Scale Studies: Malpractice Insurance for Landscape Ecologists," *Environmental Monitoring and Assessment* 36 (1995): 1–25.

4. See for example, MacDonald et al., *Monitoring Guidelines*, 1991; J. Ford, J. L. Stoddard, and C. F. Powers, "Perspectives on Environmental Monitoring: An Introduction to the U.S. EPA Long-Term Monitoring (LTM) Project," *Water, Air, and Soil Pollution* 67 (1993): 247–255; W. J. Shampine, "Quality Assurance and Quality Control in Monitoring Programs," *Environmental Monitoring and Assessment* 23, 2-3 (1993): 143–151; and Stohlgren et al., "Landscape-Scale Studies," 1–25.

5. Shampine, "Quality Assurance," 1993.

6. S. Stafford, editorial, *Environmental Monitoring and Assessment* 26 (1993): 85–89; and R. C. Wissmar, "The Need for Long-Term Stream Monitoring Programs in Forest Ecosystems of the Pacific Northwest," *Environmental Monitoring and Assessment* 26 (1993): 219–234.

7. Stohlgren et al., "Landscape-Scale Studies," 1–25.

8. W. A. Maher, P. W. Cullen, and R. H. Norris, "Framework for Designing Sampling Programs," *Environmental Monitoring and Assessment* 30 (1994): 139–162. The monitoring process presented in this section follows the framework offered in this paper. While monitoring has been described by numerous authors, this treatment is particularly clear.

9. USDI Fish and Wildlife Service, Division of Refuges, *Writing Refuge Management Goals and Objectives: A Handbook*, 602 FW 1-3 (1996).

10. G. M. Kondolf and E. R. Micheli, "Evaluating Stream Restoration Projects," *Environmental Management* 19, 1 (1995): 1–15; and E. A. Read, M. Blane, and P. Bowler, "Restoration of Coastal Sage Scrub," *Ecesis* 6, 2 (1996): 1, 4–5.

11. J. R. Kelly and M. A. Harwell, "Indicators of Ecosystem Recovery," *Environmental Management* 14, 5 (1990): 527–545.

12. R. F. Noss, "Indicators for Monitoring Biodiversity: A Hierarchical Approach," *Conservation Biology* 4, 4 (1990): 355–364.

13. Stohlgren et al., "Landscape-Scale Studies," 1–25.

14. These criteria were drawn from the following literature: J. R. Kelly and M. A. Harwell, "Indicators of Ecosystem Recovery," *Environmental Management* 14, 5 (1990): 527–545; R. F. Noss, "Indicators," 355–364; L. H. MacDonald et al., *Monitoring Guidelines*, 1991; and D. G. Silsbee and D. L. Peterson, "Planning for Implementation of Long-Term Resource Monitoring Programs," *Environmental Monitoring and Assessment* 26 (1993): 177–185.

15. For example, I. S. Zonneveld, "Principles of Bio-Indication," *Environmental*

Monitoring and Assessment 3 (1983): 207–217; and M. Kovacs, ed., *Biological Indicators in Environmental Protection* (New York: Ellis Horwood, 1992).

16. J. D. Nichols, "Extensive Monitoring Programmes Viewed as Long-Term Population Studies: The Case of North American Waterfowl," *Ibis* 133, Suppl. 1 (1991): 89–98.

17. P. B. Landres, J. Verner, and J. W. Thomas, "Ecological Uses of Vertebrate Indicator Species: A Critique," *Conservation Biology* 2, 4 (1988): 316–328; and M. L. Morrison, "Bird Populations as Indicators of Environmental Change," *Current Ornithology* 3 (1986): 429–451.

18. R. J. Hobbs, "The Role of Corridors in Conservation: Solution or Bandwagon?" *Trends in Ecology and Evolution* 7, 11 (1992): 389–392.

19. K. Green, D. Kempka, and L. Lackey, "Using Remote Sensing to Detect and Monitor Land-Cover and Land-Use Change," *Photogrammetric Engineering & Remote Sensing* 60, 3 (1994): 331–337.

20. "Active adaptive management," or "experimental management," is described in this chapter. The practice of adaptive management also includes "passive adaptive management," an approach in which a single strategy is implemented and monitored.

21. For example, see L. H. Gunderson, C. S. Holling, and S. S. Light, eds., *Barriers and Bridges to the Renewal of Ecosystems and Institutions* (New York: Columbia University Press, 1995); Lee, *Compass and Gyroscope*, 1993; and Walters, *Adaptive Management*, 1986.

22. R. L. Keeney, "Decision Analysis: An Overview," *Operations Research* 30, 5 (1982): 803–838; L. A. Maguire, "Decision Analysis in Conservation Biology," in G. K. Meffe and C. R. Carroll, *Principles of Conservation Biology* (Sunderland, Mass.: Sinauer Associates, 1994), 327–329; and B. Taylor, L. Kremsater and R. Ellis, *Adaptive Management of Forests in British Columbia* (Victoria, Canada: British Columbia Ministry of Forests, Forest Practices Branch, 1997).

23. For a discussion of the roles of science and politics in adaptive management, see Lee, *Compass and Gyroscope*, 1993.

24. J. Innes, J. Gruber, M. Neuman, and R. Thompson, *Coordinating Growth and Environmental Management Through Consensus Building* (Berkeley: California Policy Seminar, 1994).

25. Taylor et al., *Adaptive Management*, 1997.

26. Lee, *Compass and Gyroscope*, 1993.

27. K. N. Lee, "Deliberately Seeking Sustainability in the Columbia River Basin," in L. H. Gunderson, C. S. Holling, and S. S. Light, eds., *Barriers and Bridges to the Renewal of Ecosystems and Institutions* (New York: Columbia University Press, 1995), 214–238; and M. J. Wieringa, and A. G. Morton, "Hydropower, Adaptive Management, and Biodiversity," *Environmental Management* 20, 6 (1996): 831–840.

Glossary

Abiotic: Nonliving; usually referring to the physical and chemical components of the environment such as water, rocks, and mineral soil.

Adaptive management: A systematic approach to improving management by implementing policy decisions as scientific experiments that test predictions and assumptions. The experiments are designed to enhance ecosystem understanding, and the results are incorporated into management practices. This approach can also be used in the implementation of conservation plans.

Allele: An alternative form of a gene. Alleles for blue eyes, brown eyes, and green eyes, for example, may exist in a population as different forms of the eye color gene.

Allozyme: A form of enzyme produced by a particular allele. Allozymes are used in electrophoresis to indicate which alleles are present in an individual.

Biodiversity: The full range of variety and variability within and among living organisms, and the ecological complexes in which they occur; it encompasses diversity at all scales, including genetic, population, community, and landscape.

Biological integrity: A quality referring to the condition of an ecosystem, includes the presence of all appropriate components and patterns, and the occurrence of all processes at appropriate rates.

Biological scale: The level of resolution perceived or considered on a biological hierarchy; examples include organism, population, species, community, and landscape.

Biosphere reserve: A reserve model developed by the United Nation's Man and the Biosphere Program, containing an inviolate core area for ecosystem protection, a surrounding buffer zone in which nondestructive human activities are permitted, and a transition zone in which human activities of greater impact are permitted. Three goals of a biosphere reserve are conservation, education, and sustainable human development.

Biotic: Pertaining to life or living organisms; caused or produced by or comprising living organisms.

Buffer zone: An area of lower ecological value, surrounding or adjacent to an area of higher ecological value, whose purpose is to reduce the risk of impacts to the latter area. A transition zone between a reserve and adjoining lands.

Coarse filter/fine filter approach: A two-tiered approach to conservation developed by The Nature Conservancy. The coarse filter is used first to protect representative portions of each community, with emphasis on rare and threatened communities. The fine filter is used to protect additional elements of biodiversity such as rare or threatened species.

Community: The species that occur together at a particular place and time.

Community scale: The level of resolution in a biological hierarchy pertaining to community components, patterns, and processes; examples of community scale attributes include species, vegetation structure, and succession.

Component: A part of a system; when referring to biodiversity, a component is a part of an ecosystem and can exist at any scale.

Connectivity: The state of being functionally connected, allowing the movement of organisms, materials, or energy.

Conservation biology: The integrative field of biology that studies the dynamics of diversity, scarcity, and extinction.

Corridor: A linear part of a reserve network that differs from the surrounding landscape matrix.

Dispersal: The one-way movement of individuals or propagules away from their home areas.

Disturbance: A relatively abrupt change in ecosystem structure or composition caused by natural events such as fires, storms, or flooding, or human-caused events such as logging or road building.

Disturbance regime: The size, frequency, intensity, and timing of disturbances characteristic of an ecosystem type.

DNA: Deoxyribonucleic acid; the carrier of genetic information in all living organisms.

Ecosystem: A holistic concept of plants, animals, fungi, and microorganisms and their associated nonliving environment interacting as an ecological unit.

Ecosystem attribute: A characteristic of an ecosystem; an ecosystem component, pattern, or process occurring at any scale.

Ecosystem management: The integration of ecological, economic, and social principles to manage biological and physical systems in a manner that safeguards the ecological sustainability, natural diversity, and productivity of the landscape.

Ecotone: An overlap zone between two communities that is influenced by both communities.

Edge effects: The ecological changes that occur at the boundaries of ecosystems, including variations in microclimate, influences from adjacent communities and land uses, and an altered species composition. Edges between communities often contain more species than either of the communities separately. Greater amounts of edge habitat resulting from landscape fragmentation reduce habitat available to interior species.

Edge species: A species found only or primarily near the perimeter of a vegetation patch or in other ecosystems strongly influenced by edge effects.

Effective population size: The number of individuals in a population that can contribute reproductively to the next generation.

Electrophoresis: A process by which the gene products of an individual organism are separated by an electrical field in a gel medium and then stained so that they may be identified and classified. Used to infer genetic structure, diversity, and relationships within and among populations.

Endemic: Native to a particular place and found only there.

Endpoints: Factors that are the objects of a monitoring program and about which information is desired. Information on the status of a combination of endpoints is used to evaluate ecological conditions. Other closely correlated indicator variables are frequently measured instead of an endpoint if the endpoint is too difficult or expensive to measure directly.

Exotic species: Nonnative species that occur in an area as a result of deliberate or accidental introductions.

Gap analysis: A method of assessing the protection status of biodiversity, based on the representation of species and natural communities in lands managed for conservation.

Genetic diversity: The amount of genetic variation within and among the populations of a species; the lowest level of biodiversity.

Genetic drift: Random changes in the genetic constitution of a population due to chance processes alone.

Genetic scale: The level of resolution in a biological hierarchy pertaining to genetic components, patterns, and processes; examples of genetic scale attributes include alternate forms of alleles, the genetic structure of a population, and inbreeding depression.

Geographic information system (GIS): A database for geographically referenced information that is organized in thematic layers and linked to other nonspatial data.

Habitat fragmentation: The process by which habitats are subdivided into smaller patches, resulting in increased isolation of the patches and a loss of total habitat area.

Heterozygosity: An index of genetic diversity measuring the proportion of genes at which the average individual has two different alleles.

Home range: The area around an animal's home that is used for feeding and other daily activities.

Hotspot: An area of unusually high species richness or endemism, a priority for conservation.

Inbreeding depression: A reduction in fertility and offspring survival due to reduced genetic diversity within an individual; inbreeding depression typically follows a rapid increase in inbreeding in a population where inbreeding normally does not occur.

Indicator: An ecosystem component, pattern, process, or impact that is measured to assess the condition of a particular aspect of the environment.

Interbreeding: Breeding between the individuals of different populations.

Interior species: A species that is adapted to conditions deep within an unfragmented vegetation patch and unable to exist at the perimeter.

Keystone species: A species that plays a pivotal role in an ecosystem and upon which a large part of the community depends.

Landscape: A heterogeneous land area composed of interacting ecosystems that are repeated in a similar form throughout.

Landscape ecology: The study of the structure, function, and change in a heterogeneous land area composed of interacting ecosystems.

Landscape matrix: The most extensive and connected ecosystem type in a landscape, which often plays the dominant role in landscape processes.

Landscape scale: The level of resolution in a biological hierarchy pertaining to landscape components, patterns, and processes; examples of landscape scale attributes include communities, connectivity, and wildfires.

Metadata: Information about data, generally regarding the source(s), lineage, content, structure, quality, and availability of the dataset.

Metapopulation: A set of partially isolated populations of the same species connected by dispersing individuals. Dispersal allows interbreeding and recolonization of sites where neighboring populations have become extinct.

Migration: The seasonal movement of animals between separate areas.

Minimum viable population: The smallest isolated population that has a specified percentage of the chance of survival for a specified period of time, given foreseeable impacts.

Model: A simplified verbal, graphic, or mathematical description used to help understand a complex object or process.

Monitoring: The periodic measurement or observation of ecosystem components, patterns, or processes to determine ecological conditions. Monitoring indicates the extent and magnitude of change and may also involve identifying the causes of change. Monitoring is used to assess the implementation or effects of a plan, project, management practice, or policy; to detect ecological trends; to evaluate models; to improve understanding of ecosystems; and to establish baseline datasets.

Patch: A nonlinear surface area differing in appearance and function from its surroundings.

Pattern: Configuration; the structure or arrangement of ecosystem components.

Pixel: An abbreviation for "picture element"; the smallest area of resolution in a digital image. Pixel size affects data accuracy and precision since the entire area of the pixel receives the same classification.

Polymorphism: An index of genetic diversity measuring the proportion of genes in a population that occurs in alternative forms.

Population: A group of interbreeding individuals of a species inhabiting a given area.

Population scale: The level of resolution in a biological hierarchy pertaining to population components, patterns, and processes; examples of population scale attributes include population size, distribution, and growth rate.

Population viability analysis: A comprehensive analysis of the genetic, demographic, and environmental factors affecting the survival of a population, usually applied to small populations at risk of extinction.

Process: A series of actions, changes, or functions that bring about a result; in ecology, an interaction including two or more components of an ecosystem that can exist at any scale.

Range of variability: The range over which an ecosystem attribute may vary in a given period of time. The range is estimated from historical data and modeling and is influenced by societal values.

Remote sensing: Techniques involving instruments attached to airplanes or satellites that measure electromagnetic energy emitted or reflected from the earth. The information may be processed as satellite imagery or digital data, as aerial photographs, or as videography.

Reserve: An area maintained for the preservation of the ecosystems contained within it.

Reserve network: A system of nature reserves that are functionally connected to provide greater protection than the individual reserves could provide by themselves.

Riparian zone: An interface zone between terrestrial and aquatic ecosystems exhibiting gradients in community structure and ecological processes of these two ecosystem types. Functionally, riparian zones are three dimensional areas of direct interaction with aquatic ecosystems, extending outward from the channel to the limits of flooding and upward into the canopy of streamside vegetation.

Spatial scale: The level of spatial resolution perceived or considered. Also, the ratio of the size of a unit on a map to its true size.

Specialist species: A species that is adapted to and depends on a narrow range of resources.

Species: The basic unit of classification, consisting of a population or series of populations of closely related and similar organisms. In sexually reproducing organisms, a population or series of populations of organisms that freely interbreed with one another under natural conditions, but not with members of other species.

Species diversity: The variety of species inhabiting a given area and the relative abundance of those species.

Species richness: The number of species within a defined area or community. For biodiversity purposes, it is the number of native species that is significant.

Spectral signature: The intensity of radiation characteristic of a landscape element at a combination of bands of the electromagnetic spectrum; used in the classification of satellite imagery.

Succession: The natural, sequential change in the composition of a vegetation community over time.

Temporal scale: The level of temporal resolution, or the time period, perceived or considered.

Bibliography

Airola, T. M. "Emerging Technologies: Digital Aerial Photography—An Overview." In J. M. Scott, T. H Tear, and F. W. Davis, eds. *Gap Analysis: A Landscape Approach to Biodiversity Planning*. Bethesda, Md.: American Society for Photogrammetry and Remote Sensing, 1996.

Allen, T. F. H., and T. W. Hoekstra. "The Confusion Between Scale-Defined Levels and Conventional Levels of Organization in Ecology." *Journal of Vegetation Science* 1 (1990): 5–12.

Allen, T. F. H., and T. B. Starr. Hierarchy: Perspectives for Ecological Complexity. Chicago: University of Chicago Press, 1982.

Allen, W. A. "The Great Flood of 1993." *BioScience* 43, 11 (1993): 732–737.

Allendorf, F. W. "Isolation, Gene Flow, and Genetic Differentiation Among Populations." In C. M. Schonewald-Cox, S. M. Chambers, B. MacBryde, and L. Thomas, eds. *Genetics and Conservation*. Menlo Park, Calif.: Benjamin/Cummings Publishing Co., 1983.

Amos, B., and A. Rus Hoelzel. "Applications of Molecular Genetic Techniques to the Conservation of Small Populations." *Biological Conservation* 61 (1992): 133–144.

Anderson, J. E. "A Conceptual Framework for Evaluating and Quantifying Naturalness." *Conservation Biology* 5, 3 (1991): 347–352.

Aronson, J., C. Floret, E. Le Floc'h, C. Ovalle, and R. Pontanier. "Restoration and Rehabilitation of Degraded Ecosystems in Arid and Semiarid Regions. I. A View from the South." *Restoration Ecology* 1 (1993): 8–17.

Austin, M. P. "Vegetation: Data Collection and Analysis." In C. R. Margules and M. P. Austin, eds. *Nature Conservation: Cost Effective Biological Surveys and Data Analysis*. Australia: CSIRO, 1991.

Barling, R. D., and I. Moore. "Role of Buffer Strips in Management of Waterway Pollution: A Review." *Environmental Management* 18, 4 (1994): 543–558.

Barrett, S. C. H., and J. R. Kohn. "Genetic and Evolutionary Consequences of Small Population Size in Plants: Implications for Conservation." In D. A. Falk and K. E. Holsinger, eds. *Genetics and Conservation of Rare Plants*. New York: Oxford University Press, 1991.

Bartolome, J. W. "Local Temporal and Spatial Structure." In L. F. Huenneke and H. Mooney, eds. *Grassland Structure and Function: California Annual Grassland.* Dordrecht, The Netherlands: Kluwer Academic Publishers, 1989.

Baudry, J., and H. G. Merriam. "Connectivity and Connectedness: Functional Versus Structural Patterns in Landscapes." In K. Schreiber, ed. *Connectivity in Landscape Ecology: Proceedings of the Second International Seminar of the International Association for Landscape Ecology, Munster, Germany, 1987.* Paderborn, Germany: Ferdinand Schoningh, 1988.

Begon, M., J. L. Harper, and C. R. Townsend, eds. *Ecology: Individuals, Populations, and Communities.* Second edition. Boston, Mass.: Blackwell Scientific Publications, 1990.

Behler, J. "Spying on Spotties." *Wildlife Conservation* (September/October 1996): 39–45.

Beier, P. "Determining Minimum Habitat Areas and Habitat Corridors for Cougars." *Conservation Biology* 7, 1 (1993): 94–108.

———. "Dispersal of Juvenile Cougars in Fragmented Habitat." *Journal of Wildlife Management* 59, 2 (1995): 228–237.

Bennett, A. F., K. Henein, and G. Merriam. "Corridor Use and the Elements of Corridor Quality: Chipmunks and Fencerows in a Farmland Mosaic." *Biological Conservation* 68 (1994): 155–165.

Blower, J. G., L. M. Cook, and J. A. Bishop. *Estimating the Size of Animal Populations.* London, England: George Allen and Unwin, 1981.

Bolsinger, C. L. *The Hardwoods of California's Timberlands, Woodlands, and Savannas.* USDA Forest Service General Research Bulletin PNW-RB-148. Portland, Ore.: USDA Forest Service, 1988.

Botkin, D. B. *Discordant Harmonies: A New Ecology for the Twenty-first Century.* New York: Oxford University Press, 1990.

Botkin, D. B., W. S. Broeker, L. G. Everett, J. Shapiro, and J. A. Wiens. The Future of Mono Lake: Report of the Community and Organization Research Institute "Blue Ribbon Panel" for the Legislature of the State of California. Report No. 68. Riverside: University of California Water Resources Center, 1988.

Botkin, D. B., D. A. Woodby and R. A. Nisbet. "Kirtland's Warbler Habitats: A Possible Early Indicator of Climatic Warming." Biological Conservation 56 (1991): 63–78.

Brittingham, M., and S. Temple. "Have Cowbirds Caused Forest Songbirds to Decline?" *BioScience* 33, 1 (1983): 31–35.

Brussard, P. F. "The Current Status of Conservation Biology." *Bulletin of the Ecological Society of America* 66 (1985): 9–11.

Byrne, R., S. Mensing, and E. Edlund. *Long-Term Changes in the Structure and Extent of California Oaks.* Sacramento: California Department of Forestry and Fire Protection, 1993.

Campbell, N. A. *Biology.* Menlo Park: Benjamin/Cummings Publishing Co., Inc., 1987.

Campbell, P. R. *Population Projections for States by Age, Race, and Sex, 1993–2020.* U.S. Bureau of the Census, Current Population Reports, P25-1111. Washington, D.C.: U.S. Government Printing Office, 1994.

Caraher, D., and W. H. Knapp. "Assessing Ecosystem Health in the Blue Mountains." In USDA Forest Service. *Silviculture: From the Cradle of Forestry to Ecosystem Management.* General Technical Report SE-88. Asheville, N.C.: USDA Forest Service Southeastern Forest Experiment Station, 1995.

Caughley, G. "Directions in Conservation Biology." *Journal of Animal Ecology* 63 (1994): 215–244.

Cherrill, A. J., C. McClean, A. Lane, and R. M. Fuller. "A Comparison of Land Cover Types in an Ecological Field Survey in Northern England and a Remotely Sensed Land Cover Map of Great Britain." *Biological Conservation* 71 (1995): 313–323.

Clarke, R. *The Handbook of Ecological Monitoring.* New York: Oxford University Press, 1986.

Colwell, R. N., ed. *Manual of Remote Sensing.* Second edition. Falls Church, Va.: American Society of Photogrammetry, 1983.

Congalton, R. G., and K. Green. "The ABCs of GIS: An Introduction to Geographic Information Systems." *Journal of Forestry* 90, 11 (1992): 13–20.

Cooperrider, A. Y., R. J. Boyd, and H. R. Stuart, eds. *Inventory and Monitoring of Wildlife Habitat.* Denver, Colo.: U.S. Department of the Interior, Bureau of Land Management Service Center, 1986.

Courtemanch, D. L. "Bridging the Old and New Science of Biological Monitoring." *Journal of the North American Benthological Society* 13, 1 (1994): 117–121.

Crowe, R. E. "Applications of Gap Analysis Data in the Mojave Desert of California." In J. M. Scott, T. H. Tear, and F. W. Davis, eds. *Gap Analysis: A Landscape Approach to Biodiversity Planning.* Bethesda, Md.: American Society for Photography and Remote Sensing, 1996.

Davis, G. E. "Design Elements of Monitoring Programs: The Necessary Ingredients for Success." *Environmental Monitoring and Assessment* 26 (1993): 99–105.

———. "Design of a Long-Term Ecological Monitoring Program for Channel Islands National Park, California." *Natural Areas Journal* 9, 2 (1989): 80–89.

Delcourt, H. R., P. A. Delcourt, and T. Webb, III. "Dynamic Plant Ecology: The Spectrum of Vegetational Change in Space and Time." *Quaternary Science Reviews* 1 (1983): 153–175.

Diamond, J. M. "The Island Dilemma: Lessons of Modern Biogeographic Studies for the Design of Natural Reserves." *Biological Conservation* 7 (1975): 129–146.

Dingle, H. *Migration: The Biology of Life on the Move.* New York: Oxford University Press, 1996.

Draggan, S., J. J. Cohrssen, and R. E. Morrison, eds. *Environmental Monitoring, Assessment and Management: The Agenda for Long-Term Research and Development.* New York: Praeger, 1987.

Ehrlich, P. R., and A. H. Ehrlich. "The Value of Biodiversity." *Ambio* 21, 3 (1992): 219–226.

Ehrlich, P. R., and D. D. Murphy. "Monitoring Populations on Remnants of Native Vegetation." In D. A. Saunders, G. W. Arnold, A. A. Burbidge, and A. J. M. Hopkins, eds. Nature Conservation: The Role of Remnants of Native Vegetation. Chipping Norton, New South Wales, Australia: Surrey Beatty and Sons, 1987.

Estes, J. A., and J. F. Palmisano. "Sea Otters: Their Role in Structuring Near-Shore Communities." *Science* 185 (1974): 1058–1060.

Fabos, J. G. *Planning the Total Landscape: A Guide to Intelligent Land Use.* Boulder, Colo.: Westview Press, 1978.

Falk, D. A. "The Theory of Integrated Conservation Strategies for Biological Diversity." In R. S. Mitchell, C. J. Sheviak, and D. J. Leopold, eds. *Ecosystem Management: Rare Species and Significant Habitats.* Proceedings of the Fifteenth Annual Natural Areas Conference. New York State Museum Bulletin, 471. Albany: The University of the State of New York, 1990.

Falk, D. A., and K. E. Holsinger, eds. Genetics and Conservation of Rare Plants. New York: Oxford University Press, 1991.

Feidler, P. L., and S. K. Jain, eds. *Conservation Biology: The Theory and Practice of Nature Preservation and Management.* New York: Chapman and Hall, 1992.

Ford, J., J. L. Stoddard, and C. F. Powers. "Perspectives on Environmental Monitoring: An Introduction to the U.S. EPA Long-Term Monitoring (LTM) Project." *Water, Air, and Soil Pollution* 67 (1993): 247–255.

Forman, R. T. T. "The Beginnings of Landscape Ecology in America." In I. S. Zonneveld and R. T. T. Forman, eds. *Changing Landscapes: An Ecological Perspective.* New York: Springer-Verlag, 1990.

———. "Some General Principles of Landscape and Regional Ecology. *Landscape Ecology* 10, 3 (1995): 133–142.

Forman, R. T. T., and M. Godron. Landscape Ecology. New York: John Wiley & Sons, 1986.

Foster, M. L., and S. R. Humphrey. *Effectiveness of Wildlife Crossings in Reducing Animal/Auto Collisions on Interstate 75, Big Cypress Swamp, Florida.* Tallahassee: Florida Department of Transportation, 1992.

Frank, Neil. "Building Toward Disaster." Address to the Eleventh Annual Symposium of the International Association of Landscape Ecology, Galveston, Texas, March 28, 1996.

Frankel, O. H., and M. E. Soulé, *Conservation and Evolution.* New York: Cambridge University Press, 1981.

Franklin, I. R. "Evolutionary Change in Small Populations." In M. E. Soulé, and B. A. Wilcox, eds. *Conservation Biology: An Evolutionary-Ecological Perspective.* Sunderland, Mass.: Sinauer Associates, 1980.

Franklin, J. F. "Preserving Biodiversity: Species in Landscapes. Response to Tracy and Brussard." *Ecological Applications* 4 (1994): 208–209.

———. "Scientific Basis for New Perspectives in Forests and Streams." In R. J. Naiman, ed. *Watershed Management: Balancing Sustainability and Environmental Change.* New York: Springer-Verlag, 1992.

Franklin, J. F., K Cromack, W. Denison, et al. Ecological Characteristics of Old-Growth Douglas-Fir Forests. USDA Forest Service General Technical Report PNW-118. Portland, Ore.: Pacific Northwest Forest and Range Experiment Station, 1981.

Freemark, K. "Assessing Effects of Agriculture on Terrestrial Wildlife: Developing a Hierarchical Approach for the U.S. EPA." *Landscape and Urban Planning* 31 (1995): 99–115.

Fritts, S. H., and L. N. Carbyn. "Population Viability, Nature Reserves, and the Outlook for Gray Wolf Conservation in North America." *Restoration Ecology* 3, 1 (1995): 26–38.

Geiger, R. *The Climate Near the Ground.* Cambridge, Mass.: Harvard University Press, 1965.

Gentry, A. H. "Endemism in Tropical Versus Temperate Plant Communities." In M. E. Soulé, ed. *Conservation Biology: The Science of Scarcity and Diversity.* Sunderland, Mass.: Sinauer Associates, 1986.

George, R. J., D. J. McFarlane, and R. J. Speed. "The Consequences of a Changing Hydrologic Environment for Native Vegetation in South Western Australia." In D. A. Saunders, J. Craig, and L. Mattiske, eds. *Nature Conservation 4: The Role of Networks.* Chipping Norton, New South Wales Australia: Surrey Beatty and Sons, 1995.

Getting, I. A., "The Global Positioning System." *IEEE Spectrum* 30, 12 (1993): 36–47.

Gilbert, F. S. "The Equilibrium Theory of Island Biogeography: Fact of Fiction?" *Journal of Biogeography* 7 (1980): 209–235.

Gilpin, M. E. "The Genetic Effective Size of a Metapopulation." *Biological Journal of the Linnean Society* 42 (1991): 165–175.

Gilpin, M. E., and M. E. Soulé. "Minimum Viable Populations: Processes of Species Extinction." In M. E. Soulé, ed. Conservation Biology: The Science of Scarcity and Diversity. Sunderland, Mass.: Sinauer Associates, 1986.

Goldingay, R., and H. Possingham. "Area Requirements for Viable Populations of the Australian Gliding Marsupial *Petaurus australis. Biological Conservation* 73 (1995): 161–167.

Goldsmith, F. B., ed. *Monitoring for Conservation and Ecology.* New York: Chapman and Hall, 1991.

Golley, E. B., D. Petrusewicz, and R. Ryskorski, eds. *Small Mammals. Their Productivity and Population Dynamics.* Cambridge, England: Cambridge University Press, 1975.

Green, K., D. Kempka, and L. Lackey. "Using Remote Sensing to Detect and Monitor Land-Cover and Land-Use Change." *Photogrammetric Engineering & Remote Sensing* 60, 3 (1994): 331–337.

Greig-Smith, P. W. "Intensive Study Versus Extensive Monitoring in Pesticide Field Trials." In L. Somerville and C. H. Walker, eds. *Pesticide Effects on Terrestrial Wildlife.* London, England: Taylor and Francis, 1990.

Grumbine, R. E. *Ghost Bears: Exploring the Biodiversity Crisis.* Washington, D.C.: Island Press, 1992.

———. "Viable Populations, Reserve Size, and Federal Lands Management: A Critique." *Conservation Biology* 4, 2 (1990): 127–134.

Gunderson, L. H., C. S. Holling, and S. S. Light, eds. *Barriers and Bridges to the Renewal of Ecosystems and Institutions.* New York: Columbia University Press, 1995.

Hamburg, S. P., and C. V. Cogbill. "Historic Decline of Red Spruce Populations and Climatic Warming." *Nature* 331, 4 (1988): 428–430.

Hamrick, J. L., M. J. W. Godt, D. A. Murawski, and M. D. Loveless. "Correlations Between Species Traits and Allozyme Diversity: Implications for Conservation Biology." In D. A. Falk and K. E. Holsinger, eds. *Genetics and Conservation of Rare Plants.* New York: Oxford University Press, 1991.

Hanes, T. "California Chaparral." In M. G. Barbour and J. Major, eds. *Terrestrial Vegetation of California.* Sacramento: California Native Plant Society, 1977.

Hanski, I., and M. Gilpin. "Metapopulation Dynamics: Brief History and Conceptual Domain." *Biological Journal of the Linnean Society* 42 (1991): 73–88.

Harestad, A. S., and F. L. Bunnell. "Home Range and Body Weight—A Reevaluation." *Ecology* 60, 2 (1979): 389–402.

Harris, L. D. "An Everglades Regional Biosphere Reserve." *Florida Fish and Wildlife News* 4, 2: (1990): 12–15.

———. *The Fragmented Forest: Island Biogeography Theory and the Preservation of Biotic Diversity.* Chicago, Ill.: University of Chicago Press, 1984.

Harris, L. D., and P. B. Gallagher. "New Initiatives for Wildlife Conservation: The Need for Movement Corridors." In G. Mackintosh, ed. Preserving Communities and Corridors. Washington, D.C.: Defenders of Wildlife, 1989.

Hart, D. D. "Building a Stronger Partnership Between Ecological Research and Biological Monitoring." *Journal of the North American Benthological Society* 13, 1 (1994); 110–116.

Heinselman, M. L. "Fire Intensity and Frequency as Factors in the Distribution and Structure of Northern Ecosystems." In H. A. Mooney et al., Technical Coordinators. *Proceedings of the Conference, Fire Regimes, and Ecosystem Properties, December 11–15, 1978, Honolulu, Hawaii.* USDA Forest Service General Technical Report WO-26. USDA Forest Service, 1981.

Hinds, W. T. "Towards Monitoring of Long-Term Trends in Terrestrial Ecosystems." *Environmental Conservation* 2, 1 (1984): 11–18.

Hirsch, A. "Monitoring Cause and Effects—Ecosystem Changes." In D. L. Worf, ed. *Biological Monitoring for Environmental Effects.* Lexington, Mass.: Lexington Books, 1980.

Hobbs, R. J. "Can Revegetation Assist in the Conservation of Biodiversity in Agricultural Areas?" *Pacific Conservation Biology* 1 (1993): 29–38.

———. "Disturbance Regimes in Remnants of Natural Vegetation." In D. A. Saunders, G. W. Arnold, A. A. Burbidge, and A. J. M. Hopkins, eds. *Nature Conservation: The*

Role of Remnants of Native Vegetation. Chipping Norton, New South Wales, Australia: Surrey Beatty and Sons, 1987.

———. "Dynamics of Vegetation Mosaics: Can We Predict Responses to Global Changes?" *Ecoscience* 1 (1994): 346–356.

———. "The Effects of Landscape Fragmentation on Ecosystem Processes in the Western Australian Wheatbelt." *Biological Conservation* 64 (1993): 193–201.

———. "Remote Sensing of Spatial and Temporal Dynamics of Vegetation." In R. J. Hobbs and H. A. Mooney, eds. *Remote Sensing of Biosphere Functioning.* New York: Springer-Verlag, 1990.

———. "The Role of Corridors in Conservation: Solution or Bandwagon?" *Trends in Ecology and Evolution* 7, 11 (1992): 389–392.

Hobbs, R. J., and L. F. Huenneke. "Disturbance, Diversity, and Invasion: Implications for Conservation." *Conservation Biology* 6, 3 (1992): 324–333.

Hobbs, R. J., and H. A. Mooney. "Spatial and Temporal Variability in California Annual Grassland: Results from a Long-Term Study." *Journal of Vegetation Science* 5 (1994): 1–13.

Hobbs, R. J., and D. A. Norton. "Toward a Conceptual Framework for Restoration Ecology." Restoration Ecology 4, 2 (1996): 93–110.

Hoehne, L. M. "The Groundlayer Vegetation of Forest Islands in an Urban-Suburban Matrix." In R. L. Burgess and D. M. Sharpe, eds. *Forest Island Dynamics in Man-Dominated Landscapes.* New York: Springer-Verlag, 1981.

Hopper, S. D. "The Use of Genetic Information in Establishing Reserves for Nature Conservation." In R. C. Szaro and D. W. Johnston, eds. *Diversity in Managed Landscapes.* New York: Oxford University Press, 1996.

Hough, J. "Biosphere Reserves: Myth and Reality." *Endangered Species Update* 6, 1/2 (1988): 1–4.

Hough, M. *Cities and Natural Process.* New York: Routledge, 1995.

———. *City Form and Natural Process: Towards a New Urban Vernacular.* New York: Van Nostrand Reinhold, 1984.

———. "Nature and the City." *Landscape Architecture* 79, 7 (1989): 41–43.

Huenneke, L. F. "Ecological Implications of Genetic Variation in Plant Populations." In D. A. Falk and K. E. Holsinger, eds. *Genetics and Conservation of Rare Plants.* New York: Oxford University Press, 1991.

Hunsaker, C. T., and D. E. Carpenter, eds. *Ecological Indicators for the Environmental Monitoring and Assessment Program.* EPA 600/3-90/060. Research Triangle Park, N.C.: U.S. Environmental Protection Agency, Office of Research and Development, 1990.

Hunter, M. L., Jr. *Fundamentals of Conservation Biology.* Cambridge, Mass.: Blackwell Science, 1996.

Hunter, M. L., G. L. Jacobson, Jr., and T. Webb, III. "Paleoecology and the Coarse-Filter Approach to Maintaining Biological Diversity." *Conservation Biology* 2, 4 (1988): 375–385.

Innes, J., J. Gruber, M. Neuman, and R. Thompson. *Coordinating Growth and Envi-*

ronmental Management Through Consensus Building. Berkeley: California Policy Seminar, 1994.

IPCC (International Panel on Climate Change). *Climate Change, the IPCC Scientific Assessment*. Cambridge, Mass.: Cambridge University Press, 1990.

Jackman, T. R., and D. B. Wake. "Evolutionary and Historical Analysis of Protein Variation in the Blotched Forms of Salamanders of the *Ensatina* Complex (Amphibia: Plethodontidae)." *Evolution* 48, 3 (1994): 876–897.

Jensen, D. B., M. S. Torn, and J. Harte. *In Our Own Hands: A Strategy for Conserving California's Biological Diversity*. Berkeley: University of California Press, 1993.

Jones, K. B. "Data Types." In A. Y. Cooperrider, R. J. Boyd, and H. R. Stuart, eds. *Inventory and Monitoring of Wildlife Habitat*. Denver, Colo.: USDI Bureau of Land Management, Service Center, 1986.

Jongman, R. "Ecological Networks in Europe: Congruent Developments." *Landschap*. Special Issue on the Planning of Ecological Networks (1995): 123–130.

Karr, J. R. "Biological Monitoring and Environmental Assessment: A Conceptual Framework." *Environmental Management* 11, 2 (1987): 249–256.

Keeley, J. E., ed. *Interface Between Ecology and Land Development in California*. Los Angeles: Southern California Academy of Sciences, 1993.

Keeney, R. L. "Decision Analysis: An Overview." *Operations Research* 30, 5 (1982): 803–838.

Kelly, J. R., and M. A. Harwell. "Indicators of Ecosystem Recovery." *Environmental Management* 14, 5 (1990): 527–545.

Keystone Center. "Final Consensus Report on the Keystone Policy on Biological Diversity on Federal Lands." Keystone, Colo.: Keystone Center, 1991.

Kilgore, B. M. "Fire in Ecosystem Distribution and Structure: Western Forests and Scrublands." In H. A. Mooney et al., Technical Coordinators. *Proceedings of the Conference, Fire Regimes, and Ecosystem Properties, December 11–15, 1978, Honolulu, Hawaii*. USDA Forest Service General Technical Report WO-26. USDA Forest Service, 1981.

Knapp, P. A. "Secondary Plant Succession and Vegetation Recovery in Two Western Great Basin Ghost Towns." *Biological Conservation* 60, 2 (1992): 81–89.

Kondolf, G. M., and E. R. Micheli. "Evaluating Stream Restoration Projects." *Environmental Management* 19, 1 (1995): 1–15.

Kovacs, M., ed. *Biological Indicators in Environmental Protection*. New York: Ellis Horwood, 1992.

Kucera, C. L. "Grasslands and Fire." In H. A. Mooney et al., Technical Coordinators. *Proceedings of the Conference, Fire Regimes, and Ecosystem Properties, December 11–15, 1978, Honolulu, Hawaii*. USDA Forest Service General Technical Report WO-26. USDA Forest Service, 1981.

Kunz, T. H., C. Wemmer, and V. Hayssen. "Sex, Age, and Reproductive Condition of Mammals." In D. E. Wilson, F. R. Cole, J. D. Nichols, R. Rudran, and M. S. Foster, eds. *Measuring and Monitoring Biological Diversity: Standard Methods for Mammals*. Washington, D.C.: Smithsonian Institution Press, 1996.

Lamberson, R. H., R. McKelvey, B. R. Noon, and C. Voss. "A Dynamic Analysis of Northern Spotted Owl Viability in a Fragmented Forest Landscape." *Conservation Biology* 6, 4 (1992): 505–512.

Lande, R. "Genetics and Demography in Biological Conservation." *Science* 241 (1988): 1455–1460.

———. "Risks of Population Extinction from Demographic and Environmental Stochasticity, and Random Catastrophes." *American Naturalist* 142, 6 (1993): 911–927.

———. "Mutation and Conservation." *Conservation Biology* 9, 4 (1995): 782–791.

Landres, P. B., J. Verner, and J. W. Thomas. "Ecological Uses of Vertebrate Indicator Species: A Critique." *Conservation Biology* 2, 4 (1988): 316–328.

Langton, T. E. S., ed. *Amphibians and Roads: Proceedings of the Toad Tunnel Conference, Rendsburg, Federal Republic of Germany, 7–8 January 1989*. Shefford, England: ACO Polymer Products Ltd, 1989.

Lee, K. N. "The Columbia River Basin: Experimenting with Sustainability." *Environment* 31, 6 (1989): 6–11, 30–33.

———. *Compass and Gyroscope: Integrating Science and Politics for the Environment*. Washington, D.C.: Island Press, 1993.

———. "Deliberately Seeking Sustainability in the Columbia River Basin." In L. H. Gunderson, C. S. Holling, and S. S. Light, eds. *Barriers and Bridges to the Renewal of Ecosystems and Institutions*. New York: Columbia University Press, 1995.

Levins, R. "Extinction." In M. Gerstenhaber, ed. *Some Mathematical Questions in Biology*. Fifth Symposium on Mathematical Biology. Providence, R.I.: American Mathematical Society, 1970.

Lidicker, W. Z. "The Role of Dispersal in the Demography of Small Mammals." In E. B. Golley, D. Petrusewicz, and R. Ryskorski, eds. *Small Mammals: Their Productivity and Population Dynamics*. Cambridge, England: Cambridge University Press, 1975.

Loftis, J. C., G. B. McBride, and J. C. Ellis. "Considerations of Scale in Water Quality Monitoring and Data Analysis." *Water Resources Bulletin* 27, 2 (1991): 225–264.

Luken, J. O. *Directing Ecological Succession*. New York: Chapman and Hall, 1990.

Lyle, J. T. *Design for Human Ecosystems: Landscape, Land Use, and Natural Resources*. New York: Van Nostrand Reinhold, 1985.

———. *Regenerative Design for Sustainable Development*. New York: Wiley, 1994.

MacArthur, R. H., and E. O. Wilson. *The Theory of Island Biogeography*. Princeton: Princeton University Press, 1967.

Macdonald, D. W., and H. Smith. "Dispersal, Dispersion and Conservation in the Agricultural Ecosystem." In R. G. H. Bunce and D. C. Howard, eds. *Species Dispersal in Agricultural Habitats*. London: Belhaven Press, 1990.

MacDonald, L. H., and A. W. Smart. "Beyond the Guidelines: Practical Lessons for Monitoring." *Environmental Monitoring and Assessment* 26 (1993): 203–218.

MacDonald, L. H., A. W. Smart, and R. C. Wissmar. *Monitoring Guidelines to Evaluate Effects of Forestry Activities on Streams in the Pacific Northwest and Alaska.* EPA 910/9-91-001. Seattle, Wash.: U. S. Environmental Protection Agency, 1991.

MacKinnon, J., K. MacKinnon, G. Child, and J. Thorsell. *Managing Protected Areas in the Tropics.* Gland, Switzerland: IUCN, 1986.

Maguire, L. A. "Decision Analysis in Conservation Biology." In G. K. Meffe and C. R. Carroll., eds. *Principles of Conservation Biology.* Sunderland, Mass.: Sinauer Associates, 1994.

Maher, W. A., P. W. Cullen, and R. H. Norris. "Framework for Designing Sampling Programs." *Environmental Monitoring and Assessment* 30 (1994): 139–162.

Mainwaring, J. *An Introduction to the Study of Map Projection.* New York: St. Martin's Press, 1960.

Mantell, M. A. "The California Experiment." *National Wetlands Newsletter* 16, 5 (1994): 9–10.

Margules, C., and M. B. Usher. "Criteria Used in Assessing Wildlife Conservation Potential: A Review." *Biological Conservation* 21 (1981): 79–109.

Margules, C., A. J. Higgs, and R. W. Rafe. "Modern Biogeographic Theory: Are There Any Lessons for Nature Reserve Design?" *Biological Conservation* 24 (1982): 115–128.

Margules, C. R., and M. P. Austin, eds. *Nature Conservation: Cost-Effective Biological Surveys and Data Analysis.* Australia: CSIRO, 1991.

Margules, C. R., A. O. Nicholls, and R. L. Pressey. "Selecting Networks of Reserves to Maximize Biological Diversity." *Biological Conservation* 43 (1988): 63–76.

Marsh, W. M. *Environmental Analysis for Land Use and Site Planning.* New York: McGraw-Hill, 1978.

———. *Landscape Planning: Environmental Applications.* Reading, Mass.: Addison-Wesley Publishing Co., 1983.

Master, L. L. "Assessing Threats and Setting Priorities for Conservation." *Conservation Biology* 5, 4 (1991): 559–563.

McCarthy, J. F., and L. R. Shugart. *Biomarkers of Environmental Contamination.* Boca Raton, Fla.: Lewis Publishers, 1990.

McCullough, D.R., ed. *Metapopulations and Wildlife Conservation.* Washington, D.C.: Island Press, 1996.

McHarg, I. L. *Design with Nature.* Garden City, N.Y.: Natural History Press, 1969.

Meffe, G. K. "Genetic Approaches to Conservation of Rare Fishes: Examples from North American Desert Species." *Journal of Fish Biology* 37, Supp. A (1990): 105–112.

Meffe, G. K., and C. R. Carroll, eds. Principles of Conservation Biology. Sunderland, Mass.: Sinauer Associates, 1994.

Mejia, A. A., L. T. de Alonso, L. Brower, and D. Murphy. "Maintaining Migratory Phenomena: The Mexican Monarch Butterfly Challenge." *Society for Conservation Biology Newsletter 3* (1996): 1 and 17.

Menges, E. S. "The Application of Minimum Viable Population Theory to Plants." In D. A. Falk and K. E. Holsinger, eds. *Genetics and Conservation of Rare Plants.* New York: Oxford University Press, 1991.

Merriam. G., and A. Lanoue. "Corridor Use by Small Mammals: Field Measurement for Three Experimental Types of *Peromyscus leucopus.*" *Landscape Ecology* 4, 2/3 (1990): 123–131.

Millar, C. I., and W. J. Libby. "Restoration: Disneyland or a Native Ecosystem?" *Fremontia* 17, 2 (1989): 3–10.

———. "Strategies for Conserving Clinal, Ecotypic, and Disjunct Population Diversity in Widespread Species." In D. A. Falk and K. E. Holsinger, eds. *Genetics and Conservation of Rare Plants.* New York: Oxford University Press, 1991.

Mills, L. S., M. E. Soulé, and D. F. Doak. "The Keystone-Species Concept in Ecology and Conservation." *BioScience* 43, 4 (1993): 219–224.

Milton, S. J., R. J. Dean, M. A. du Plessis, and W. R. Siegfried. "A Conceptual Model of Arid Rangeland Degradation." *BioScience* 44, 2 (1994): 70–76.

Minnich, R. A. "Chaparral Fire History in San Diego County and Adjacent Northern Baja California: An Evaluation of Natural Fire Regimes and the Effects of Suppression Management." In S. C. Keeley, ed. *The California Chaparral: Paradigms Reexamined.* Publication 34. Los Angeles: Los Angeles County Natural History Museum, 1989.

Mooney, H. A., and J. A. Drake, eds. *Ecology of Biological Invasions of North America and Hawaii.* New York: Springer-Verlag, 1986.

Mooney, H. A., and M. Godron, eds. Disturbance and Ecosystems: Components of Response. New York: Springer-Verlag, 1983.

Moore, H. D., W. V. Holt, and G. M. Mace, eds. *Biotechnology and the Conservation of Genetic Diversity.* Symposia of the Zoological Society of London No. 64. Oxford, England: Clarendon Press, 1992.

Moritz, C., C. J. Schneider, and D. B. Wake. "Evolutionary Relationships Within the *Ensatina eschscholtzii* Complex Confirm the Ring Species Interpretation." *Systematic Zoology* 41, 3 (1992): 273–291.

Morrison, M. L. "Bird Populations as Indicators of Environmental Change" *Current Ornithology* 3 (1986): 429–451.

Morrison, M. L., and B. G. Marcot. "An Evaluation of Resource Inventory and Monitoring Program Used in National Forest Planning." Environmental Management 19, 1 (1995): 147–156.

Moyle, P. B., J. E. Williams, and E. D. Wikramanayake. *Fish Species of Special Concern in California.* Final Report Submitted to the California Department of Fish and Game, Inland Fisheries Division. Rancho Cordova: California Department of Fish and Game, 1989.

Muscutt, A. D., G. L. Harris, S. W. Bailey, and D. B. Davies. "Buffer Zones to Improve Water Quality: A Review of Their Potential Use in U.K. Agriculture." *Agriculture, Ecosystems and Environments* 45 (1993): 59–77.

Myers, W. L., and R. L. Shelton. *Survey Methods for Ecosystem Management.* New York: John Wiley, 1980.

Naiman, R. J., C. A. Johnston, and J. C. Kelley. "Alteration of North American Streams by Beaver." *BioScience* 38, 11 (1988): 753–762.

Nature Conservancy, The. *Conservation by Design: A Framework for Mission Success.* Arlington, Va.: The Nature Conservancy, 1996.

Newmark, W. D. "A Land-Bridge Island Perspective on Mammalian Extinctions in Western North American Parks." *Nature* 325, 29 (1987): 430–432.

Nichols, J. D. "Extensive Monitoring Programmes Viewed as Long-Term Population Studies: The Case of North American Waterfowl." *Ibis* 133, Suppl. 1 (1991): 89–98.

Noss, R. F. "Conservation of Biodiversity at the Landscape Scale." In R. C. Szaro and D. W. Johnston, eds. *Diversity in Managed Landscapes.* New York: Oxford University Press, 1996.

———. "Corridors in Real Landscapes: A Reply to Simberloff and Cox." *Conservation Biology* 1, 1 (1987): 159–164.

———. "From Plant Communities to Landscapes in Conservation Inventories: A Look at The Nature Conservancy (USA)." *Biological Conservation* 41 (1987): 11–37.

———. "Indicators for Monitoring Biodiversity: A Hierarchical Approach." *Conservation Biology* 4, 4 (1990): 355–364.

———. "Landscape Connectivity: Different Functions at Different Scales." In W. E. Hudson, ed. *Landscape Linkages and Biodiversity.* Washington, D.C.: Island Press, 1991.

———. "Nodes, Networks, and MUMs: Preserving Diversity at All Scales." *Environmental Management* 10, 3 (1986): 299–309.

———. "Wildlife corridors." In D. S. Smith and P. Cawood Hellmund, eds. *Ecology of Greenways: Design and Function of Linear Conservation Areas.* Minneapolis: University of Minnesota Press, 1993.

Noss, R. F., and A. Y. Cooperrider. Saving Nature's Legacy: Protecting and Restoring Biodiversity. Washington, D.C.: Island Press, 1994.

Noss, R. F., and L. D. Harris. "Nodes, Networks, and MUMs: Preserving Diversity at All Scales." *Environmental Management* 10, 3 (1986): 299–309.

Noss, R. F., S. P. Cline, B. Csuti, and J. M. Scott. "Monitoring and Assessing Biodiversity." In E. Likke, ed. *Achieving Environmental Goals: The Concept and Practice of Environmental Performance Review.* London: Belhaven Press, 1991.

Nunney, L., and K. A. Campbell. "Assessing Minimum Viable Population Size: Demography Meets Population Genetics." *Trends in Ecology and Evolution* 8, 7 (1993): 234–239.

Odum, E. P. *Fundamentals of Ecology.* Philadelphia, Pa: W.B. Saunders, 1971.

O'Neill, R. V., D. L. DeAngelis, J. B. Waide, and T. F. H. Allen. *A Hierarchical Concept of Ecosystems.* Princeton, N.J.: Princeton University Press, 1986.

Opdam, P. "Dispersal in Fragmented Populations: The Key to Survival." In R. G. H. Bunce, and D. C. Howard, eds. *Species Dispersal in Agricultural Habitats.* Irvington, N.Y.: Belhaven Press, 1990.

Osborne, L. L., and D. A. Kovacic. "Riparian Vegetated Buffer Strips in Water Quality Restoration and Stream Management." *Freshwater Biology* 29 (1993): 243–258.

Paine, R. T. "A Note on Trophic Complexity and Community Stability." *American Naturalist* 103 (1969): 91–93.

Parker, V. T. "Effect of Wet-Season Management Burns on Chaparral Regeneration: Implications for Rare Species." In T. E. Elias, ed. *Proceedings of a Conference on the Conservation and Management of Rare and Endangered Plants.* Sacramento: California Native Plant Society, 1987.

Pavlik, B. M. "Conserving Plant Species Diversity: The Challenge of Recovery." In R. C. Szaro and D. W. Johnston, eds. *Diversity in Managed Landscapes.* New York: Oxford University Press, 1996.

Phillips, J. D. "An Evaluation of the Factors Determining the Effectiveness of Water Quality Buffer Zones." *Journal of Hydrology* 107 (1989): 133–145.

Pickett, S. T. A., V. T. Parker, and P. L. Fiedler. "The New Paradigm in Ecology: Implications for Conservation Biology Above the Species Level." In P. L. Fiedler and S. K. Jain, eds. *Conservation Biology: The Theory and Practice of Nature Conservation and Management.* New York: Chapman and Hall, 1992.

Pickett, S. T. A., and P. S. White, eds. The Ecology of Natural Disturbance and Patch Dynamics. New York: Academic Press, Inc., 1985.

Pollard, E., and T. J. Yates. *Monitoring Butterflies for Ecology and Conservation.* London: Chapman and Hall, 1993.

Possingham, H. P., D. B. Lindenmayer, and T. W. Norton. "A Framework for the Improved Management of Threatened Species Based on Population Viability Analysis (PVA)." *Pacific Conservation Biology* 1 (1993): 39–45.

Rabinowitz, D., S. Cairns, and T. Dillon. "Seven Forms of Rarity and Their Frequency in the Flora of the British Isles." In M. E. Soulé, ed. *Conservation Biology: The Science of Scarcity and Diversity.* Sunderland, Mass.: Sinauer Associates, 1986.

Ranney, J. W., M. C. Bruner, and J. B. Levenson. "The Importance of Edge in the Structure and Dynamics of Forest Islands." In R. L. Burgess and D. M. Sharpe, eds. *Forest Island Dynamics in Man-Dominated Landscapes.* New York: Springer-Verlag, 1981.

Read, E. A., M. Blane, and P. Bowler. "Restoration of Coastal Sage Scrub." *Ecesis* 6, 2 (1996): 1, 4–5.

Romme, W. H., and D. G. Despain. "Historical Perspective on the Yellowstone Fires of 1988." Bioscience 39, 10 (1989): 695–699.

Romme, W. H., and D. H. Knight. "Landscape Diversity: The Concept Applied to Yellowstone Park." Bioscience 32 (1982): 664–670.

Salwasser, H., C. M. Schonewald-Cox, and R. Baker. "The Role of Interagency Cooperation in Managing Viable Populations." In M. E. Soulé, ed. *Viable Populations for Conservation.* New York: Cambridge University Press, 1987.

Saunders, D. A., G. W. Arnold, A. A. Burbidge, and A. J. M. Hopkins, eds. *Nature Conservation: The Role of Remnants of Native Vegetation.* Chipping Norton, New South Wales, Australia: Surrey Beatty and Sons, 1987.

Saunders, D. A., J. L. Craig, and E. M. Mattiske, eds. Nature Conservation 4: The Role of Networks. Chipping North, New South Wales, Australia: Surrey Beatty and Sons, 1996.

Saunders, D. A., and R. J. Hobbs, eds. *Nature Conservation 2: The Role of Corridors.* Chipping Norton, New South Wales, Australia: Surrey Beatty and Sons, 1991.

Saunders, D. A., and R. J. Hobbs, "The Role of Corridors in Conservation: What Do We Know and Where Do We Go from Here?" In D. A. Saunders and R. J. Hobbs, eds. *Nature Conservation 2: The Role of Corridors.* Chipping Norton, New South Wales, Australia: Surrey Beatty and Sons, 1991.

Saunders, D. A., R. J. Hobbs, and C. R. Margules. "Biological Consequences of Ecosystem Fragmentation: A Review." Conservation Biology 5, 1 (1991): 18–32.

Sayer, J. *Rainforest Buffer Zones: Guidelines for Protected Area Managers.* Gland, Switzerland: IUCN, 1991.

Schaal, B. A., W. J. Leverich, and S. H. Rogstad. "Comparison of Methods for Assessing Genetic Variation in Plant Conservation Biology." In D. A. Falk and K. E. Holsinger, eds. *Genetics and Conservation of Rare Plants.* New York: Oxford University Press, 1991.

Schonewald-Cox, C. M. "Conclusions: Guidelines to Management: A Beginning Attempt." In C. M. Schonewald-Cox, S. M. Chambers, B. MacBryde, and W. L. Thomas, eds. *Genetics and Conservation.* Menlo Park, Calif.: Benjamin/Cummings Publishing Co., 1983.

Schonewald-Cox, C. M., and J. W. Bayless. "The Boundary Model: A Geographical Analysis of Design and Conservation of Nature Reserves." Biological Conservation 38 (1986): 305–322.

Schonewald-Cox, C. M., and M. Buechner. "Park Protection and Public Roads." In P. L. Fiedler and S. K. Jain, eds. *Conservation Biology: The Theory and Practice of Nature Conservation and Management.* New York: Chapman and Hall, 1992.

Schonewald-Cox, C. M., S. M. Chambers, B. MacBryde, and W. L. Thomas., eds. *Genetics and Conservation: A Reference for Managing Wild Animal and Plant Populations.* Menlo Park, Calif.: Benjamin/Cummings, 1983.

Scott, J. M., T. H. Tear, and F. W. Davis, eds. *Gap Analysis: A Landscape Approach to Biodiversity Planning.* Bethesda, Md.: American Society for Photogrammetry and Remote Sensing, 1996.

Scott, T. A. "Along the Wildland Urban Interface." In J. E. Keeley, ed. *Interface Between Ecology and Land Development in California.* Los Angeles: Southern California Academy of Sciences, 1993.

Shaffer, M. L. "Determining Minimum Viable Population Sizes for the Grizzly Bear." In C. E. Meslow, ed. *International Conference on Bear Research and Management 5.* West Glacier, Mont.: International Association for Bear Research and Management, 1983.

———. "Minimum Population Sizes for Species Conservation." *Bioscience* 31, 2 (1981): 131–134.

———. "Population Viability Analysis." *Conservation Biology* 4, 1 (1990): 39–40.

Shampine, W. J. "Quality Assurance and Quality Control in Monitoring Programs." *Environmental Monitoring and Assessment* 26, 2/3 (1993): 143–151.

Short, H. L., and J. B. Hestbeck. "National Biotic Resource Inventories and Gap Analysis: Problems of Scale and Unproven Assumptions Limit a National Program." *Bioscience* 45, 8 (1995): 535–539.

Shugart, H. H., and D. C. West. "Long-Term Dynamics of Forest Ecosystems." *American Scientist* 69 (1981): 647–652.

Silsbee, D. G., and D. L. Peterson, "Planning for Implementation of Long-Term Resource Monitoring Programs." *Environmental Monitoring and Assessment* 26 (1993): 177–185.

Simberloff, D. "The Contribution of Population and Community Biology to Conservation Science." *Annual Review of Ecology and Systematics* 19 (1988): 473–511.

Simberloff, D., and L. G. Abele. "Conservation and Obfuscation: Subdivision of Reserves." *Oikos* 42, 3 (1984): 399–401.

Simberloff, D., and J. Cox. "Consequences and Costs of Conservation Corridors." *Conservation Biology* 1, 1 (1987): 63–71.

Simberloff, D., J. A. Farr, J. Cox, and D. W. Mehlman. "Movement Corridors: Conservation Bargains or Poor Investments?" *Conservation Biology* 6, 4 (1992): 493–504.

Simon, N., and P. Geroudet. *Last Survivors*. New York: World Publishing Company, 1970.

Skalski, J. R. "A Design for Long-Term Status and Trends Monitoring." *Journal of Environmental Management* 30 (1990): 139–144.

Slocombe, D. S. "Environmental Monitoring for Protected Areas: Review and Prospect." *Environmental Monitoring and Assessment* 21 (1992): 49–78.

Smith, D. S., and P. Cawood Hellmund, eds. *Ecology of Greenways: Design and Function of Linear Conservation Areas*. Minneapolis: University of Minnesota Press, 1993.

Soulé, M. E. "What Is Conservation Biology?" *Bioscience* 35, 11 (1985): 727–734.

———, ed. *Conservation Biology: The Science of Scarcity and Diversity*. Sunderland, Mass.: Sinauer Associates, 1986.

———. "Conservation: Tactics for a Constant Crisis." *Science* 253 (1991): 744–750.

———. "Land-Use Planning and Wildlife Maintenance: Guidelines for Conserving Wildlife in an Urban Landscape." *American Planning Association Journal* 57 (1991): 313–323.

———. "Thresholds for Survival: Maintaining Fitness and Evolutionary Potential." In M. E. Soulé and B. A. Wilcox, eds. *Conservation Biology: An Evolutionary-Ecological Perspective*. Sunderland, Mass.: Sinauer Associates, 1980.

———, ed. *Viable Populations for Conservation*. New York: Cambridge University Press, 1987.

Soulé, M. E., D. T. Bolger, A. C. Alberts, J. Wright, M. Sorice, and S. Hill. "Reconstructed Dynamics of Rapid Extinctions of Chaparral-Requiring Birds in Urban Habitat Islands." Conservation Biology 2, 1 (1988), 75–92.

Soulé, M. E., and D. Simberloff. "What Do Genetics and Ecology Tell Us About the Design of Nature Reserves? *Biological Conservation 35* (1986): 19–40.

Soulé, M. E., and B. A. Wilcox, eds. *Conservation Biology: An Evolutionary-Ecological Perspective.* Sunderland, Mass.: Sinauer Associates, 1980.

Spirn, A. *The Granite Garden: Urban Nature and Human Design.* New York: Basic Books, 1984.

Sprugel, D. G. "Disturbance, Equilibrium, and Environmental Variability: What Is 'Natural' Vegetation in a Changing Environment?" *Biological Conservation* 58 (1991): 1–18.

Stafford, S. "Editorial." *Environmental Monitoring and Assessment* 26 (1993): 85–89.

Star, J., and J. Estes. *Geographic Information Systems: An Introduction.* Englewood Cliffs, N.J.: Prentice-Hall, 1990.

Stebbins, R. C. *Natural History of the Salamanders of the Plethodontid Genus* Ensatina. Berkeley: University of California Publications in Zoology 54, 1954.

Steiner, F. *The Living Landscape: An Ecological Approach to Landscape Planning.* New York: McGraw-Hill, 1991.

Stohlgren, T. J., D. Binkley, T. T. Veblen, and W. L. Baker. "Attributes of Reliable Long-Term Landscape-Scale Studies: Malpractice Insurance for Landscape Ecologists." *Environmental Monitoring and Assessment* 36 (1995): 1–25.

Stout, B. B. "The Good, the Bad, and the Ugly of Monitoring Programs: Defining Questions and Establishing Objectives." *Environmental Monitoring and Assessment* 26 (1993): 91–98.

Swanson. F. J., J. A. Jones, D. O. Wallin, and J. H. Cissel. "Natural Variability–Implications for Ecosystem Management." In USDA Forest Service. *Ecosystem Management: Principles and Applications.* Eastside Forest Ecosystem Health Assessment, Volume II. Portland, Ore.: USDA Forest Service Pacific Northwest Experiment Station, 1993.

Sycamore Associates. *Guidelines for Management of Genetic Resources in the California State Park System.* Lafayette, Calif.: Sycamore Associates, 1992.

Taylor, B., L. Kremsater, and R. Ellis. *Adaptive Management of Forests in British Columbia.* Victoria, Canada: British Columbia Ministry of Forests, Forest Practices Branch, 1997.

Terborgh, J. "Keystone Plant Resources in the Tropical Forest." In M. E. Soulé, ed. *Conservation Biology: The Science of Scarcity and Diversity.* Sunderland, Mass.: Sinauer Associates, 1986.

Thayer, R. L., Jr. *Gray World, Green Heart: Technology, Nature, and the Sustainable Landscape.* New York: John Wiley & Sons, 1994.

Thomas, C. D. "What Do Real Population Dynamics Tell Us About Minimum Viable Population Sizes? *Conservation Biology* 4, 3 (1990): 324–327.

Thomas, J. W., E. D. Forsman, J. B. Lint, E. C. Meslow, B. R. Noon, and J. Verner. *A*

Conservation Strategy for the Northern Spotted Owl. 1990-791-171/20026. Washington, D.C.: U. S. Government Printing Office, 1990.

Tolle, T., and R. L. Czaplewski. "An Interagency Monitoring Design for the Pacific Northwest Forest Ecosystem Plan." In J. E. Thompson, compiler. *Analysis in Support of Ecosystem Management.* Analysis Workshop III, April 10–13, 1995. Fort Collins, Colo.: USDA Forest Service, Ecosystem Management Analysis Center, 1995.

Tracy, C. R., and P. F. Brussard. "Preserving Biodiversity: Species in Landscapes." *Ecological Applications* 4, 2 (1994): 205–207.

Turner, M. G. "Landscape Ecology: The Effect of Pattern on Process." *Annual Review of Ecology and Systematics* 20 (1989): 171–197.

———, ed. *Landscape Heterogeneity and Disturbance.* New York: Springer Verlag, 1987.

Turner, M. G., R. H. Gardner, V. H. Dale, and R. V. O'Neill. "Predicting the Spread of Disturbance Across Heterogeneous Landscapes." *Oikos* 55 (1989): 121–129.

Turner, M. G., W. H. Romme, R. H. Gardner, R. V. O'Neill, and T. K. Kratz. "A Revised Concept of Landscape Equilibrium: Disturbance and Stability on Scaled Landscapes." *Landscape Ecology* 8, 3 (1993): 213–227.

UNESCO. *Task Force on Criteria and Guidelines for the Choice and Establishment of Biosphere Reserves.* Man and the Biosphere Report No. 22. Paris, France: UNESCO, 1974.

———. "Action Plan for Biosphere Reserves." *Nature and Resources* 20, 4 (1984): 11–22.

Urban, D. L., R. V. O'Neill, and H. H. Shugart, Jr. "Landscape Ecology: A Hierarchical Perspective Can Help Scientists Understand Spatial Patterns." *BioScience* 37, 2 (1987): 119–127.

USDA Forest Service. *French Gulch Environmental Assessment, Deerlodge National Forest.* Philipsburg: Mont.: USDA Forest Service, 1992.

USDI Fish and Wildlife Service, Division of Refuges. "Writing Refuge Management Goals and Objectives: A Handbook." 602 FW 1-3. USDI Fish and Wildlife Service, 1996.

Van der Ryn, S., and S. Cowan. *Ecological Design.* Washington, D.C.: Island Press, 1996.

Verner, J., M. L. Morrison, and C. J. Ralph, eds. *Wildlife 2000: Modeling Habitat Relationships of Terrestrial Vertebrates.* Madison: The University of Wisconsin Press, 1986.

Vitousek, P. M. "Biological Invasions and Ecosystem Properties: Can Species Make a Difference?" In H. A. Mooney and J. A. Drake, eds. *Ecology of Biological Invasions of North America and Hawaii.* New York: Springer-Verlag, 1986.

Vos, C. D., and P. Opdam, eds. *Landscape Ecology of a Stressed Environment.* New York: Chapman and Hall, 1993.

Walker, J. L., and W. D. Boyer. "An Ecological Model and Information Needs Assessment for Longleaf Pine Ecosystem Restoration." In USDA Forest Service. *Silvicul-ture: From the Cradle of Forestry to Ecosystem Management.* General Technical Report SE-88. Asheville, N.C.: USDA Forest Service Southeastern Forest Experiment Station, 1995.

Walters, C. *Adaptive Management of Renewable Resources.* New York: MacMillan Publishing Co., 1986.

Weise, D. R., and R. E. Martin, Technical Coordinators. *The Biswell Symposium: Fire Issues and Solutions in Urban Interface and Wildland Ecosystems.* February 15–17, 1994, Walnut Creek, California. General Technical Report PSW-GTR-158. Albany, Calif.: USDA Forest Service Pacific Southwest Research Station, 1995.

Wells, M. P., and K. E. Brandon. "The Principles and Practice of Buffer Zones and Local Participation in Biodiversity Conservation." *Ambio* 22, 2/3 (1993): 157–162.

Westoby, M., B. Walker, and I. Noy-Meir. "Opportunistic Management for Rangelands Not at Equilibrium." *Journal of Range Management* 42 (1989): 266–274.

White, P. S. "Pattern, Process and Natural Disturbance in Vegetation." *The Botanical Review* 45, 3 (1979): 229–285.

Wieringa, M. J., and A. G. Morton. "Hydropower, Adaptive Management, and Biodiversity." *Environmental Management* 20, 6 (1996): 831–840.

Wilcove, D. S. "Nest Predation in Forest Tracts and the Decline of Migratory Songbirds." *Ecology* 66 (1985): 1211–1214.

Wilcove, D. S., C. H. McLellan, and A. P. Dobson. "Habitat Fragmentation in the Temperate Zone." In M. E. Soulé, ed. Conservation Biology: The Science of Scarcity and Diversity. Sunderland, Mass.: Sinauer Associates, 1986.

Wilson, D. E., F. R. Cole, J. D. Nichols, R. Rudran, and M. S. Foster, eds. *Measuring and Monitoring Biological Diversity: Standard Methods for Mammals.* Washington, D.C.: Smithsonian Institution Press, 1996.

Wilson, E. O. *The Diversity of Life.* Cambridge, Mass.: Harvard University Press, 1992.

Wilson, E. O., and E. O. Willis. "Applied Biogeography." In M. L. Cody and J. M. Diamond, eds. Ecology and Evolution of Communities. Cambridge, Mass.: Harvard University Press, 1975.

Wissmar, R. C. "The Need for Long-Term Stream Monitoring Programs in Forest Ecosystems of the Pacific Northwest." *Environmental Monitoring and Assessment* 26 (1993): 219–234.

Wright, S. *Evolution and the Genetics of Populations*, vol. 3, *Experimental Results and Evolutionary Deductions.* Chicago, Ill.: University of Chicago Press, 1977.

Zonneveld, I. S. "Principles of Bio-Indication." *Environmental Monitoring and Assessment* 3 (1983): 207–217.

Zonneveld, I. S., and R. T. T. Forman, eds. Changing Landscapes: An Ecological Perspective. New York: Springer-Verlag, 1990.

Index